I0415701

Tactical-Level Logistics

U.S. Marine Corps

PCN 143 000072 00

To Our Readers

Changes: Readers of this publication are encouraged to submit suggestions and changes that will improve it. Recommendations may be sent directly to Commanding General, Marine Corps Combat Development Command, Doctrine Division (C 42), 3300 Russell Road, Suite 318A, Quantico, VA 22134-5021 or by fax to 703-784-2917 (DSN 278-2917) or by E-mail to **morgannc@mccdc.usmc.mil**. Recommendations should include the following information:

- Location of change
  Publication number and title
  Current page number
  Paragraph number (if applicable)
  Line number
  Figure or table number (if applicable)
- Nature of change
  Add, delete
  Proposed new text, preferably double-spaced and typewritten
- Justification and/or source of change

Additional copies: A printed copy of this publication may be obtained from Marine Corps Logistics Base, Albany, GA 31704-5001, by following the instructions in MCBul 5600, *Marine Corps Doctrinal Publications Status.* An electronic copy may be obtained from the Doctrine Division, MCCDC, world wide web home page which is found at the following universal reference locator: **http://www.doctrine.usmc.mil**.

Unless otherwise stated, whenever the masculine or feminine gender is used, both men and women are included.

DEPARTMENT OF THE NAVY
Headquarters United States Marine Corps
Washington, D.C. 20380-1775

13 June 2000

FOREWORD

1. PURPOSE

Marine Corps Warfighting Publication (MCWP) 4-11, *Tactical-Level Logistics*, provides the doctrinal basis for the planning and execution of ground and aviation logistic support for Marine air-ground task force (MAGTF) operations at the tactical level of war. It establishes standard terms of reference for tactical logistics and combat service support operations and provides guidance for developing local Fleet Marine Force standing operating procedures. MCWP 4-11 expands on MCWP 4-1, *Logistics Operations*, and provides detailed guidance to Marine Corps logisticians for the conduct of tactical-level logistics.

2. SCOPE

This manual is intended for commanders and their staffs who are responsible for planning and conducting logistic support at the tactical level of war. The secondary audience is commanders and staff officers who require logistical support or who will benefit from a greater understanding of logistical support at the tactical level.

3. SUPERSESSION

Fleet Marine Force Manual 4-1, *Combat Service Support Operations*, dated 12 July 1993.

4. CERTIFICATION

Reviewed and approved this date.

BY DIRECTION OF THE COMMANDANT OF THE MARINE CORPS

J.E. Rhodes

J. E. RHODES
Lieutenant General, U.S. Marine Corps
Commanding General
Marine Corps Combat Development Command

DISTRIBUTION: 143 000072 00

Tactical-Level Logistics

Table of Contents

Appendices

Chapter 1

Fundamentals

Logistics is defined as "the science of planning and carrying out the movement and maintenance of forces. In its most comprehensive sense, those aspects of military operations which deal with: a. design and development, acquisition, storage, movement, distribution, maintenance, evacuation, and disposition of materiel; b. movement, evacuation, and hospitalization of personnel; c. acquisition or construction, maintenance, operation, and disposition of facilities; and d. acquisition or furnishing of services." (Joint Publication [JP] 1-02, *Department of Defense Dictionary of Military and Associated Terms*)

Logistics is a fundamental element of Marine air-ground task force (MAGTF) expeditionary operations. Marine expeditionary forces provide self-contained and self-sustained forces that have everything necessary to accomplish the mission—from individual equipment to expeditionary airfields and medical treatment facilities. These forces are structured to meet a wide range of contingency operations and possess the logistic capabilities needed to initiate an operation, sustain forces, and reconstitute for follow-on missions.

Effective logistic support must be viewed from the perspectives of supported (e.g., ground combat element) and supporting (e.g., combat service support element) organizations. It emphasizes the need for detailed planning and close integration of logistic capabilities of both supported combat units and supporting combat service support units.

Combat service support (CSS) is defined as "the essential capabilities, functions, activities, and tasks necessary to sustain all elements of operating forces in theater at all levels of war. Within the national and theater logistic systems, it includes but is not limited to that support rendered by service forces in ensuring the aspects of supply, maintenance, transportation, health services, and other services required by aviation and ground combat troops to permit those units to accomplish their missions in combat. Combat service support encompasses those activities at all levels of war that produce sustainment to all operating forces on the battlefield." (JP 1-02) CSS in the Marine Corps is a function or tasking associated with a unit that, by table of organization (T/O) and table of equipment (T/E), is organized, equipped, and trained as a CSS organization to perform CSS operations.

1001. Levels of War

Military operations require specific logistic support which is based on the strategic, operational, or tactical levels of war.

a. Strategic

"The level of war at which a nation, often as a member of a group of nations, determines national or multinational (alliance or coalition) security objectives and guidance, and develops and uses national resources to accomplish those objectives. Activities at this level establish national and multinational military objectives; sequence initiatives; define limits and assess risks for the use of military and other instruments of national power; develop global plans or theater war plans to achieve these objectives; and provide military forces and other capabilities in accordance with strategic plans." (JP 1-02)

b. Operational

"The level of war at which campaigns and major operations are planned, conducted, and sustained to accomplish strategic objectives within theaters or areas of operations. Activities at this level link tactics and strategy by establishing operations objectives needed to accomplish the strategic objectives sequencing events to achieve the operational objectives, initiating actions, and applying resources to bring about and sustain these events. These activities imply a broader dimension of time or space than do tactics; they ensure the logistic and administrative support of tactical forces, and provide the means by which tactical successes are exploited to achieve strategic objectives." (JP 1-02)

c. Tactical

"The level of war at which battles and engagements are planned and executed to accomplish military objectives assigned to tactical units or task forces. Activities at this level focus on the ordered arrangement and maneuver of combat elements in relation to each other and to the enemy to achieve combat objectives." (JP 1-02)

1002. The Logistic Continuum

Strategic, operational, and tactical logistics parallel and complement the levels of war. Strategic logistics supports the organizing, training, and equipping of forces needed to further the national interest. Operational logistics links tactical requirements and strategic capabilities to accomplish operational goals and objectives. Tactical logistics includes organic unit capabilities and combat service support activities required to support military operations.

Effective tactical logistic support results from the proper employment of logistic capabilities within the MAGTF concept of operations and scheme of maneuver. Commanders and logisticians must carefully integrate logistic considerations into operations planning and execution. Tactical-level logistic capabilities are a primary element of a self-sufficient MAGTF, which is supported externally through the logistic activity at the strategic and operational levels. Figure 1-1 depicts the continuum of logistic support through the levels of war.

1003. Strategic Logistics

Strategic logistic capabilities are generated based on guidance from the National Command Authorities and logistic requirements identified by the operating forces. The combatant command and staff plan and oversee logistics from a theater strategic perspective. They assign execution responsibilities to Service components unless a joint or multinational functional command is formed to perform theater strategic logistic functions. The joint staff and combatant commanders generate and move forces and materiel into theater and areas of operations where operational logistic concepts are employed.

1004. Operational Logistics

Operational logistics connects the logistic efforts of the strategic level with those of the tactical level. The Marine component commander is responsible for conducting operational logistics and coordinating operational logistic support with tactical logistic operations. The component commander may assign operational-level logistic tasks to the combat service support element and aviation combat element commanders in addition to their tactical logistic responsibilities. In larger operations, a Marine logistic command may be

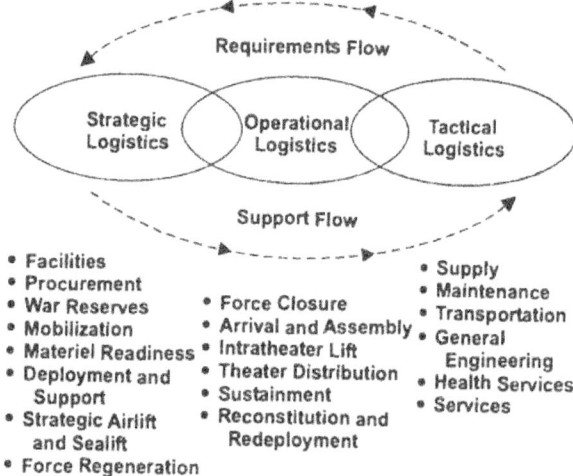

Figure 1-1. The Logistic Continuum.

established to conduct operational-level logistic tasks.

To provide operational-level support to tactical operations, Commander, Marine Corps Forces (COMMARFOR), may establish a Marine logistics command (MLC). The MLC would be responsible for establishing the theater support structure to facilitate arrival, assembly, reception, staging, onward movement, and integration operations. In addition, the MLC could provide operational logistic support to Marine Corps forces as the Marine component commander's operational-level logistic agency in theater. Normally, COMMARFOR assigns the MLC mission to a specific force service support group (FSSG). The COMMARFOR also assigns additional resources, based on the operational situation, theater geography, and infrastructure requirements, to the FSSG for the conduct of theater-supported logistic operations.

1005. Tactical Logistics

Effective logistic support is a command responsibility. The MAGTF commander must plan and coordinate tactical logistics within the MAGTF and coordinate with higher headquarters for the operational-level logistic support necessary to sustain MAGTF operations. Subordinate element commanders are responsible for the efficient employment of organic logistic capabilities, while the combat service support element (CSSE) commander is also responsible for executing CSS operations in support of the entire MAGTF.

All elements of the MAGTF execute tactical logistics to some degree by employing organic capabilities. The initial source of logistic support available to any unit is its own organic capabilities. Organic capabilities are defined in T/Os and T/Es. The CSSE, possessing capabilities beyond those found in the other MAGTF elements, conducts CSS operations to provide any additional logistic support the other MAGTF elements require.

1006. Functions and Subfunctions of Tactical Logistics

Marine Corps tactical-level logistics encompasses all of the logistic support activities performed at the tactical-level of war, to include combat service support. Tactical logistics is normally categorized in six functional areas: supply, maintenance, transportation, general engineering, health services, and services. See table 1-1, on page 1-4.

a. Supply

Supply is a cyclic process of acquiring and issuing materiel to supported units. This materiel may be consumable or durable materiel, components, and end items. See MCWP 4-11.7, *MAGTF Supply Operations*, for additional information. Logisticians normally calculate requirements for each class and subclass of supply. See table 1-2, on page 1-5.

b. Maintenance

Maintenance involves those actions taken to keep materiel in serviceable condition (preventive maintenance) and actions required to return materiel to serviceable condition (corrective maintenance). Maintenance tasks are grouped by levels of support that determine assignment of maintenance responsibilities. Tables 1-3 and 1-4, on page 1-6, depict the levels of support as they are defined for ground equipment and aviation equipment, respectively; tactical logistic maintenance levels are highlighted. See MCWP 4-11.4, *Maintenance Operations*, for additional information.

Table 1-1. Functions and Subfunctions of Tactical Logistics.

Supply	Maintenance	Transportation
Determination of requirements	Inspection and classification	Embarkation
Procurement	Service, adjustment, and tuning	Landing support
Storage	Testing and calibration	Port and terminal operations
Distribution	Repair	Motor transport
Salvage	Modification	Air delivery
Disposal	Rebuilding and overhaul	Freight/passenger transportation
	Reclamation	Materials handling equipment
	Recovery and evacuation	
General Engineering	**Health Services**	**Services**
Engineer reconnaissance	Health maintenance	Command services:
Horizontal/vertical construction	Casualty collection	● Personnel administration
Facilities maintenance	Casualty treatment	● Religious ministries support
Demolition and obstacle removal	Temporary casualty holding	● Financial management
Explosive ordnance disposal	Casualty evacuation	● Communications
Bridging		● Billeting
		● Messing
		● Band
		● Morale, welfare, and recreation
		CSS services:
		● Disbursing
		● Postal services
		● Exchange services
		● Security support
		● Legal services support
		● Civil affairs support
		● Graves registration

Table 1-2. Classes of Supply.

Class	Description	Subclass
I	Subsistence, which includes rations and gratuitious health and welfare items.	A–air (in-flight rations), C–combat rations, R–refrigerated subsistence, and S–nonrefrigerated.
II	Minor end items, which include clothing, individual equipment, tentage, organizational tool sets and tool kits, hand tools, and administrative and housekeeping supplies and equipment.	B–ground support materiel, E–general supplies, F–clothing and textiles, M–weapons, and T–industrial supplies (e.g., bearings, block and tackle, cable, chains, wire rope, screws, bolts, studs, steel rods, plates, bars).
III	Petroleum, oils, and lubricants, which include petroleum fuels, lubricants, hydraulic and insulating oils, preservatives, liquid and compressed gases, bulk chemical products, coolants, de-icing and antifreeze compounds and the components and additives of such products, and coal.	A–air and W–ground (surface).
IV	Construction, which includes construction materiel, installed equipment, and all fortification or barrier materiel.	
V	Ammunition of all types, which includes chemical, biological, radiological, and special weapons, bombs, explosives, mines, fuzes, detonators, pyrotechnics, missiles, rockets, propellants, and other associated items.	A–air and W–ground.
VI	Personal demand items and nonmilitary sales items.	
VII	Major end items, which are the final combination of end products assembled and configured in their intended form and ready for use (e.g., launchers, tanks, mobile machine shops, and vehicles).	A–air, B–ground support materiel (includes power generators and construction, barrier, bridging, firefighting, petroleum, and mapping equipment), D–administrative vehicles (commercial vehicles used in administrative motor pools), G-electronics, K–tactical vehicles, L–missiles, M–weapons, and N-special weapons.
VIII	Medical materiel, which includes medical-unique repair parts.	A–medical and/or dental materiel and B–blood and blood products.
IX	Repair parts, which include components and kits, assemblies, and subassemblies (reparable and nonreparable) required for maintenance support of all equipment.	A–air, B–ground support materiel, D–administrative vehicles, G–electronics, K–tactical vehicles, L–missiles, M–weapons, N–special weapons, and T–industrial supplies.
X	Nonmilitary materiel, which includes materiel to support nonmilitary programs (e.g., agriculture and economic development), that is not included in classes I-IX.	

Table 1-3. Levels and Echelons of Ground Equipment
Maintenance.

Levels of Maintenance	Echelons of Maintenance[1]
Organizational—Authorized at, performed by, and the responsibility of the using unit. Consists of cleaning, servicing, inspecting, lubricating, adjusting, and minor repair.	First—Limited action performed by crew or operator as prescribed by applicable manuals. Second—Limited action above the operator level performed by specialist personnel in the using unit.
Intermediate—Performed by designated agencies in support of the using unit or, for certain items of equipment, by specially authorized using units. Includes repair of subassemblies, assemblies, and major end items for return to lower echelons or to supply channels.	Third—Component replacement usually performed by specially trained personnel in owning or CSS units. Fourth—Component and end item overhaul and rebuilding performed by CSS units at semipermanent or fixed sites.
Depot—Major overhaul and complete rebuilding of parts, subassemblies, assemblies, and end items.	Fifth—End item overhaul and rebuilding performed by industrial-type activities using production line techniques, programs, and schedules.

[1]Equipment technical manuals and stock lists specify echelon of repair for each item.

Table 1-4. Levels of Aviation Equipment Maintenance
Activities.

Levels of Maintenance	Maintenance Activities
Organizational	Tactical and training squadrons, Marine Corps air stations with aircraft assigned.
Intermediate	Marine aviation logistics squadrons (MALS).
Depot	Naval aviation depots, contract maintenance depot activities. Each MALS has limited depot-level capability.

c. Transportation

Transportation is moving from one location to another using railways, highways, waterways, pipelines, oceans, and airways. Throughput is the amount of cargo and personnel passed through the transportation systems. The transportation system includes the means and the controls for managing the transportation means. The transportation subfunctions are generally applicable to all levels of support, although the means, methods, control, and management procedures employed at each level will vary. Although transportation is discussed as a logistic function, at the tactical level, transportation is a combat support function. Combat organizations use organic, attached, and supporting transportation assets for tactical movement.

d. General Engineering

General engineering is distinct from combat engineering. General engineering is typically considered a CSS function (e.g., engineer support battalion), while combat engineering is considered a combat support function (e.g., combat engineer battalion). General engineering assets at the tactical level may be used to reinforce or augment combat engineer organizations in specific situations for mobility, countermobility, or survivability tasks. These assets are normally in general support of the MAGTF for a wide range of tasks. These tasks often involve more detailed planning and preparation and higher standards of design and construction than typical combat engineer tasks.

e. Health Services

Health services support (HSS) seeks to minimize the effect that wounds, injuries, and disease have on unit effectiveness, readiness, and morale. HSS is accomplished by a preventive-medicine program that initially safeguards personnel against potential health risks and by the establishment of a system that provides medical support from the point of wounding, injury, or illness through evacuation. See MCWP 4-11.1, *Health Service Support Operations*, for additional information.

f. Services

The services function provides for the effective administration, management, and employment of military organizations. Services subfunctions are essentially administrative in nature. These are categorized as either command services, which are services provided to Marines by their individual commands, or CSS services, which are services provided by a CSS unit.

1007. Tactical Logistic Support External to the Marine Air-Ground Task Force

Cross-Service support is appropriate when there are standing Department of Defense (DOD) procedures for common-item support (e.g., for material managed by the Defense Logistics Agency [DLA]) or there are existing inter-Service support agreements (ISSAs) (e.g., for the U.S. Army to provide line-haul transportation to Marine Corps forces in certain theaters). Commanders of unified commands have directive authority for logistics by which they may authorize cross-Service support within their theater. Coalition, bilateral, and/or host nation support agreements authorize specified support across national lines. Requests for cross-Service or cross-national logistic support are coordinated by the Marine component commander.

1008. Combat Service Support Installations

The CSSE established fixed installations to build up logistic capabilities in support of the MAGTF. These installations are physical locations either aboard ship or ashore. Their number, location, and specific capabilities are dictated by the concept of CSS, which is based on the MAGTF mission and concept of operations. The MAGTF concept of operations must address the requirement to defend and protect the following CSS installations and facilities, as required.

a. Beach Support Area

In amphibious operations, the beach support area (BSA) is "the area to the rear of a landing force or elements thereof, established and operated by shore party units, which contains the facilities for the unloading of troops and materiel and the support of the forces ashore; it includes facilities for the evacuation of wounded, enemy prisoners of war, and captured materiel." (JP 1-02)

The BSA is one of the first CSS installations established ashore during an amphibious operation and maritime prepositioning force (MPF) operations involving in-stream offload. It is established by the shore party group or team, but the CSSE commander may eventually disestablish it or consolidate it as part of the combat service support area (CSSA). In some situations, the BSA may be the only CSS installation ashore; in other situations, it may be one of several CSS installations.

b. Landing Zone Support Area

The landing zone support area is "a forward support installation which provides minimum essential support to the helicopterborne assault forces of the Marine air-ground task force. It can expand into a combat service support area but it is most often a short term installation with limited capabilities, normally containing dumps for rations, fuel, ammunition, and water only; maintenance is limited to contact teams and/or support teams." (MCRP 5-12C)

This CSS installation is established to support helicopterborne assault elements. It is established by the CSSE when a buildup of supplies or other CSS capabilities is anticipated. When a logistic buildup is not planned, the supported unit is responsible for helicopter support team (HST) operations associated with support of the helicopterborne force.

c. Combat Service Support Area

A CSSA is "an area ashore that is organized to contain the necessary supplies, equipment, installations, and elements to provide the landing force with combat service support throughout the operation." (JP 1-02)

The CSSEs operate CSSAs in accordance with the CSSE operation order (OPORD). Because CSSAs are primary targets, the landing force must plan for their defense. The BSAs or landing zone support areas are often developed into CSSAs when the CSSE establishes the necessary CSS capabilities in the installation to support sustained operations.

d. Force Combat Service Support Area

An force combat service support area (FCSSA) is "the primary combat service support installation established to support MAGTF operations ashore. Normally located near a beach, port, and/or airfield, it usually contains the command post of the combat service support element commander and supports other combat service support installations." (MCRP 5-12C)

The FSSG establishes an FCSSA near a beach, seaport, and/or airfield to support other CSS installations and to provide support not available at forward installations. Normally, the FCSSA contains the command post of the FSSG commander.

e. Repair and Replenishment Point

A repair and replenishment point is "a combat service support installation, normally in forward areas near the supported unit, established to support a mechanized or other rapidly moving force.

It may be either a prearranged point or a hastily selected point to rearm, refuel, or provide repair services to the supported force." (MCRP 5-12C)

Normally, a CSSD establishes a repair and replenishment point in support of a mechanized or other rapidly moving force. It may be either a prearranged point or a hastily selected point at which to rearm, refuel, or provide repair services to the supported force. Depending on the size of the supported force, the CSSD may establish multiple points.

Although the main body of the CSSD normally follows in trace of the advancing mechanized force, repair and replenishment points are normally in forward areas near the supported unit. This presents some unique command and control problems because CSS assets can become scattered over a wide area. The CSSD can also select repair and replenishment points farther to the rear of the mechanized force. Optimally, however, the CSS unit minimizes handling of supplies by having vehicles from the rear make deliveries directly to the users at repair and replenishment points.

f. Forward Arming and Refueling Point

A forward arming and refueling point (FARP) is a temporary facility organized, equipped, and deployed by an aviation commander to rapidly refuel and rearm simultaneously. The aviation combat element (ACE) commander may establish a FARP to support the force scheme of maneuver.

The FARP locations are selected where natural camouflage and terrain features can hide equipment and aircraft. Good drainage and room for tactical dispersion (helicopter servicing, fueling, arming) are of primary importance. Towns and villages are usually ideal locations because they provide hard land for easy movement of aircraft and wheeled vehicles, intersecting road networks, and excellent night operation capabilities.

After selection of the site, preloaded supplies (e.g., refueling equipment, bladders, ammunition) can be transported to the site by truck along with material handling equipment and personnel. Helicopters may be used for rapid, initial emplacement of the FARP. Resupply may be accomplished by air or surface transportation. Under certain situations, a combination of aerial and ground-established FARPs may be operationally desirable. The FARPS are usually established in or near the forward assembly areas. Locations and routes to and from FARPs should be masked from radar detection. Because of the volume of air traffic and its importance to helicopter operations, FARPs should be kept beyond medium artillery range. To minimize this threat, FARPs must be displaced often when they are located farther forward.

g. Airfields

The availability of existing airfields within or close to the MAGTF objective area is a key planning consideration. ACE fixed-wing aircraft may require runway surfaces as long as 10,000 feet. Helicopter, short takeoff, vertical landing, and tilt-rotor aircraft runway requirements are considerably less.

Fixed-wing aircraft can operate from runways as short as 4,000 feet by reducing fuel and ordnance loads and by using arresting gear. Additionally, less developed strips can be enhanced with expeditionary airfield equipment. If required and if time permits, a complete expeditionary airfield can be installed.

(1) Expeditionary Airfields. An expeditionary airfield is a prefabricated and portable airfield. The effort (e.g., material, engineer support, operational guidance, security) required for the installa-

tion and operation of an expeditionary airfield may require the support of all elements of the MAGTF. When deployed, it provides the capability to launch and recover MAGTF helicopters and fixed-wing aircraft under all weather conditions. Expansion of expeditionary airfield facilities into a strategic expeditionary landing field (SELF) allows the support and maintenance for a complete wing-sized ACE. The SELF has parking and taxiways to accommodate the Air Mobility Command and Civil Reserve Air Fleet aircraft. Small expeditionary airfields are constructed by the Marine wing support squadron (MWSS). Larger airfields may require the MWSS to be augmented by the FSSG engineer support battalion or naval construction forces. The Navy mobile construction battalion provides augmentation to the FSSG and MWSS, or, if required, it assumes full responsibility for construction of the expeditionary airfield.

(2) Bare Base Expeditionary Airfields. Bare base expeditionary airfields provide the capability for using an existing airfield or road network to establish an expeditionary airfield. A bare base expeditionary airfield is established in place of a full expeditionary airfield due to the extensive embarkation or construction requirements associated with the full expeditionary airfield. The bare base expeditionary airfield concept calls for the use of available concrete and/or asphalt-surfaced facilities. This concept involves embarking only those assets that are necessary for conducting air operations (e.g., airfield lighting or marking, landing aids, arresting gear). Bare base kits have been established to support all expeditionary airfields.

(reverse blank)

Chapter 2

Organizations, Capabilities, and Responsibilities

Commanders, staff officers, and logisticians at all levels must understand the logistic and CSS capabilities of the MAGTF in order to plan effectively for the tactical phases of expeditionary operations. This chapter discusses Marine Corps organization, MAGTF and task organizations' logistic capabilities, and commanders and staff officers' roles and responsibilities for planning and directing tactical-level logistic support.

Section I. Marine Corps Organization

The Marine Corps is structurally organized into four categories: Headquarters, Marine Corps; the Marine Corps Reserve; the supporting establishment; and the operating forces. These structural organizations have inherent logistic capabilities and responsibilities at the strategic, operational, and tactical levels of war.

2101. Headquarters, Marine Corps

Headquarters, Marine Corps, is responsible for strategic logistics. The Commandant ensures that Marine Corps forces (MARFOR) under the command of a combatant commander or joint task force (JTF) commander are trained, equipped, and prepared logistically to undertake assigned missions.

2102. Marine Corps Reserve

The Marine Corps Reserve is organized under the Commander, Marine Corps Forces Reserve (MARFORRES). The MARFORRES consists of a combined-arms force with a division, a wing, and a force service support group. The logistic and combat service support capabilities resident in the MARFORRES are comparable to the capabilities of the active forces. The MARFORRES possesses the graves registration capability and

the bulk of the bridging capability for the Marine Corps. See MCWP 4-1, *Logistics Operations*, and Marine Corps Reference Publication (MCRP) 5-12D, *Organization of Marine Corps Forces*, for more information.

2103. Supporting Establishment

The Marine Corps supporting establishment consists of those personnel, bases, and activities that support the Marine Corps operating forces. This establishment consists of many bases and stations. In addition, it includes the Marine Corps Materiel Command, the Marine Corps Recruiting Command, the Marine Corps Combat Development Command, as well as all training activities and formal schools. The supporting establishment provides logistic support vital to the combat readiness of the Marine Corps.

2104. Operating Forces

Marine Corps Forces, Pacific (MARFORPAC), and Marine Corps Forces, Atlantic (MARFORLANT), are component commands. These MARFORs are operating forces under combatant command of designated unified commanders for joint operations. Normally, MARFORPAC and MARFORLANT retain support responsibility for MAGTFs that are provided to a joint force commander (JFC). The MARFORPAC and the MARFORLANT may deploy a headquarters element to the JFC. This element exercises administrative control over assigned MAGTFs as a Service component commander. In the absence of a headquarters element from a Marine component command, the senior MAGTF commander in theater may assume the responsibilities of Service component commander. Independent of the Service component arrangement, MARFORPAC and MARFORLANT coordinate operational-level logistic requirements that affect the employment of MAGTFs. Marine and Navy operating forces are assigned to type commanders for the purposes of training, employment, and logistic support. Fleet Marine Forces (FMF) Atlantic and FMF Pacific are type commands. A type command is an administrative subdivision of a fleet or force into ships or units of the same type. Commander, MARFORPAC (COMMARFORPAC), is also the Commanding General, FMF Pacific; and Commander, MARFORLANT (COMMARFOR-LANT) is also the Commanding General, FMF Atlantic. Commander, Naval Air Atlantic (COM-NAVAIRLANT); Commander, Naval Air Pacific (COMNAVAIRPAC); and Commander, Naval Air Reserve (COMNAVAIRRESFOR) are the type commanders for Marine Corps aircraft and aviation support equipment.

Section II. Marine Air-Ground Task Force Organization

The MAGTF is the principal Marine Corps organization for all missions across the range of military operations. It is composed of forces task-organized under a single commander capable of responding rapidly to a contingency anywhere in the world.

2201. Core Elements

The types of forces in the MAGTF are functionally grouped into four core elements: a command element (CE), an aviation combat element (ACE), a ground combat element (GCE), and a combat service support element (CSSE). See figure 2-1. These core elements are categories of forces, not formal commands. The basic structure of the MAGTF never varies, though the number, size, and type of Marine Corps units comprising each of its four elements will always be mission dependent.

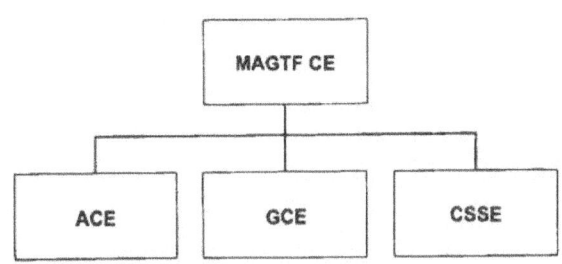

Figure 2-1. Marine Air-Ground Task Force.

2202. Marine Air-Ground Task Forces

The five types of MAGTFs are the Marine expeditionary force (MEF), Marine expeditionary brigade (MEB), Marine expeditionary unit (MEU), special purpose MAGTF (SPMAGTF), and air contingency MAGTF.

a. Marine Expeditionary Force

The MEF is the largest MAGTF and the principal Marine Corps warfighting organization, particularly for larger crises or contingencies. It is task-organized around a permanent command element and normally contains one or more Marine force service support groups, Marine divisions, and Marine aircraft wings. The MEF is capable of missions across the range of military operations, including amphibious assault and sustained operations ashore. It can operate from a sea base and/or a land base. It may contain other Service or foreign military forces assigned or attached to the MAGTF.

The MEF can also task-organize MAGTFs to conduct a specific mission. Typically, a combat service support detachment (CSSD) is the task-organized CSSE for the following MAGTFs:

- The SPMAGTF is a MAGTF that is organized, trained, and equipped with narrowly focused capabilities. It is designed to accomplish a specific mission, often of limited scope and duration. It may be any size, but normally it is a relatively small force—the size of a MEU unit or smaller. It may contain other Service or foreign military forces assigned or attached to the MAGTF.

- The air contingency MAGTF is an on-call, combat-ready MAGTF that deploys by airlift. Air contingency MAGTFs vary in size based on mission requirements and the availability of airlift. Because they deploy by air, they have a limited organic logistic capability and require an arrival airfield. Air contingency MAGTFs usually are activated to respond to developing crises. They may deploy independently or in conjunction with other expeditionary forces.

b. Marine Expeditionary Brigade

The MEB is a mid-sized MAGTF that provides combatant commanders with an extremely flexible expeditionary force. Commanded by a general officer, a MEB is normally built around a GCE of a reinforced infantry regiment. Its ACE consists of a Marine aircraft group with fixed- and rotary-wing squadrons. The CSSE is a brigade service support group (BSSG) organized to provide the full spectrum of CSS to the MEB. As an expeditionary force, the MEB is capable of rapid deployment and employment via amphibious shipping, strategic airlift and/or sealift, marrying with maritime or geographical prepositioning force assets, or any combination thereof. The MEB is a complete fighting force. It is a MAGTF that has been task-organized for the mission and is capable of self-sustainment for 30 days. It can function alone, as a logical follow-on force to the MEU, as part of a joint task force, or as the lead element of a MEF.

c. Marine Expeditionary Unit

The MEU is task-organized normally around a battalion landing team, reinforced helicopter squadron, and a MEU service support group (MSSG). Capable of limited combat operations, it provides an immediate reaction capability for crisis situations.

Section III. Marine Expeditionary Force Organizations and Capabilities

The MEF's tactical logistic capabilities include the organic logistic personnel and equipment arrayed in the various units that comprise the MAGTF element and the CSS capabilities associated with the CSSE. The primary mission of the CSSE is to provide combat service support throughout the MAGTF. Generally, each MEF consists of a permanent CE, an FSSG, a Marine division, and a Marine aircraft wing. When the MEF deploys, it may be reinforced with more capabilities than it possesses in garrison, such as an additional division in the GCE or an FSSG in the CSSE.

2301. Force Service Support Group

The FSSG is the MEF CSSE. It is a grouping of functional battalions that provide tactical-level ground logistic support to all elements of the MEF. See figure 2-2. In addition, the FSSG may be tasked to provide operational-level logistic support to the Marine component of a joint command. The FSSG embodies the fundamental principle—economy of operations through centralization of logistic resources and

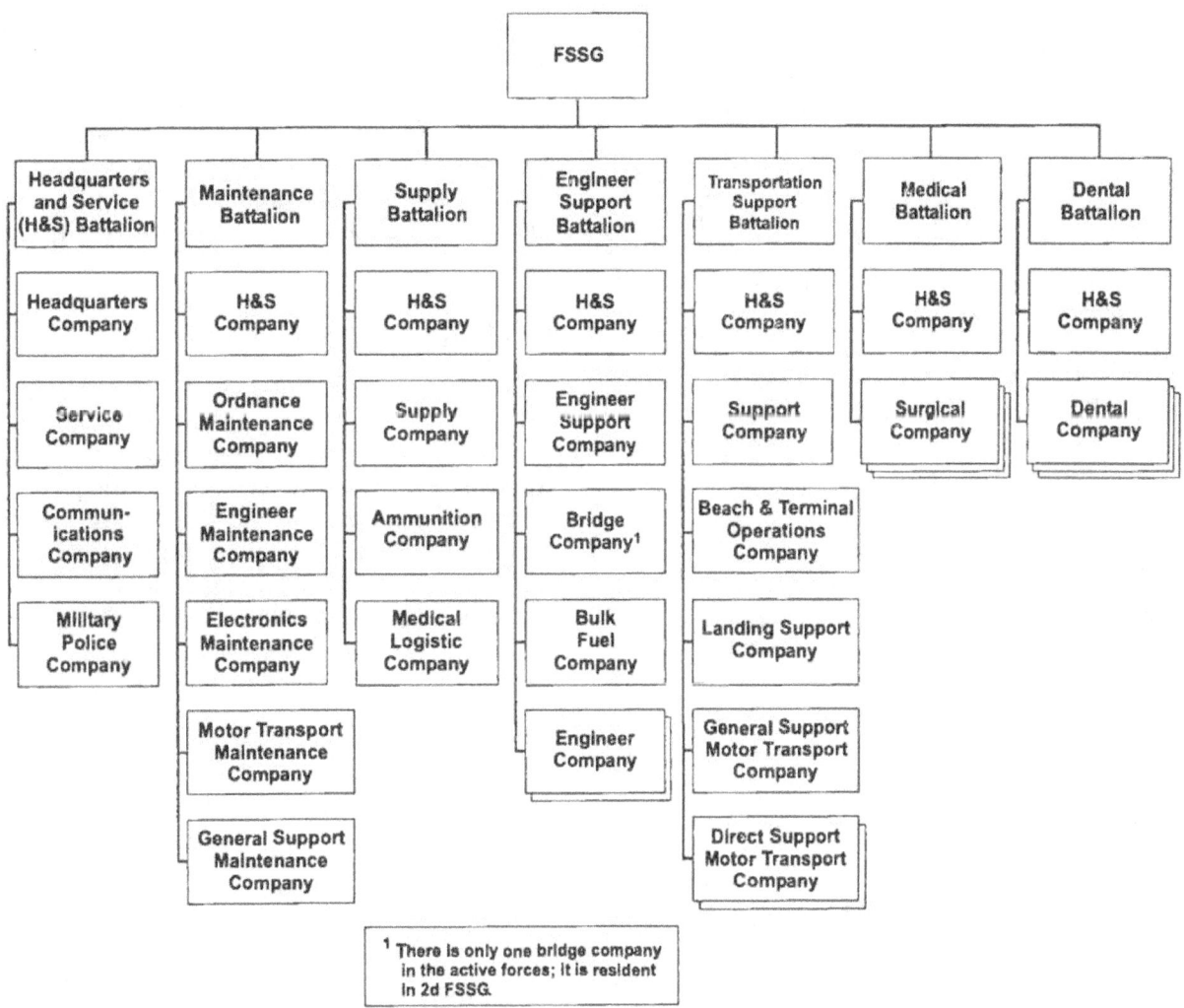

Figure 2-2. Force Service Support Group.

decentralization of support operations. The FSSG organizations are structured to provide task-organized groups to support independently deployed battalions, regiments, MAGTFs, and/or geographically separated units.

a. Headquarters and Service Battalion

The headquarters and service (H&S) battalion provides command and control, administration, services, communications, and security support to the FSSG. It also coordinates CSS to other MAGTF elements. The battalion is self-supporting in supply, organizational maintenance, health services, communications, and transportation for its command and administrative functions. It provides communications for the FSSG CE and subordinate CSSEs. In addition, the battalion provides messing for itself, and the maintenance, supply, and motor transport battalions. The H&S battalion is organized into headquarters, military police, services, and communications companies. See figure 2-3.

(1) Headquarters Company. The headquarters company provides command and control (C2), administration, and command support functions for the H&S battalion, the FSSG, and the CSSE CEs. The H&S battalion's supply, health services, and messing capabilities are resident in this company. The headquarters company transports its administrative and command sections and performs organizational maintenance on organic equipment.

(2) Communications Company. The communications company provides communications support to the FSSG CEs and those subordinate

CSSEs without organic communications capabilities. The company is capable of organic transportation support for administrative and command functions. It performs organizational maintenance on its equipment, except for test equipment, and conducts third echelon maintenance on the battalion's ground communications and electronics critical low-density equipment.

(3) Military Police Company. The military police company provides security support, enemy-prisoner-of-war (EPW) control, and law-and-order operations for the MEF. The company is capable of organic transportation support for administrative and command functions. It also performs organizational maintenance on organic equipment.

(4) Service Company. The service company provides general support services support for the MEF. It also provides administrative and disbursing support for U.S. Navy personnel assigned to the MEF. The company contains the nucleus for initial active duty civil affairs support. It is capable of performing organizational maintenance on organic equipment.

b. Maintenance Battalion

The maintenance battalion provides intermediate-level, third and fourth echelon maintenance support for tactical ordnance, engineer, motor transport, communications-electronics, and general support equipment of the MEF. It also evacuates equipment to repair facilities. The battalion is self-supporting in supply, organizational maintenance, and transportation of command and administrative elements. The maintenance battalion is

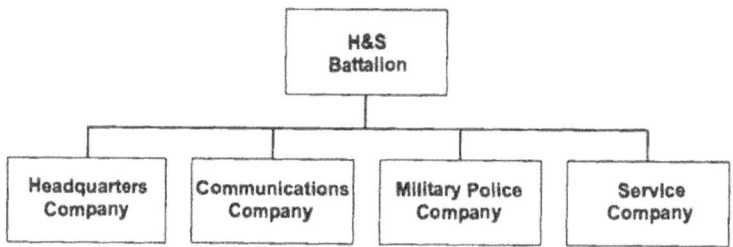

Figure 2-3. Headquarters and Service Battalion.

organized into H&S, ordnance, engineer, electronics, motor transport, and general support maintenance companies. See figure 2-4.

(1) Headquarters and Service Company. H&S company provides C2, administration, and command support functions for the maintenance battalion. It is capable of organic supply and first echelon maintenance on organic equipment. It provides second echelon maintenance on the battalion's ordnance and motor transport equipment, except for motor transport equipment belonging to general support maintenance and motor transport maintenance companies. The H&S company is capable of organic transportation support for administrative and command functions.

(2) Ordnance Maintenance Company. The ordnance maintenance company provides third and fourth echelon maintenance support for the MEF's Marine Corps-furnished ordnance equipment. The company is capable of organic transportation support for its administrative and command functions. It also conducts first echelon maintenance on organic equipment and second echelon maintenance on ordnance equipment.

(3) Engineer Maintenance Company. The company provides third and fourth echelon maintenance support for MEF engineering equipment and second echelon and intermediate maintenance on fabric. It conducts first echelon maintenance on organic equipment and second echelon maintenance on engineer assets. The company is capable of organic transportation support for its adminis-

trative and command functions and of transportation support to evacuate heavy engineer items.

(4) Electronics Maintenance Company. The electronics maintenance company provides third and fourth echelon maintenance support for the ground communications-electronics equipment of a MEF and the evacuation of ground communications-electronics equipment to repair facilities. It conducts first echelon maintenance on organic equipment and second echelon maintenance on organic ground communications-electronics equipment and ordnance equipment, except for infantry weapons. The company is capable of organic transportation support for its administrative and command functions.

(5) Motor Transport Maintenance Company. The motor transport maintenance company provides third and fourth echelon maintenance support for MEF motor transport equipment. It conducts first echelon maintenance on organic equipment and second echelon maintenance on battalion motor transport equipment, except for those items belonging to the H&S and general support maintenance companies. In addition, the company provides transportation support to effect evacuation of heavy motor transport equipment. The company is capable of organic transportation support for its administrative and command functions.

(6) General Support Maintenance Company. The general support maintenance company provides third and fourth echelon maintenance support, including component rebuilding for MEF

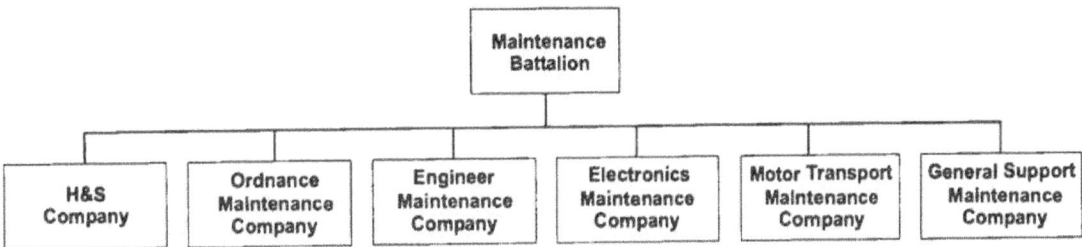

Figure 2-4. Maintenance Battalion.

ground equipment, except for communications-electronic equipment and fire control components. It conducts organizational and intermediate maintenance on organic equipment. In addition, the company is capable of organic transportation support for its administrative and command functions.

c. Supply Battalion

The supply battalion provides general supply support, except for bulk liquids and Navy-funded stock and programs, for sustaining MAGTF operations. The battalion provides organizational and intermediate maintenance on medical and dental equipment. It also provides packing, preservation, and packaging capabilities. The battalion is self-supporting in administration, organic supply, organizational maintenance, and transportation for its command and administrative functions. The supply battalion is organized into H&S, supply, ammunition, and medical logistic companies. See figure 2-5.

(1) Headquarters and Service Company. The H&S company of the supply battalion provides C2, administration, and command support functions for the supply battalion and general subsistence supply support to the MEF, including packing, preservation, and packaging capabilities. The battalion's organic supply and internal transportation capabilities are resident in this company. The H&S company has organic capabilities to provide transportation for its administrative and command functions and to perform organizational maintenance on its equipment.

(2) Supply Company. The supply company provides general supply support, including supply management and control, to sustain the operations

of the MEF. The company provides support for class II, class III (except for bulk), and classes IV, VI, VII, and IX items. The company has organic capabilities to provide transportation for its administrative and command functions and to conduct first echelon maintenance on its equipment.

(3) Ammunition Company. The ammunition company provides general class V supply support to the MEF. The company has organic capabilities to provide transportation for its administrative and command functions and to conduct first echelon maintenance on its equipment.

(4) Medical Logistic Company. Medical logistic company provides general supply and maintenance support for medical and dental (class VIII) materiel. The company has organic capabilities to provide transportation for its administrative and command functions and to conduct first echelon maintenance on its equipment. The company provides organic and intermediate maintenance on equipment held by the medical logistic company and conducts intermediate maintenance on equipment held by other units.

d. Engineer Support Battalion

The engineer support battalion provides general engineering support of an expeditionary nature, including survivability, countermobility, and mobility enhancements. This support includes explosive ordnance disposal (EOD), horizontal and vertical construction, utilities support, engineer reconnaissance, and general supply support incident to the handling, storing, and dispensing of bulk class I (water) and bulk class III and III(A) items. The battalion has organic capabilities for administration, organizational maintenance, messing, engineering support, single-channel

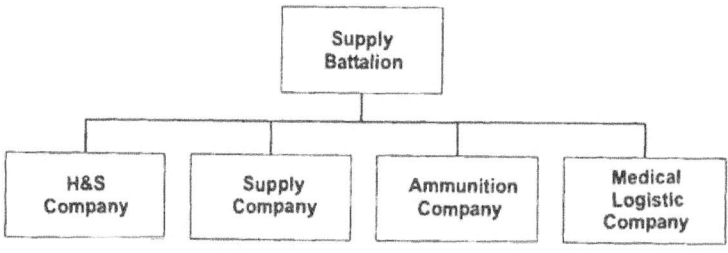

Figure 2-5. Supply Battalion.

communications, supply, and transportation for its command and administrative elements. The engineer support battalion is organized into H&S, engineer support, bridge, and bulk fuel companies, as well as three engineer companies. See figure 2-6.

(1) Headquarters and Service Company. The H&S company provides C2, administration, and command support functions for the engineer support battalion and EOD support for the MEF. The battalion's organic supply, single-channel communications, chaplain, medical, and messing capabilities are resident in this company. The H&S company has organic capabilities to provide transportation for its administrative and command functions and to perform first echelon maintenance on organic equipment. It also provides second echelon maintenance on ordnance, surveying, and communications-electronics equipment.

(2) Engineer Support Company. The engineer support company provides bath, laundry, potable water supply, and mobile electric power to the MEF. It also provides maintenance support for specified equipment that is organic to the battalion, transportation and services support, as well as general support and reinforcing heavy equipment augmentation to the battalion's engineer companies. The company is capable of first echelon maintenance on organic equipment and second echelon maintenance on organic equipment (except for communications-electronics), ordnance, EOD, and bulk fuel equipment. It is also capable of third echelon maintenance on bridge equipment and boats.

(3) Bridge Company. The bridge company provides bridging support to enhance tactical mobility. The company has organic capabilities to provide transportation for its organic administrative and command functions and to conduct organizational maintenance on its equipment.

(4) Bulk Fuel Company. The bulk fuel company provides general support class III supply support. The company has organic capabilities to provide transportation for its administrative and command functions and to conduct organizational maintenance on bulk fuel system-specific equipment.

(5) Engineer Companies. Engineer companies provide general engineering support of a deliberate nature. The companies have organic capabilities to provide transportation for their administrative and command functions and to conduct organizational maintenance on their equipment (except for communications, ordnance, EOD, and bulk fuel items).

e. Transportation Support Battalion

Transportation support battalion provides motor transport, air delivery, and landing support for the MEF. Landing support provides for ship-to-shore movement during amphibious, maritime prepositioning force (MPF) operations, and subsequent terminal operations to permit throughput of supplies, equipment, and personnel. Motor transport support includes medium- and heavy-lift transportation support. The battalion has organic capabilities to provide for its administration, supply, communications, and transportation of command

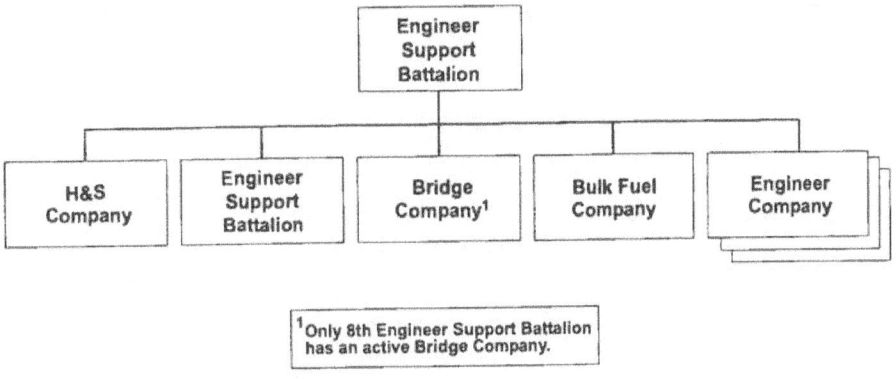

Figure 2-6. Engineer Support Battalion.

and administrative elements. Having a limited engineering capability, the battalion conducts organizational maintenance on organic equipment, third echelon maintenance on motor transport and engineering equipment, and intermediate maintenance on air delivery equipment. The support battalion is organized into H&S, support, beach and terminal operations, landing support, general support motor transport, and two direct support motor transport companies. See figure 2-7.

(1) Headquarters and Service Company. The H&S company of the support battalion provides C2, administration, and command support functions for the battalion. The battalion's organic supply, communications, and organizational maintenance for ordnance and communications-electronic equipment are resident in this company. The H&S company has the organic capability to provide transportation for its administrative and command functions.

(2) Support Company. The support company provides materials handling equipment (MHE) and container handling support. The company has the organic capability to provide transportation for its administrative and command functions. It is also capable of organizational maintenance on its landing support equipment (LSE), second and third echelon maintenance on motor transport assets, and first through third echelon maintenance on engineer equipment organic to the battalion.

(3) Beach and Terminal Operations Company. The beach and terminal operations company provides general transportation support in coordinating throughput operations. The company provides air delivery support and coordinates transportation support in throughput operations at designat-

ed ports, beaches, railheads, airheads, cargo terminals, dumps, and depots. The company has organic capabilities to provide transportation for its administrative and command functions and to conduct first echelon maintenance on its equipment and organizational and intermediate maintenance on air delivery equipment.

(4) Landing Support Company. The landing support company provides C2 for throughput operations in support of surface and/or helicopter assault operations. This company provides the MAGTF's with shore party teams or groups, helicopter support teams (HSTs), departure airfield control groups (DACGs), port operations group (POG), and/or arrival airfield control groups (AACGs). The company has organic capabilities to provide transportation for its administrative and command functions and to conduct first echelon maintenance on its equipment.

(5) General Support Motor Transport Company. The general support company provides general medium- and heavy-lift transportation support. The company is capable of first echelon maintenance on organic equipment.

(6) Direct Support Motor Transport Companies. Direct support companies provide direct and general medium- and heavy-lift transportation support. The companies are capable of first echelon maintenance on organic equipment.

f. Medical Battalion

The medical battalion conducts initial resuscitative HSS. It is the only source of organic Marine Corps medical support above the aid station level. In addition to initial resuscitative surgical inter-

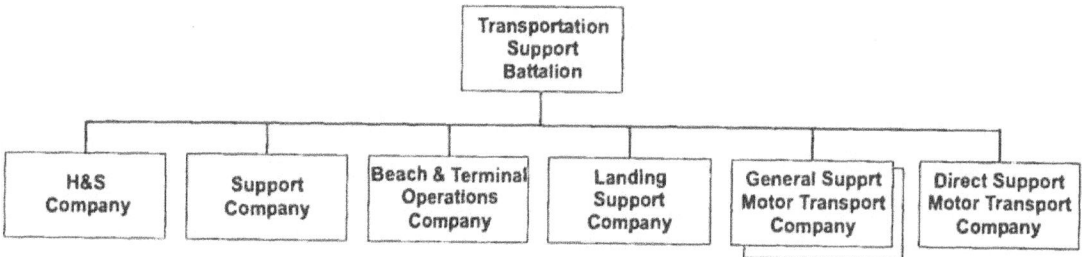

Figure 2-7. Transportation Support Battalion.

vention, the battalion provides temporary casualty holding, ground evacuation support to forward medical elements, and preventive medical support. It has organic capabilities to provide its supplies and to perform organizational maintenance on its equipment and first echelon maintenance on medical equipment. The battalion can transport its command and administrative elements, evacuate casualties from forward areas, and transfer patients to medical treatment facilities (MTFs) in rear areas. The medical battalion is organized into an H&S company and three surgical companies. See figure 2-8.

(1) Headquarters and Service Company. The H&S company provides the medical battalion's C2, command support functions, and shock-trauma capabilities. The H&S company is capable of organic supply and intermediate maintenance on organic equipment. In addition, the company has the organic capability to transport its command and administrative elements.

(2) Surgical Companies. Each of the surgical companies can support regimental-sized operations. The surgical company provides MTFs for resuscitative surgery, medical treatment, and temporary holding of casualties.

g. Dental Battalion

The dental battalion has organic supplies. It is capable of organizational maintenance on organic equipment and third echelon maintenance on dental equipment. In addition, it is capable of transporting its command and administrative elements.

It is organized into an H&S company and three dental companies. See figure 2-9.

(1) Headquarters and Service Company. The H&S company provides the dental battalion's C2 and command support functions. The company is capable of transporting its command and administrative elements.

(2) Dental Companies. The dental companies provide dental services to the major subordinate elements of the MEF. These companies have organic capabilities to provide transportation for their administrative and command functions.

2302. Marine Division

While the Marine division depends on the FSSG for extensive CSS, the division is structured with a significant array of organic logistic capabilities, which should be utilized before requesting support from the FSSG. The division consists of a headquarters battalion, infantry regiments, an artillery regiment, a tank battalion, an assault amphibian battalion, a combat engineer battalion, and a light armored reconnaissance (LAR) battalion (figure 2-10, on page 2-12). See MCWP 5-12D for additional information.

a. Headquarters Battalion

The headquarters battalion is capable of self-administration, organic supply support, food service support, first and second echelon maintenance on

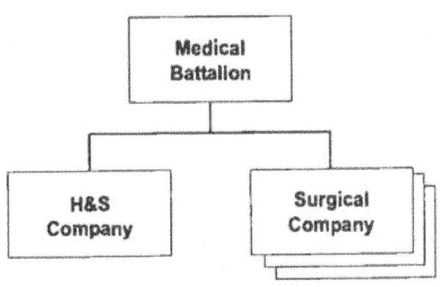

Figure 2-8. Medical Battalion.

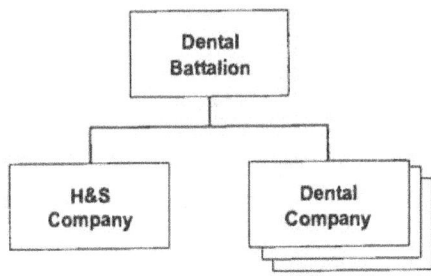

Figure 2-9. Dental Battalion.

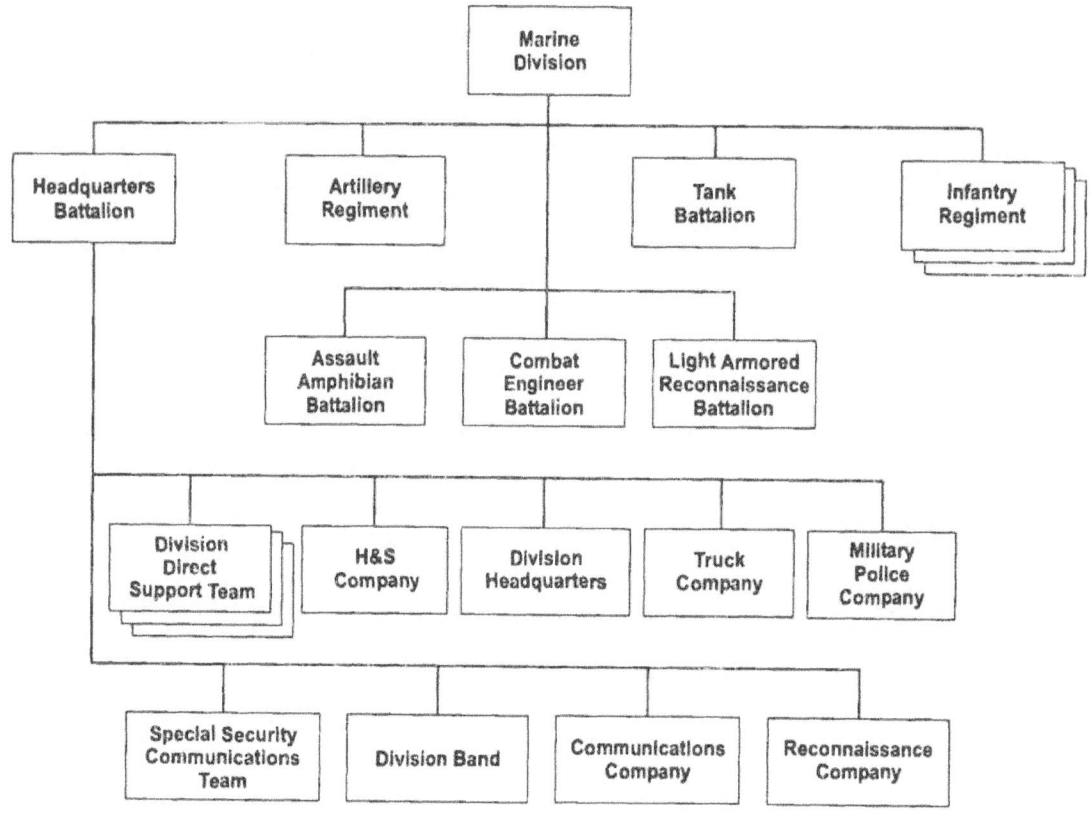

Figure 2-10. Marine Division.

all organic equipment, and third echelon maintenance on communications-electronics equipment. The battalion's medical services provide routine and emergency medical care. The battalion's truck company provides general motor transport support to the division.

b. Infantry Regiment

The infantry regiment is capable of self-administration, organic supply support, food service support, as well as first and second echelon maintenance on all organic equipment. It has a limited transportation capability (high mobility, multipurpose wheeled vehicles [HMMWVs]). The regimental medical platoon can establish a regimental aid station to provide routine and emergency medical care. The regiment's infantry battalions are capable of self-administration, organic supply, food service support, first and second echelon maintenance on organic equipment and weapons, and limited transportation (HMMWVs). The regiment's battalion medical

platoons establish battalion aid stations that provide routine and emergency medical care.

c. Artillery Regiment

The artillery regiment is capable of organic supply support, self-administration, food service support, routine and emergency medical services support, first and second echelon maintenance on organic equipment (except fire control), third and fourth echelon maintenance on electronics systems, and fourth echelon maintenance on weapons-loading radar equipment. The regiment, as a whole, has significant organic logistic capability for short-term self-sufficiency, but requires extensive CSS, especially fuel and ammunition, for sustained operations. The regiment's artillery battalions are capable of self-administration, organic supply support, food service support, medical services that provide routine and emergency support, and first and second echelon maintenance on organic equipment (except fire control). The regiment's artillery units are capable of moving their personnel, equipment, and a limited quantity of supplies.

d. Tank Battalion

The tank battalion is capable of self-administration, organic supply support, food service support, and medical services that provide routine and emergency medical care. The battalion has significant organic logistic capabilities for short-term self-sufficiency, but requires extensive CSS, especially fuel and ammunition, for sustained operations. The battalion's tank companies conduct first and second echelon maintenance on all organic equipment. The battalion provides second echelon maintenance on motor transport equipment and third echelon maintenance on tanks, tank-mounted weapons, and tube-launched, optically tracked, wire-command link guided missile (TOW) systems. The battalion possesses a significant amount of motor transport equipment.

e. Assault Amphibian Battalion

Assault amphibian battalion is capable of self-administration, organic supply support, food service support, and medical services that provide routine and emergency medical care. The assault amphibian battalion has significant organic logistic capabilities for short-term self-sufficiency, but for sustained operations, it requires extensive CSS, especially fuel and ammunition. The battalion conducts second echelon maintenance on motor transport equipment and third echelon maintenance on amphibious assault vehicles, mounted weapons, and communications equipment. The battalion possesses a significant amount of motor transport equipment. The battalion's assault amphibian companies conduct first and second echelon maintenance on its equipment.

f. Combat Engineer Battalion

The combat engineer battalion is capable of self-administration, organic supply support, food service support, and medical services that provide routine and emergency medical care. It conducts first and second echelon maintenance on all organic engineering, motor transport, and communications equipment. The battalion has significant organic logistic capabilities for short-term self-

sufficiency, but requires extensive CSS, especially fuel, for sustained operations.

g. Light Armored Reconnaissance Battalion

The LAR battalion is capable of self-administration, organic supply support, food service support, and medical services that provide routine and emergency medical care. It conducts first and second echelon maintenance on all organic equipment and third echelon maintenance on light-armored vehicles. In addition, the battalion has motor transportation capability. The battalion has organic logistic capabilities for short-term self-sufficiency, but requires extensive CSS, especially fuel and ammunition, for sustained operations.

2303. Marine Aircraft Wing

The MAW possesses organic aviation and ground logistic capabilities. It employs organic aircraft-specific aviation supply, maintenance, and services capabilities in direct support of aircraft squadrons and groups. Although the MAW has its own aviation ground support capabilities, it depends on the FSSG for ground CSS and delivery of aviation bulk commodities. The MAW is organized into a Marine wing headquarters squadron (MWHS), fixed- and rotary-wing Marine aircraft groups (MAGs), a Marine air control group (MACG), and a Marine wing support group (MWSG). A notional garrison MAW is depicted in figure 2-11.

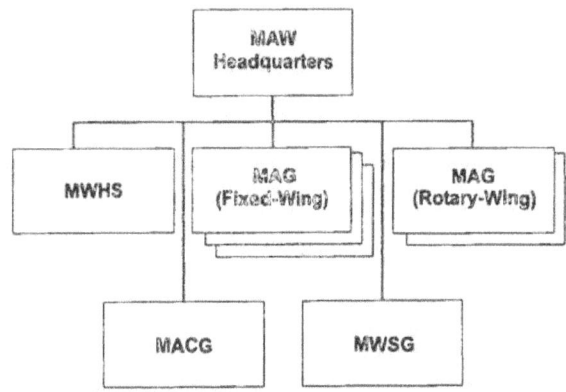

Figure 2-11. Marine Aircraft Wing.

a. Marine Wing Headquarters Squadron

The MWHS provides command, administrative, and supply support for a MAW headquarters and certain elements of the MACG.

b. Marine Wing Support Group

The MWSG, via its Marine wing support squadrons, provides all essential aviation ground support to fixed- and rotary-wing components of an ACE. The group is organized into a headquarters, two fixed-wing support squadrons, and two rotary-wing support squadrons. See figure 2-12.

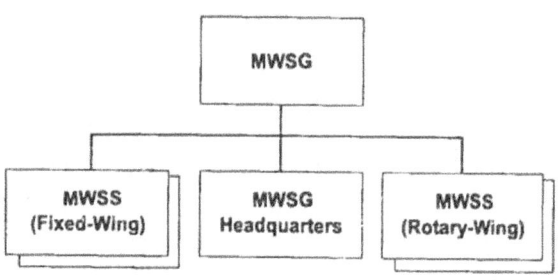

Figure 2-12. Marine Wing Support Group.

(1) MWSG Headquarters. The MWSG headquarters performs administrative, C2, religious ministries support, and coordination functions. It conducts organic supply, first echelon maintenance on all assigned equipment, and second echelon maintenance on nuclear, biological, and chemical (NBC) defense equipment.

(2) Marine Wing Support Squadrons. Marine wing support squadrons (MWSSs) are designated either fixed-wing or rotary-wing and provide the same capabilities with the exception of the operation of M-21 aircraft recovery equipment which is found in a fixed-wing MWSS. The MWSS is self-supporting in administration. It provides second echelon maintenance for organic motor transport and engineering equipment except for those items that belong to the MACG. It conducts organizational maintenance on organic engineering, communications and motor transport equipment, and weapons. It also conducts third echelon and limited fourth echelon maintenance on expeditionary airfield systems equipment. In addition, MWSSs

provide the following essential aviation ground support to an ACE:

- Internal airfield communications.
- Weather service.
- Expeditionary airfield service.
- Aircraft rescue and firefighting.
- Aviation and ground refueling.
- Essential engineering service.
- Motor transport support.
- Field messing support.
- Medical service.
- Personnel training.
- NBC defense.
- Security and law enforcement.
- Air base commandant functions.
- EOD support.

c. Marine Aircraft Group

The MAG is an administrative and tactical headquarters. It is the smallest aviation unit designated for independent operations with no outside assistance except access to a source of supply. There are two types of MAGs: fixed-wing and rotary-wing. The MAG is self-administrating and capable of performing routine and emergency support. MAGs are organized into several aircraft squadrons that perform organizational maintenance on assigned aircraft and a Marine aviation logistic squadron (MALS).

The MALS is capable of self-administration, routine and emergency medical care, first echelon maintenance on organic equipment, and second echelon maintenance on infantry weapons. In addition, it provides the following aviation logistic support (e.g., aviation-peculiar maintenance and supply) for the subordinate units of either a fixed- or rotary-wing MAG:

- Conducts intermediate maintenance on aircraft and aeronautical equipment.
- Provides aircraft supply support.
- Assembles and distributes class V(A) ammunition (requires motor transport support from the MWSS for distribution).

- Manufactures cryogenics.
- Provides supply support to the MWSS expeditionary airfield and weather sections.

d. Marine Air Control Group

The MACG provides, operates, and maintains the Marine air command and control system (MACCS). The MACG is capable of routine and self-administration and emergency medical care. It has sufficient organic motor transport equipment for routine operations. The MACG is capable of performing organic supply functions and operates secondary reparable floats for MACCS-peculiar ground electronics equipment. Squadrons of the group perform organizational maintenance and different levels of intermediate maintenance on a wide variety of equipment.

Section IV. Marine Expeditionary Brigade Organizations and Capabilities

The MEB is the mid-sized MAGTF and is normally commanded by a brigadier general. The MEB bridges the gap between the MEU and the MEF. The MEB is a task-organized MAGTF normally composed of a CE, a reinforced infantry regiment, a composite MAG, and a BSSG. With 30 days of sufficient supplies for sustained operations, the MEB is capable of conducting amphibious assault operations and MPF operations. During potential crisis situations, a MEB may be forward deployed afloat for an extended period to provide an immediate combat response. A MEB can operate independently or serve as the advance echelon of a MEF. The MEB CE is embedded in the MEF CE and is identified by line number for training and rapid deployment.

2401. Combat Service Support Element

The BSSG is the CSSE for the MEB. The FSSG provides MSSGs with the necessary personnel and equipment to accomplish their missions. The MSSGs provide the MEU with the following CSS:

- Supply support.
- Maintenance support.
- Transportation support.
- Deliberate engineering support.
- Medical and dental services.
- Automated information processing support.

- Utilities support.
- Landing support (port and airfield support operations).
- Disbursing services.
- Legal services.
- Postal services.
- Accompanying supplies (classes I, II, III[B], IV, V[W], and IX) necessary to support the MEU for 30 days.

2402. Aviation Combat Element

The MEB composite MAG generally receives ground tactical logistic support from a composite MWSS (fixed-wing [FW])/(rotary-wing [RW]) or both MWSS(RW) and MWSS(FW), depending on the number of airfields ashore. Normally, the aviation maintenance support for MEB aircraft is provided by the aviation intermediate maintenance department (AIMD) of the general purpose amphibious assault ships and the aviation logistics support ship (TAVB).

2403. Ground Combat Element

The GCE consists of a reinforced infantry regiment. Specific reinforcements vary but generally include artillery, reconnaissance, light armor, tanks, antiarmor, amphibious vehicles, and combat engineer detachments. The GCE has limited logistic capability organic to the various elements.

Section V. Marine Expeditionary Unit Organizations and Capabilities

The MEU is the MAGTF routinely forward deployed for presence and quick response to a developing contingency. The MEU is organized and equipped to provide a rapidly deployable, sea-based capability with 15 days of self-sustainment. The MEU may serve as an enabler for larger missions in the event that the situation or mission requires additional capabilities or resources.

2501. Combat Service Support Element

The MSSG is the CSSE for the MEU. The FSSG provides MSSGs with the necessary personnel and equipment to accomplish their missions. The MSSGs provide the MEU with the following CSS:

- Supply support.
- Maintenance support.
- Transportation support.
- Deliberate engineering support.
- Medical and dental services.
- Automated information processing support.
- Utilities support.
- Landing support (port and airfield support operations).
- Disbursing services.
- Legal services.

- Postal services.
- Accompanying supplies (classes I, II, III[B], IV, V[W], and IX) necessary to support the MEU for 15 days.

2502. Aviation Combat Element

The MEU ACE generally consists of a medium-lift helicopter squadron reinforced with several heavy-lift helicopters and AV-8B attack aircraft. Aerial refueling support is provided by a shore-based aerial refueling detachment. Normally, the aviation maintenance support for MEU aircraft is provided by the aviation intermediate maintenance department (AIMD) of the general purpose amphibious assault ship on which the ACE is embarked. The MALS augments the ship's capabilities with personnel and materiel. If the MEU ACE is directed ashore, the ship operating offshore or a MALS deployed ashore provides intermediate-level support.

2503. Ground Combat Element

The GCE consists of a reinforced infantry battalion that forms a battalion landing team (BLT). Specific reinforcements vary but generally include artillery, reconnaissance, light armor and/or tanks, antiarmor, amphibious vehicles, and combat engineer detachments. The GCE has limited logistic capability organic to the various elements.

Section VI. Task Organizations

Logistic and CSS organizations, units, and sections within larger organizations are either permanently organized or task-organized. Task-organizing is basic to the concept of the MAGTF. It is the process by which commanders organize the forces under their command to meet the requirements of the mission. MAGTFs have a wide range of capabilities that are further enhanced by task-organizing. This gives commanders the ability to respond to different types and intensities of contingency situations. Task organizations are used in garrison at the operational and tactical levels to provide support at widely separated locations.

2601. Combat Service Support Organizations

The FSSG commanders form temporary task organizations when existing organizations and command relationships are inadequate for a particular situation. Task-organizing allows FSSG commanders to tailor their forces to provide the specific type and scope of logistic support required by the supported unit, the mission, and the tactical situation. The decision to task-organize is based on the priorities of the MAGTF commander and those of the supported organizations. The FSSG commander may assign personnel and units missions in support of another commander or may coordinate with the MAGTF commander to attach the units to another organization.

a. Combat Service Support Group

A combat service support group (CSSG) is a task organization of CSS assets, similar in size and capability to a BSSG. A CSSG is formed to provide CSS to a large GCE task force, reinforce regiment, or composite MAG conducting independent operations or geographically separated from the MEF. A CSSG is capable of task-organizing subordinate CSSDs. Currently 1st FSSG has CSSG-1

established to support 7th Marines (Rein) at Twentynine Palms, California and 3d FSSG has CSSG-3 established to support 3d Marines (Rein) and the Aviation Support Element at Kaneohe Bay, Hawaii.

b. Combat Service Support Detachment

A CSSD is a separate task organization of combat service support assets formed for the purpose of providing rearming, refueling, and/or repairing capabilities to the MAGTF or designated subordinate elements (e.g., a battalion conducting independent operations or an aircraft squadron operating at a remote airfield). Normally, the combat service support element provides the CSSD command element.

Establishing CSSDs enables a CSS commander to provide logistic support to a wide array of supported units. Each CSSD can be tailored to meet the specific logistic requirements of supported units across the MAGTF. When formed, CSSDs are assigned numeric designators based on the following sequence:

- 1st FSSG: 11-19 and 51-59.
- 2d FSSG: 21-29 and 61-69.
- 3d FSSG: 31-39 and 71-79.
- 4th FSSG: 41-49 and 81-89.

c. Combat Service Support Operations Center

The combat service support operations center (CSSOC) is the CSSE commander's agency to control and coordinate the day-to-day operations of the organization. The CSSOC focuses on meeting the needs of supported units. During combat operations, FSSGs, MSSGs, and CSSDs operate CSSOCs 24 hours a day to monitor and record the status of CSS operations. The CSSOC is discussed further in chapter 3.

2602. Movement Control Organizations

At the direction of COMMARFOR, the MEF activates a series of movement control agencies, both at the operational and tactical levels. These organizations help the MAGTF commander move forces to deploy and/or redeploy. These movement control organizations function in the same manner during both peacetime and periods of conflict.

These organizations are staffed and equipped by permanent units. For smaller MAGTFs, movement control organizations may be no more than one or two individuals in the S-4. Subordinate movement control organizations at the battalion, squadron, regiment, and air group levels may function temporarily while their organizations are moving. See chapter 3 for a comprehensive discussion of the command and control of movement control operations.

a. Force Movement Control Center

The force movement control center (FMCC) provides the MEF commander with the ability to control and coordinate all deployment activities. The FMCC coordinates with the U.S. Transportation Command (USTRANSCOM) and the transportation operating components regarding transportation requirements, priorities, and allocations. The operating components are the Military Sealift Command (MSC), Air Mobility Command (AMC), and Military Traffic Management Command (MTMC).

The FMCC directs the deployment support activities of the division, MAW, FSSG, and deploying MAGTFs and units and/or detachments. It also coordinates with supporting organizations and/or commands to meet the deploying MAGTF commander's priorities. Normally, the FMCC includes both operation and logistic representation, but the actual structure of the FMCC is determined by the size and complexity of the MAGTF deployment. Movement control throughout the MEF commander's assigned battlespace is a major consideration for planning and executing the

single battle. The MEF commander may therefore direct the FSSG commander to develop and execute the MEF movement control plan. The FSSG commander uses the logistic movement control center (LMCC) to accomplish these tasks.

b. Logistic Movement Control Center

The principle focus of the LMCC is to allocate, schedule, and coordinate ground transportation requirements based on the MEF commander's priorities. It requires significant augmentation to exercise command, control, and enforcement over movement control. The LMCC supports the planning and execution of MAGTF movements and reports directly to the FMCC. The LMCC may be augmented by base, station, host nation, or other organizations. Separate LMCCs support units or elements moving from separate geographic areas.

Following the MAGTF movement schedule when activated, the LMCC controls and coordinates all equipment augmentation, Marine Corps and commercial transportation, movement scheduling, materials handling equipment, and other movement support from origin to ports of embarkation. In addition, it coordinates activities with base and station operations support groups and directs the efforts of the DACGs and AACGs, port operations groups, beach operations groups, and unit movement control centers.

c. Unit Movement Control Center

Every deploying unit down to battalion, squadron, and company level activates a unit movement control center (UMCC). UMCCs may consist of a single individual. The UMCC—

- Ensures that units are prepared for embarkation.
- Directs marshaling.
- Coordinates assets.
- Identifies additional support requirements.
- Coordinates the movement of forces to aerial ports of embarkation (APOEs) and surface ports of embarkation (SPOEs), as directed by the LMCC.

d. Departure Airfield Control Group and Arrival Airfield Control Group

The AACGs and DACGs are formed from the FSSG support battalion and respond to LFSP or LMCC direction.

A DACG is responsible for receiving deploying equipment from units at the APOE and for coordinating with the Air Force airlift control element. DACGs ensure that cargo and personnel are properly prepared for air shipment and positioned at the ready line.

AACGs operate in the aerial port of debarkation (APOD). They ensure that cargo and personnel are properly unloaded from aircraft and pass through the APOD.

2603. Maritime Prepositioning Force Organizations

The arrival of the MPF and its assembly into a fighting force are critical operational concerns of the MEF in general and the FSSG in particular. The MEF forms a number of temporary organizations whose purpose is to transform the cargo and personnel of an MPF into a viable combat force.

a. Survey, Liaison, and Reconnaissance Party

The survey, liaison, and reconnaissance party (SLRP) is a self-sustaining task organization formed from the MAGTF and Navy support element (NSE). It conducts reconnaissance, establishes liaison with in-theater authorities, and initiates preparations for the arrival of the main body of the fly-in echelon and the maritime prepositioning ships squadron. The SLRP normally deploys to the arrival and assembly area (AAA) under MAGTF cognizance.

b. Offload Preparation Party

The offload preparation party (OPP) is a temporary task organization that consists of maintenance technicians, embarkation specialists, and equipment operators drawn from all elements of the MAGTF and the NSE. It prepares equipment on board the maritime prepositioning ships (MPS) for debarkation in the AAA. The OPP can join the MPS before sailing, during transit, or on arrival in the AAA. Ideally, the OPP boards the MPS 96 hours before arrival in the AAA.

c. Arrival and Assembly Operations Group

The arrival and assembly operations group (AAOG) is a temporary task organization that controls and coordinates the arrival and assembly operations of maritime prepositioning forces. Normally, the AAOG deploys as an element of the advance party and initiates operations at the arrival airfield. The AAOG is formed from elements of the MAGTF and liaison personnel from the NSE during an MPF operation. The AAOG controls the following four subordinate throughput organizations:

- POG is responsible for preparing the port prior to arrival of the MPS and for the throughput of equipment and supplies as they are offloaded from the ships.
- Beach operations group (BOG) organizes and develops the beach area as necessary to support the offload and throughput of equipment and supplies.
- AACG is responsible for the control and coordination of the offload of airlifted units and equipment at the airfield.
- Movement control center (MCC) plans, schedules, routes, and controls the movement of personnel, equipment, and supplies from the port, beach, or airfields to the unit assembly areas.

2604. Amphibious Ship-to-Shore Movement Organizations

a. Navy Control Organization

The Navy is responsible for control of the ship-to-shore movement of both waterborne and helicopterborne assault forces. The structure of the Navy control organization varies depending on the scope of the operation and number and type of beaches and helicopter landing zones (HLZs). The TACLOG is the Marine agency for advising and assisting the Navy control organization regarding landing force requirements during the ship-to-shore movement.

(1) Control for Waterborne Movement. The following officers are responsible for controlling waterborne ship-to-shore movements:

- **Central Control Officer.** Normally aboard the ATF flagship, the central control officer directs the movement of all scheduled waves. After scheduled waves have landed, the central control officer continues to coordinate movement to and from the beach until unloading is complete. The central control ship is normally some distance seaward of the line of departure.

- **Primary Control Officer.** The senior Navy commander appoints a primary control officer for each transport organization that lands a regimental landing team across a colored beach or a geographically separated beach. From aboard the primary control ship, this officer directs movement to and from a colored beach. The primary control ship is usually near the line of departure.

(2) Control for the Helicopterborne Movement. The senior Navy commander, through the tactical air officer, controls helicopters during the ship-to-shore movement. Control agencies include the tactical air control center (TACC) and HDCs. These agencies control helicopters to meet both tactical and logistic requirements. They also coordinate the movement of helicopters with other aircraft movement. The helicopter control system must be flexible and responsive to the requirements of the tactical situation. See NWP 3-02.1/FMFM 1-8; FMFM 5-40, *Offensive Air Support*; and MCWP 3-24, *Assault Support*.

b. Landing Force Control Organization

The landing force control organization interfaces with the Navy control organization to keep it apprised of landing force requirements and priorities

as well as to advise on transportation methods and phasing of serials. Although the exact structure of the landing force control organization varies, it is usually composed of the landing force operations center, landing force support party, and tactical-logistical group.

(1) Landing Force Operations Center. During the initial phases of the amphibious operation, the landing force operations center (LFOC) is the MAGTF commander's command post afloat. Normally, the LFOC is located in the vicinity of ATF's combat information center. The LFOC maintains communications with the LFSP elements and with the landing force TACLOG, which functions as the landing force liaison with the Navy control organization through the central control officer. From the LFOC, the MAGTF commander—

- Monitors the progress of the ship-to-shore movement and operations ashore.
- Controls assigned assault units.
- Communicates with subordinate commanders.

(2) Landing Force Support Party. The ship-to-shore movement is a complex evolution that generates intensive activity under combat conditions. The LFSP is a temporary landing force organization composed of Navy and landing force elements tasked to provide initial combat support and CSS to the landing force during the ship-to-shore movement. Its mission is to support the landing and movement of troops, equipment, and supplies across the beaches and into HLZs. The LFSP facilitates the smooth execution of the landing plan. It is specifically task-organized to facilitate a rapid buildup of combat power ashore by ensuring an organized and uniform flow of personnel, equipment, and supplies over the beach in support of the landing force scheme of maneuver.

(3) Tactical-Logistical Group. At the landing force level, the TACLOG is composed of representatives from the MAGTF G-3/S-3 and G-4/S-4. The TACLOG advises the Navy control organization of the ship-to-shore movement requirements to meet the tactical requirements ashore and to assist in identifying support resources. To provide this advice, the TACLOG—

- Keeps abreast of which serials have landed.
- Monitors the command, tactics, and logistical nets to anticipate requirements ashore for serials.
- Provides the central control officer with advice on the priority of landing additional serials.
- Recommends modes of transportation for serials, when appropriate.

The TACLOGs subordinate to the landing force TACLOG are established by each subordinate commander in the landing force. A subordinate TACLOG may also be established aboard the helicopter transport group commander's ship to provide liaison for the helicopterborne force. These subordinate TACLOGs coordinate duties between the Navy control organization, the landing force, and the landing force TACLOG.

c. Naval Beach Group

The naval beach group is "a permanently organized naval command within an amphibious force comprised of a commander and staff, a beachmasters unit, an amphibious construction battalion, and an assault craft unit, designed to provide an administrative group from which required naval tactical components may be made available to the attack force commander and to the amphibious landing force commander to support the landing of one division (reinforced)." (JP 1-02)

This group task-organizes beach party teams and/or groups for specific tasks. It can make limited beach improvements to help in the landing and the evacuation of casualties and EPWs. For additional information on the naval beach group, refer to NWP 3-02.14 and JP 3-02, *Joint Doctrine for*

Amphibious Operations. The naval beach group is an administrative organization that provides—

- A beach party.
- Pontoon causeway teams.
- Self-propelled pontoon barges.
- Elements for lighterage or transfer line operations.
- Warping tug teams for tending causeways and salvage.
- Ship-to-shore bulk fuel elements.
- Underwater wire communications from the primary control ship to the beach.

d. Other Navy Landing Support Assets

(1) Medical Regulating Center. The medical regulating center remains up to date on all medical capabilities. It coordinates the efforts of the medical regulating section, which maintains an up-to-date listing of the medical capabilities of ships in the objective area and advises the HDC and/or primary control officer on the status of CRTSs. For further information, refer to MCWP 4-11.1.

(2) Navy Cargo Handling and Port Group. The Navy cargo handling and port group supervises the planning for and unloading of MSC or MSC-chartered ships used in amphibious operations. Additional information is available in JP 3-02.2, NWP 3-02.3/FMFM 1-5, *Maritime Prepositioning Force (MPF) Operations,* and NWP 3-02.1/FMFM 1-8.

(3) Sea-Air-Land Teams. Sea-air-land (SEAL) teams clear obstacles from the beach. The SEAL team serves as the hydrographic section of the beach party. If it is assigned with the advance force early in the operation, it reports to the beach party commander for direction.

Section VII. Logistic Staff Responsibilities

The logistics staff officer (J-4/G-4/S-4) is the commander's principal assistant for logistics and the focal point for policy formation and overall logistic coordination within the organization and between the organization and supported and/or supporting commands. Logistic officers coordinate logistic planning and operations. These officers also initiate and maintain continuous liaison with other organizational elements, higher headquarters, other Services, and allied forces throughout the planning and execution of military operations.

This section identifies and discusses the duties, responsibilities, and functions of principal logistic staff officers, both internal and external to the MAGTF. See tables 2-1 and 2-2, on page 2-24.

Table 2-1. Officers Responsible for CE, ACE, GCE, and CSSE Logistics.

General Staff	Chief of Staff	Manpower or Personnel Staff Officer	Operations Staff Officer	Logistics Staff Officer	Aviation Logistics Officer	Comptroller
special staff officer (logistics)	provost marshal staff judge advocate chaplain	adjutant personnel officer morale, welfare, and recreation officer postal officer disbursing officer legal officer	civil affairs officer CSSE - ground supply support coordinator - ground maintenance support coordinator - transportation support coordinator - engineer support coordinator - medical support officer - dental support officer - support officers for services functions	ground supply officer aviation supply officer fiscal officer maintenance management (ground equipment) officer ordnance officer aviation ordnance officer engineer airfield services officer motor transport officer strategic mobility officer embarkation officer surgeon (medical) dental officer food services officer	aviation supply officer aviation maintenance officer aviation ordnance officer avionics officer	disbursing officer fiscal officer USN budget and accounting officer USMC budget and accounting officer

1. Individual commands may vary based on the commander's preference and/or availability of personnel.

2. Normally, staff structure at lower levels parallels staff structure at the element level.

3. Aviation logistics, supply, maintenance, ordnance, and avionics officers are unique to ACE and MAW headquarters. In ACEs based on a single aircraft group or composite squadron, these posts are normally assumed as additional duties by the commanding officer of the assigned host MALS and the squadron or detachment staff.

4. The staff judge advocate and the legal officer coordinate legal functions within the command and between the command and the CSSE legal services support section.

5. If the command does not have a comptroller the disbursing officer or fiscal officer assumes the comptroller's duties.

6. In the CSSE, the G-3/S-3, through functional-area support officers, is responsible for ground CSS operations in support of the MAGTF. The CSSE G-3/S-3 normally does not supersede the cognizant staff officers (e.g., G-1/S-1, G-4/S-4, etc.) for internal support of the CSSE.

7. The aviation ordnance officer and strategic mobility officer are assigned to MEF common equipment facilities.

8. The supply officer, under the cognizance of the G-4/S-4, may also be designated as the fiscal officer.

9. The USMC and USN budget and accounting officers are unique to the ACE.

Table 2-2. CE, ACE, GCE, and CSSE Tactical-Level Logistic Responsibilities.

General Staff	Chief of Staff	Manpower or Personnel Staff Officer	Operations Staff Officer	Logistics Staff Officer	Aviation Logistics Officer	Command, Control, Communications, and Computers Systems Officer	Comptroller
supply				ground supply (aviation supply)	aviation supply		
maintenance				ground maintenance	aviation maintenance		
transportation				transportation			
general engineering				general engineering			
health services				health services			
Services CSS services	security legal	disbursing postal exchange legal graves registration	civil affairs CSSE - disbursing - postal - exchange - security - legal services - graves registration				
command services	religious ministries	band personnel administration morale, welfare, and recreation		financial management billeting messing		communications and information services	financial management

1. Individual commands may vary based on the commander's preference and/or availability of personnel.

2. Normally, staff structure at lower levels parallels staff structure at the element level. However, at lower levels special staff responsibilities may be assigned as additional duties rather than as primary duties.

3. The aviation logistics officer is unique to ACE and MAW headquarters. In ACEs based on a single aircraft group or composite squadron, this posts is normally assumed as additional duties by the commanding officer of the assigned host MALS and the squadron or detachment staff.

4. The staff judge advocate and the legal officer coordinate legal functions within the command and between the command and the CSSE legal services support section.

5. In the CSSE, the G-3/S-3, through functional-area support officers, is responsible for ground CSS operations in support of the MAGTF. The CSSE G-3/S-3 normally does not supersede the cognizant staff officers (e.g., G-1/S-1, G-4/S-4, etc.) for internal support of the CSSE.

6. At a MEF common equipment facility, the logistics officer is responsible for aviation supply.

7. The logistics officer is responsible for financial management if the command does not have a comptroller.

8. The supply officer, under the cognizance of the G-4/S-4, may also be designated the fiscal officer.

2701. Joint Task Force

Normally, MAGTFs operate as part of a joint or combined task force. A MEF may serve as the nucleus for such a task force, especially when a MEU is already in theater as the result of forward deployment. In such cases, the Marine Corps Service component commander may be tasked to provide the JTF headquarters nucleus; the MEU would become the initial logistic capability on site. The JTF commander requires direct connectivity with the commander in chief (CINC) and with the entire JTF. Work with non-Department of Defense, international and local agencies, as well as all components of the JTF requires enhanced C2, liaison, and support for logistics. The MAGTF G-4/S-4 may become the J-4 for the JTF and perform the following functions:

- Formulate logistic plans.
- Coordinate and supervise—
  - Supply.
  - Maintenance.
  - Repair.
  - Evacuation.
  - Transportation.
  - Engineering.
  - Salvage.
  - Procurement.
  - Health services.
  - Mortuary affairs.
  - Communications systems.
  - Host nation support.
  - Other related logistic activities.
- Understand the established policies of the other military Services operating as part of the JTF.
- Advise the commander of the logistical support that can be provided for proposed courses of action (COAs).
- Formulate policies to ensure effective logistic support for all forces in the command.
- Coordinate the execution of the commander's policies and guidance.
- Establish an MLSE to coordinate multinational logistic operations.

2702. Marine Forces

When conducting sustained operations ashore, Marine forces are usually part of a joint or combined force, and the COMMARFOR is subordinate to the JFC. The MAGTF commander may serve as COMMARFOR and must comply with operational direction from the JFC. The COMMARFOR must be capable of coordinating combat, combat support, and CSS activity with adjacent units from other Services and allied nations as well as exercising operational control over assigned forces. Consequently, the MAGTF G-4/S-4 must be able to execute operational logistic functions. The COMMARFOR G-4 is responsible for the following functions:

- Advising the commander and operations staff officer (G-3) on the support required to sustain campaigns and major operations.
- Identifying requirements and coordinating the distribution of resources with the strategic base.
- Anticipating tactical logistic requirements.
- Maximizing the overall effect of support so that the deployment and employment of the force are balanced.
- Planning and supervising the establishment and operation of intermediate and forward support bases. Supervising the reception, staging, onward movement, and integration of Marines reaching the theater.
- Coordinating with joint, other Service, and host nation agencies for logistic support.
- Planning and supervising the reconstitution and redeployment of the MAGTF for follow-on missions.

2703. Marine Air-Ground Task Force

The MAGTF G-4/S-4 is responsible for the following functions:

- Advising the commander and the G-3/S-3 on the readiness status of major equipment and weapons systems.
- Developing policies and identifying requirements, priorities, and allocations for logistic support.
- Integrating organic logistic operations with logistic support from external commands or agencies.

- Coordinating and preparing the logistic and CSS portions of plans and orders.
- Supervising the execution of the commander's orders regarding logistics and CSS.
- Ensuring that the logistic support concept supports the overall concept of operations and the scheme of maneuver by identifying and resolving support deficiencies.
- Collating the support requirements of subordinate organizations by identifying the support requirements that can be satisfied with organic resources and passing unsatisfied requirements to the appropriate higher and/or external command.
- Supervising some command services, such as messing and, as directed, billeting and financial management functions.
- Coordinating with the amphibious task force (ATF) N-4 and the MAGTF G-4/S-4 for aviation-peculiar support under the ACE G-4/S-4 cognizance.

2704. Combat Service Support Organization

The ground-common or aviation-peculiar logistic support CSS organization G-3/S-3 coordinates with supported organizations for their support requirements. The G-3/S-3 is responsible for—

- Coordinating with both the G-3/S-3 and G-4/S-4 of the supported organizations to identify support requirements and to develop estimates of supportability for their concepts of operations.
- Recommending the task organization of supporting CSSDs based on guidance from higher headquarters, the concepts of operation, and schemes of maneuver of the supported organizations.

- Coordinating and supervising execution of the command's logistic support operations and providing liaison elements to the supported commands. (The CSSE is the primary agency for nonaviation-peculiar logistic support operations in the MAGTF and the ACE is responsible for aviation-peculiar support.)
- Coordinating with the G-3/S-3 of the supported organizations during the development of their concepts of operations and schemes of maneuver to ensure that they are supportable.

2705. Aviation Logistics Department and Marine Aviation Logistics Squadron

The assistant chief of staff of the aviation logistics department (ALD) and the commanding officer of the MALS optimize aircraft readiness by coordinating intermediate and depot-level maintenance, ordnance, supply, and avionics support for operational squadrons. They perform the following functions:

- Determine aircraft-specific logistic support requirements, assign priorities, and allocate logistic resources for the ACE; develop the level of support with Navy activities when resources are to be provided by the Navy.
- Integrate the capabilities of the ACE logistic support organizations with the MAGTF G-3/S-3/G-4/S-4, the CSSE G-3/S-3, and the ACE G-3/S-3/G-4/S-4.
- Coordinate aviation-peculiar support with the ATF N-4 and the MAGTF G-4/S-4.
- Prepare and supervise applicable portions of the ACE operation order (OPORD) and/or operation plan (OPLAN) relating to logistic functions.

Chapter 3

Command and Control

"Command and control is the means by which a commander recognizes what needs to be done and sees to it that appropriate actions are taken." (MCDP 6). Through effective tactical-level logistic command and control, commanders recognize and prioritize critical logistic requirements and direct the appropriate logistic and CSS response. This chapter describes procedures, responsibilities, and systems that are the means for executing tactical logistic and CSS command and control in the MAGTF.

Command and control processes assist commanders in dealing with the following influences on warfare:

- **Uncertainty.** Commanders seek to clearly identify support requirements for tactical-level logistic and CSS operations. Absolute certainty will never be achieved in the dynamic situations that are characteristic of warfare. Commanders reduce uncertainty by employing a fully integrated planning process, prioritizing requirements, ensuring redundancy and flexibility in their plans, as well as maintaining situational awareness.
- **Time.** There will rarely be enough time available to complete all desired planning and preparation for logistic operations, especially at the tactical level. Therefore, the planning, decision, execution, and assessment (PDE&A) cycle must be tailored to function effectively in the time available. The PDE&A is facilitated by a continuous exchange of information between all command echelons and functional activities and by exchange of liaison officers.
- **Tempo.** It is essential to maintain a constant, uninterrupted operational rhythm that leaves insufficient time for the enemy to react. To assist in maintaining a command's operational tempo, logisticians must anticipate support required and balance this with other battlespace activities. For example, attacks should not be interrupted or delayed because units need resupply or because CSSDs are using critical main supply routes. To maximize operational tempo in this way, logisticians must participate fully in the operations planning process, stay updated on the status of battlespace activities, and prepare to conduct support operations.

Command and control for tactical-level logistics is focused on monitoring, directing, and executing logistic operations in support of tactical operations. Tactical logisticians establish and maintain communications links to higher, adjacent, and supporting and/or supported commands to ensure MAGTF elements can pass logistic information. (See figure 3-1, on page 3-2.)

3001. Establishing Command and Control

The MAGTF commander exercises command and control over MAGTF logistics. The commander evaluates logistic requirements based on subordinate organizations' capabilities, mission, and concept of operations. Based on this logistic evaluation, the MAGTF commander provides guidance to subordinate commanders. Typically, the guidance addresses three primary areas: requirements, priorities, and allocations. The subordinate commanders employ organic logistic resources to support their respective elements and then identify requirements beyond their organic capabilities to the CSSE.

The CSSE commander assigns support missions to subordinate elements based on the tactical situation, the supported unit's needs, and CSSE capabilities. The CSSE commander coordinates mission assignments with the MAGTF commander and supported unit commanders.

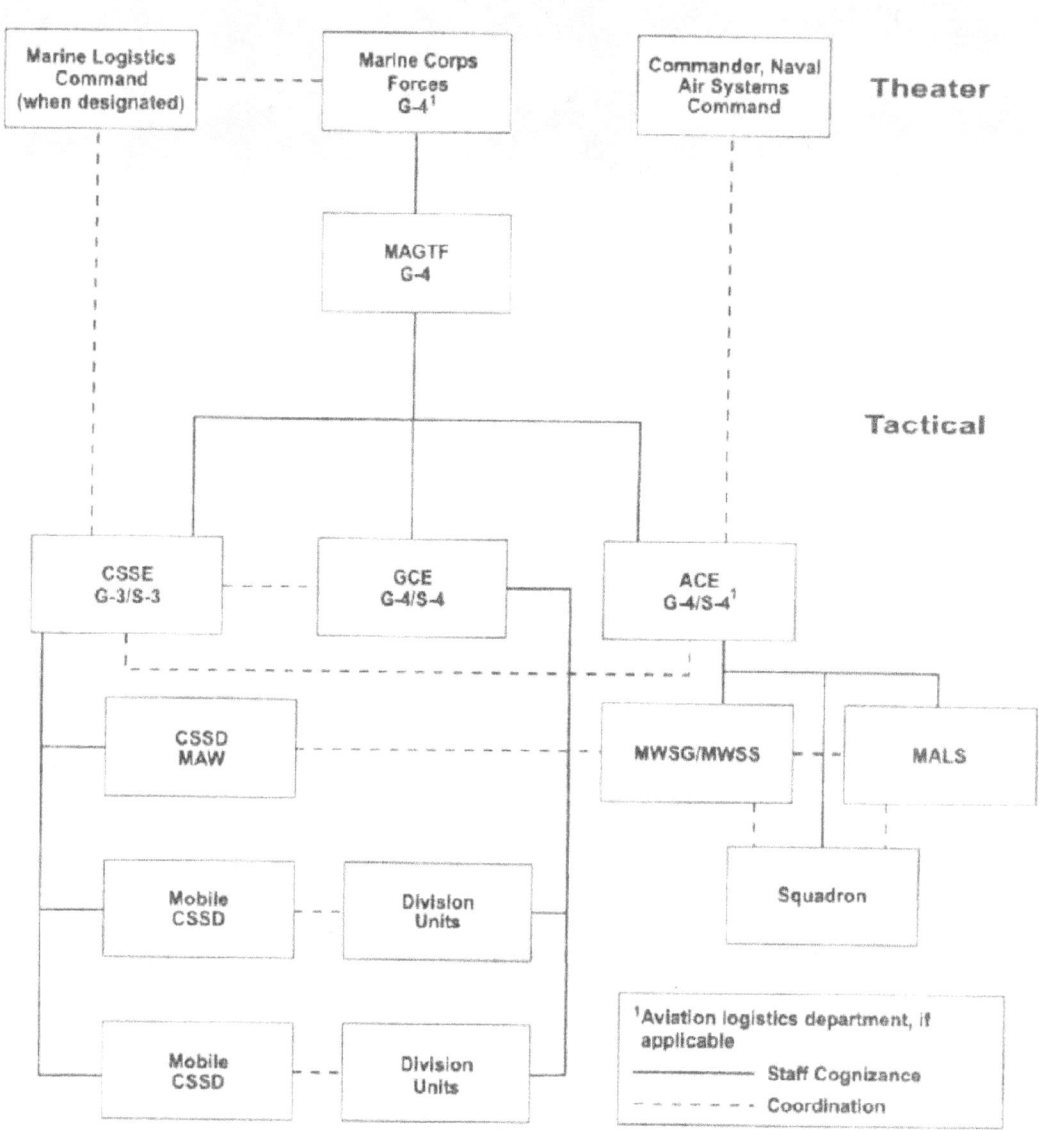

Figure 3-1. Staff Cognizance of Tactical-Level Logistics.

a. Task Organization

By task-organizing, the commander retains centralized control and provides for decentralized execution, which promotes responsiveness. Existing T/Os and T/Es provide logistic capabilities within most organizations, but the majority of the MAGTF's tactical-level logistic capability is contained within CSS units. The MAGTF commander organizes assets to optimize support for the main effort and to continue support of the whole force. Task-organization considerations can be found in appendix A.

b. Command Relationships

CSS units provide support to the other elements of the MAGTF via either a general or direct support relationship. In a support relationship, the CSS unit, while responsive to the needs of the supported unit, remains under the command of its parent organization. The CSS commander retains control over subordinate units, which enhances centralized command and control and decentralized execution. While this is the normal method, it is not the only method. Both permanent and task-organized CSS units can be attached to other organizations. The MAGTF commander may direct the CSSE commander to attach CSS units to GCE or ACE units. The CSSE commander retains responsibility for supporting CSS units attached to other units but cannot assign or change their mission.

c. Mission Assignments

A primary means of maintaining command and control over logistic units is the assignment of formal missions, particularly when CSS units function in a support relationship. The formalized mission structure helps by standardizing the responsibilities associated with each mission and allows the commander to tailor logistics to the tactical situation.

3002. Logistic and Combat Service Support Missions

Formal missions may be either standard or nonstandard. Standard missions are direct support and general support. A nonstandard mission is any mission other than one of the standard missions. Formal missions dictate relationships, responsibilities, and C2 procedures. They facilitate planning for future operations by providing for on-order tasks. They also simplify the planning and execution of MAGTF operations.

a. Inherent Responsibilities

Formal missions dictate specific responsibilities for both the supporting unit and the supported unit. Mission assignments establish the CSS unit's relationship to the supported unit as well as to other CSS units. A CSS unit or organization with a direct support mission—

- Responds to CSS requests in priority from—
  - Supported unit.
  - Higher CSS headquarters.
  - Own units.
- Provide liaison personnel to the supported unit.
- Establishes communications with—
  - Supported unit.
  - Higher CSS headquarters.
- Is positioned by the supported unit.

A CSS unit or organization with a general support mission—

- Responds to CSS requests in priority from—
  - Higher CSS headquarters.
  - Supported unit.
  - Own units.
- Establishes liaison with the supported unit(s).
- Establishes communications with—
  - Supported unit(s).
  - Higher CSS headquarters.
- Is positioned by higher CSS headquarters.

(1) Priority of Response. For each mission, the priority of response tells the supporting commander precisely who has priority of services. Support priorities are the primary distinction between standard missions.

(2) Liaison. The supporting commander decides what type(s) of liaison to use. See paragraph 3007.

(3) Communications. Communications between the supporting and supported units is essential. The supporting commander, with the concurrence of the parent headquarters, decides what type of communications to use.

(4) Positioning. Positioning is not simply locating facilities on the ground. It includes the authority to displace facilities to new locations. The CSSE commander has the responsibility and authority for determining the general location and the displacement time of ground-common CSS units and facilities to ensure continued support to the MAGTF. The subordinate CSS commander recommends the time for displacements and selects exact locations for new facilities when given their general locale. Because CSS units are often in areas that are under the control of other MAGTF elements, the CSSE commander must coordinate with those elements and the MAGTF

commander before establishing or moving units and facilities.

b. Mission Statement Elements

Every CSS mission statement has four essential elements. Three of these elements are mandatory and should always be included. The fourth element is optional and may be used to provide additional information and guidance.

(1) Mandatory Elements. Always include the following mission statement elements:

- Identification of the supporting unit.
- Designation of the standard mission assigned.
- Identification of the supported unit.

An example of a simplified mission statement containing only the three mandatory elements is: *CSSD-28 provides direct support to 8th Marines.*

(2) Optional Elements. If the commander anticipates a change in mission, a fourth element may be added to the mission statement to facilitate future operations. This optional element may provide a warning order or additional information or guidance necessary for continuity of operations, for example: *Be prepared to provide general support to 2d Marine Division.* The complete identity of the supported unit must always be included. This added element alerts both the supporting and supported units to expect and prepare for a change of mission.

The commander may also use the optional element to provide additional guidance. For example: *7th Engineer Support Battalion (-) provides general support to the MEF. Attach one reinforced platoon to CSSD-41, and place one platoon in direct support of MWSS-44.* Notice the CSSE commander does not select the specific subordinate elements for alternative missions. Selecting specific platoons is the prerogative of the battalion and company commanders. It is, however, within the CSSE commander's authority to direct different missions or command relationships for subordinate elements of the CSSE and to task-organize subordinate elements. The CSSE com-

mander does so in coordination with the MAGTF commander, the supported unit commander, and the CSSE's subordinate commanders.

c. Standard Missions

(1) Direct Support. Direct support is "a mission requiring a force to support another specific force and authorizing it to answer directly the supported force's request for assistance." (JP 1-02)

A CSS unit assigned a direct-support mission is immediately responsive to the needs of the supported unit. It furnishes continuous support to that unit and coordinates its operations to complement the concept of operations of the supported unit. The direct-support mission creates a one-to-one relationship between supporting and supported units. The higher headquarters of the supporting and supported units become involved only on an exception basis. The supported unit sends requests directly to the supporting unit.

A direct-support mission may be assigned to either a functional or task-organized CSS unit. A functional unit or a task-organized unit may be either a single-function unit or a multifunction unit (provides support in two or more CSS functional areas). The following are examples of direct-support missions assigned to functional and task-organized units:

- **Functional Units.** The CSSE commander may assign the direct-support mission to any functional subordinate organization (e.g., engineer or motor transport organizations).

- **Task-Organized Units.** The CSSE commander may assign the direct-support mission to a task-organized unit such as a CSSD. CSSDs are most often in direct-support. The commander must ensure that the task-organized unit has enough assets to accomplish the direct-support mission. Of particular concern is the ability to establish and maintain communications with the supported unit.

(2) General Support. A CSS unit assigned a general support mission supports the MAGTF or several units within the MAGTF under the direction of the CSSE commander.

The general support mission is the most centralized mission. CSSE commanders retain full control over their subordinate units, including establishing the priority of the units' efforts. This does not prevent supported units from dealing directly with various CSS agencies. For example, they submit requisitions directly to the supply source. However, the CSSE commander may control how and when requisitions are filled. The CSSE commander follows the priorities and allocations of the MAGTF commander. In certain cases, the MAGTF commander may stop the issue of supplies or items of equipment without prior approval of the CSSE commander. In other cases, the MAGTF commander might specify a priority of issue for certain items or may assign a specific quantity to each unit.

The MAGTF CSSE always has a general-support mission. However, CSSE commanders may assign different missions to subordinate units consistent with the requirements of the tactical situation. The concept of logistics and CSS, found in Annex D of the MAGTF OPORD, specifically addresses this topic. It tells precisely how to satisfy the requirements of a particular tactical situation. The following are examples of general support missions assigned to functional and task-organized units:

- **Functional Units.** The CSSE commander may assign the general support mission to any subordinate functional organizations. For example, the FSSG commander may give the engineer support battalion the mission of general support of the MAGTF. The battalion would provide support based on the priorities of the MAGTF commander. The CSSE commander would not assign this mission without prior coordination with and approval from the MAGTF commander.
- **Task-Organized Units.** The CSSE commander may assign the general support mission to a task-organized unit such as a CSSD or LFSP. Task-organized CSS units must have sufficient assets to perform the functions associated with

this mission. Of particular concern is the ability to establish and maintain communications and liaison with the supported unit and parent organization.

d. Nonstandard Missions

The CSSE commander normally uses the direct support and/or general support standard missions to meet the needs of the supported force. However, unique situations may dictate the selection of a nonstandard mission. The nonstandard mission must satisfy the requirements of the specific situation and requires detailed planning and coordination.

The optional fourth element of the mission statement is the operative element in the nonstandard mission. The optional element amplifies the basic mission statement and addresses unique responsibilities and relationships.

The mission statement for a nonstandard mission must contain the three mandatory elements. For example: *CSSD-28 provides general support for assigned U.S. and multinational forces.* The optional fourth element, which gives advance information on subsequent missions may also be used, as appropriate.

The mission statement above is adequate for a standard mission. For the CSSD-28 commander, however, it does not provide enough information in this particular case. With standard missions, the CSSD commander immediately knows the associated responsibilities. When assigning a nonstandard mission, the CSSE commander must also give detailed coordinating instructions to amplify the mission statement. Paragraph 3 of the CSSE OPORD should include the following items:

- Priority of response to support requests for—
  - MAGTF units (or name of specific unit).
  - Other U.S. forces.
  - Allied forces (classes I, III, and V only).
- Liaison requirements that—
  - Maintain liaison with supported Marine Corps units on a full-time basis.

- Maintain liaison with other supported units as required.
- Communications responsibilities that—
  - Establish and maintain communications with MAGTF units on a full-time basis.
  - Establish and maintain communications with other elements as required.

3003. Management Procedures in Tactical Logistic Functional Areas

The functional areas of tactical-level logistics are managed with procedures tailored to support particular functions.

a. Supply

MAGTF commanders, in particular CSSE commanders, manage the flow of support from source to consumer. Three management techniques and procedures are critical to supply support.

(1) Control. Supplies should flow by the most direct route from the source to the consumer. CSS units should handle supplies as infrequently as possible.

(a) Records. Records should include only information that is essential to control supply activities and to ensure sustainability.

(b) Stockage Objective. The stockage objective is the maximum quantity of materiel that the CSSE must have on hand to sustain current operations. It consists of the sum of stocks represented by the operating level and the safety level. The operating level is the level required to sustain operations between submission of requisitions or between the arrival of successive shipments. These quantities are based on the established replenishment period (daily, monthly, or quarterly). In combat, the replenishment period is usually shorter than during peacetime operations. The safety level is the quantity required to continue operations if there are minor delays in resupply or unpredictable changes in demand. In combat, the safety level is more critical than during peacetime.

The MAGTF commander prescribes the stockage objective for CSS installations on the basis of the recommendations of the CSSE commander. Selection of the proper stockage objective is critical for proper management of transportation and continued support of combat operations. Too high a stockage objective can place an excessive burden on handling and management systems. Too low a stockage objective can delay or even prevent combat operations.

(c) Reorder Point. The reorder point is that point at which the CSS unit must submit a requisition to maintain the stockage objective. The supply representative requisitions the stockage objective when the sum of the requisition processing time, shipping time, and safety days of supply equals the remaining days of supply based on daily consumption rates. For example:

		Days of Supply
Safety level	=	5
Reorder time	=	2
Shipping time	=	15
Reorder point	=	22

(2) Distribution Methods. The two normal methods of distribution are supply point distribution and unit distribution, but the commander typically uses a combination of the two methods.

(a) Supply Point Distribution. In point distribution, the supported unit picks up the supplies from a central point established by the supporting unit similar to getting fuel from a filling station or food from a store.

(b) Unit Distribution. In unit distribution, the supporting unit (e.g., CSSE) delivers supplies to the supported unit. The supported unit will in turn distribute the supplies to subordinate elements.

(c) Combination. Normally, the commander uses a combination of unit and supply point distribution. The commander assigns top priority for unit distribution to those units that are in contact with the enemy and have limited organic transportation. The commander gives a lower priority to engaged units with more organic transportation. The lowest priority is assigned to units that are not in contact with the enemy. When the available transport has been allocated to unit distribution, the remaining support requirements must be satisfied through supply point distribution.

(3) Replenishment Systems. Replenishment systems are either pull systems, push systems, or a combination of both systems. Selecting a replenishment system is generally based on the availability of supplies and distribution capabilities.

(a) Pull Systems. A pull system requires the consumer to submit a support request. This system provides only what the supported unit requests. Pull systems generally do not anticipate a unit's needs, which makes them less responsive and more efficient than push systems.

(b) Push Systems. Push systems use reports as the requesting document or anticipate demand based on consumption rates. For example, on-hand and usage reports submitted by the supported unit serve as the basis for resupply. The CSSE delivers sustainment based on consumption rates and the desired basic load of the unit without waiting for a requisition. Use of this method could burden the unit with more supplies than it can handle, which makes them more responsive and less efficient.

(c) Combination. The MAGTF commander should specify the most appropriate replenishment system, which is often a combination of the two methods. The decision should be based on the tactical situation, available resources, and the recommendations of the CSSE commander.

b. Maintenance

The goal of maintenance support operations is to keep equipment operational at the using unit. Sup-

porting commanders achieve this goal by balancing centralization of control with decentralization of execution.

Maintenance support procedures need to be flexible and adaptable to changing situations. For example, during the amphibious assault, both the LFSP and supported organizations have limited maintenance capabilities. Normally, the LFSP commander centralizes both control and execution of maintenance operations at the beach support area or landing zone support area. The supported organization commander centralizes control and execution of organic maintenance capabilities in the organizational train. When the CSSE and the remainder of assault organizations go ashore, maintenance capabilities increase. This permits a shift to decentralized execution of maintenance. To perform maintenance as far forward as possible, the commander must decentralize execution of essential tasks.

As a general rule, the goal in combat should be centralized control with decentralized execution to maximize responsiveness. Organizational contact teams from the owning organizations and intermediate maintenance support teams from the CSSE go forward and repair equipment whenever possible.

c. Transportation

The MAGTF commander generally centralizes control of movement at the highest level, typically assigning this responsibility to the CSSE commander. Movements should be regulated and coordinated to prevent congestion and conflicting movements over transportation routes. The transportation system must be highly adaptable to use the MAGTF's limited transportation capabilities effectively. This adaptability enables the commander to maintain continuous movement of personnel, supplies, and equipment. Commanders must maximize the efficient and effective use of transportation assets. The commander must keep equipment loaded and moving while allowing for adequate maintenance and personnel rest.

d. General Engineering

General engineering operations are not subject to unique control measures. The standard support missions and normal engineer support relationships establish the parameters within which general engineering operations are controlled.

e. Health Services

The medical regulating system is activated as necessary for monitoring and controlling the movement of patients through the casualty evacuation and health service support system. The medical regulating system is responsible for patient movement and tracking through successive levels of medical and dental care to provide the appropriate level of care. For information on medical regulating procedures, see MCWP 4-11.1; Naval Warfare Publication (NWP) 4-02.2, *Patient Movement, Part A, Naval Expeditionary Forces Medical Regulating*; and JP 4-02.2, *Joint Tactics, Techniques, and Procedures for Patient Movement in Joint Operations*.

f. Services

The services function provides for the effective administration, management, and employment of military organizations. The administrative subfunctions are categorized as either command or CSS services.

3004. Command Groups and Control Agencies

Each MAGTF element establishes sections to direct operations and control employment of their organic ground-common and aviation-peculiar logistic capabilities. Additionally, they will coordinate CSS requirements with the CSSE.

a. Aviation Ground Support Operations Center

The MWSG and/or MWSS will establish an aviation ground support operations center to control aviation ground support tasks at the ACE airfield(s). The center coordinates the activities of the airfield operations, motor transport operations, engineer operations, medical, and other services sections.

b. Combat Service Support Operations Center

The CSSE establishes a CSSOC that controls and coordinates the day-to-day operations of the CSS organization. The CSSOC focuses on meeting the needs of supported units. The CSSE operations officer supervises the day-to-day functioning of the CSSOC.

The CSSE commander establishes the CSSOC in the CSSE command post. The CSSOC continually monitors and records the status of CSS operations. The CSSOC personnel coordinate and control CSS operations according to the established policies, standing operating procedures (SOPs), and operational decisions of the commander.

The CSSOC is not a separate organization. The CSS unit's operations and communications personnel staff the CSSOC. Local SOPs govern the size and composition of the CSSOC. Generally, the commander has the following CSSOC organization configuration options:

- **Centralized CSSOC.** Figure 3-2 depicts a centralized CSSOC arrangement. An advantage to placing functional representatives for supply, maintenance, transportation, engineering, health services, and services within the CSSOC is that the watch officer has immediate access to technical advice. This option is appropriate when tactical considerations do not require dispersal. A disadvantage can be the high activity level generated by large numbers of personnel and communications in a confined facility. Higher level CSS organizations and those farther to the rear use a centralized CSSOC more frequently than do smaller units.

- **Decentralized CSSOC.** Figure 3-3 depicts a decentralized CSSOC arrangement with functional representatives placed outside the CSSOC. Smaller CSS organizations and those farther forward most often select this option. In some

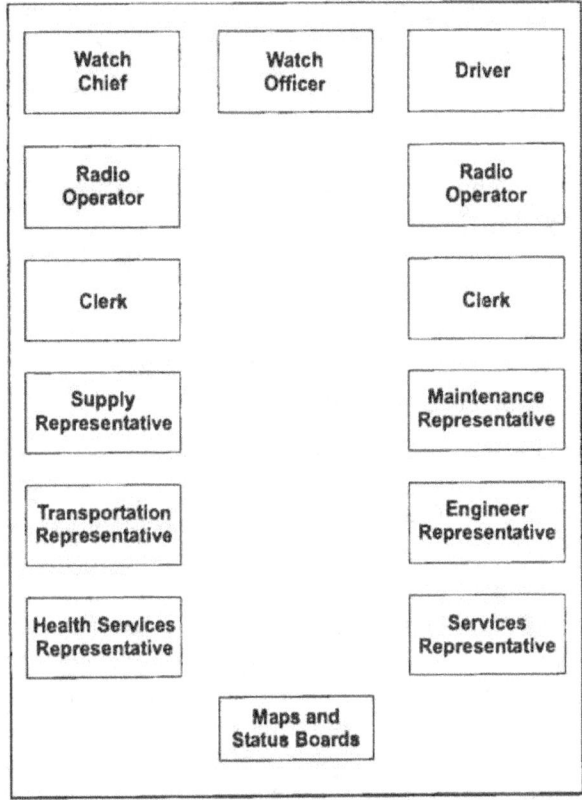

Figure 3-2. Centralized Combat Service Support Operations Center Configuration.

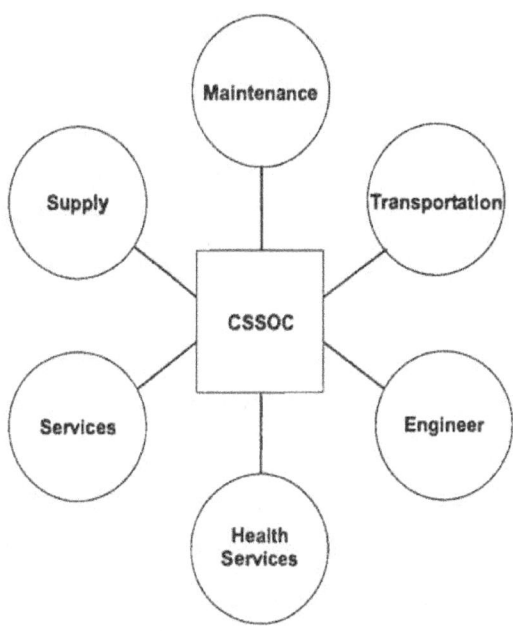

Figure 3-3. Decentralized Combat Service Support Operations Center Configuration.

situations, the CSS unit will not have enough personnel or skills to operate a centralized CSSOC. In other cases, dispersion is a tactical necessity that weighs against centralization.

The CSSOC controls the CSS request net(s) and the CSSA local net(s). The CSSOC has hotlines to subordinates, supported units, and higher headquarters, and it may have teletype or data links. Normal CSSOC functions include the following:

- Receiving and recording operational reports from subordinate units.
- Maintaining current plots of the friendly and enemy situation and displaying the information in the CSSOC.
- Preparing and submitting operational reports to higher headquarters.
- Providing dedicated communications channels for control of CSS operations.
- Transmitting orders and decisions.

- Monitoring the progress of ground-common CSS operations and reporting significant events and incidents to the commander.
- Advising interested staff sections of events or information of immediate concern to them.
- Serving as the principal point of contact for liaison personnel from senior, supported, or adjacent units.
- Maintaining a rear area security (RAS) overlay that depicts preplanned targets, active security measures for CSS installations, and main supply routes within the rear area.
- Coordinating security of CSS installations and main supply routes within the rear area with higher and adjacent elements of the MAGTF.

3005. Communications

Commanders must establish communications with higher, adjacent, and subordinate commands to promote situational awareness and to direct and coordinate military operations. Following the MAGTF communications plan, commanders establish single-purpose and general-purpose nets and/or frequencies for the control of MAGTF and/or element operations, logistic and CSS operations, and general administrative support.

The communications plan must specify the means for requesting and coordinating ground-common and aviation-peculiar logistic support. In addition, the plan must designate the primary and alternate means for logistic communications.

The CSS request net is the most important communications net for day-to-day ground-common CSS operations. The request net is a direct link between the CSS unit and the supported organizations. Each CSSD establishes a CSS request net. Supported organizations enter the net to pass routine or emergency support requests. The CSSE also establishes a CSS request net between itself and its subordinate CSSDs. CSS units use these nets to pass reports, requests, and orders. Supported unit logistic officers should monitor the CSS request net to assess the status of CSS units and to facilitate anticipation of requirements.

3006. Logistic Information Management

Logistic command and control manages the process of providing resources to support the warfighter; information management is a principal tool in this process. Tactical-level logistic information management ranges from manual methods to employment of sophisticated automated systems.

a. Organic Capabilities

Most Marine Corps organizations down to company levels have organic information systems capabilities to manage their personnel, logistic, and training responsibilities. Each organization has one or more computers to support data input to Marine Corps information systems. In addition, MAGs possess a variety of computer hardware suites and software applications for submitting input to and receiving output from Navy support systems.

The communications and information systems officer (G-6/S-6) supervises the command's communications and information systems support operations. The G-6/S-6 is responsible for the technical direction, control, and coordination of communications and information systems support tasks. The G-6/S-6 section works closely with the functional users of automated information system (AIS) to ensure its efficacy.

b. Information Systems Functional User Responsibilities

Functional users of information operate the information systems supporting their functional area. Functional users include every staff section that is supported by communications and information systems. Consequently, all staff principals have functional user responsibilities for the functional areas over which they have staff cognizance. For example, the logistics staff officer has functional user responsibilities for the Asset Tracking Logistics and Supply System (ATLASS). Functional user responsibilities include—

- Serving as the primary point of contact for issues affecting information systems supporting the functional area.
- Conducting the following routine information system administration:
  - Assigning user identification, passwords, and privileges.
  - Performing data and/or file storage and management.
  - Conducting system backups.
- Coordinating with the G-6/S-6 to ensure that adequate hardware, software, trained personnel, and procedures are in place before implementing a new system or system modification.
- Coordinating with the G-6/S-6 to develop and maintain user training programs for communications and information systems.
- Identifying to the G-6/S-6 information system support requirements.
- Identifying to the G-6/S-6 specific communications requirements, including requirements to interface with other information systems and potential interface problems.

• Complying with applicable communications and information systems security measures.

• Reporting malfunctions and outages and coordinating with the G-6/S-6 to restore service.

• Designating an information management officer for the staff section.

c. Marine Air-Ground Task Force Information Systems

Each MAGTF element has computers and required software to support data input for standard logistic information systems as well as to operate related C2 systems. These logistic information systems include manpower, supply, maintenance, transportation, embarkation, disbursing, and aviation-peculiar systems.

(1) Global Command and Control System. The Global Command and Control System (GCCS) is a flexible, evolutionary, interoperable joint command, control, communications, computers, and intelligence (C4I) system. Ultimately, GCCS will connect joint and upper echelon Service systems down to the battalion level and move information both horizontally and vertically. GCCS encompasses the policies, procedures, personnel, AISs, common communications paths, and common switches that are necessary to plan, deploy, sustain, and employ forces.

GCCS provides joint operation planning and execution capabilities and facilitates the deployment and redeployment of Marine Corps forces by using one of the following systems:

• Joint Operation Planning and Execution System (JOPES) is a DOD-directed, Joint Chiefs of Staff (JCS)-specified system for preparing and executing joint OPLANs. This system enables supported commanders, supporting commanders, and USTRANSCOM to manage the deployment of forces and follow-on sustainment for both training and contingencies. The JOPES is one of the first applications incorporated into GCCS. The GCCS and MAGTF C4I systems must be compatible.

• Global Status of Resources and Training System (GSORTS) provides information on the readiness status of units with respect to personnel, equipment, and training.

(2) Global Combat Support System. The Global Combat Support System (GCSS) is not a discrete system but is rather an over-arching capability. Its goal is to provide universal access to information and interoperability of that information within logistics and other support functions. It will share this information with other C2 systems to contribute to the CINC's common operational picture. GCSS consists of applications and shared data in a common operating environment linked through a global network. Ultimately, the GCSS will include near real-time C2 of the logistic pipeline from battlefield to sustaining base—one fused picture of combat support to the warfighter and a closed link between operational C2 and logistics C2.

(3) Marine Corps Training, Exercise, and Employment Program. The Marine Corps Training, Exercise, and Employment Program (MCTEEP) is the Marine Corps operational training, exercise, and employment schedule that Marine Corps operating forces update and maintain by using automated systems. The program is used to schedule training and normal routine exercises.

(4) Marine Air-Ground Task Force II/Logistics Automated Information System. This family of systems supports Marine Corps ground-common logistic data requirements. The MAGTF II system is the primary tool for defining and tailoring a MAGTF and for providing updates to JOPES to support force deployment, planning, and execution. The following MAGTF II/Logistics Automated Information Systems (LOGAISs) provide functional logistic management for sustainment and distribution:

• Marine Air-Ground Task Force Deployment Support System II (MDSS II) enables commanders at various echelons of a MAGTF to build and maintain a data base containing force and equipment data that reflects how the MAGTF is configured for deployment. This data can be maintained during normal day-to-day garrison activities and updated during plan development and execution.

- Transportation Coordinator's Automated Information for Movements System (TC-AIMS) is one of the primary MAGTF II/LOGAISs that provides functional logistic sustainment and distribution management. It provides automated support for motor transport control, planning of support, and coordination of overland movement and convoys. It manages day-to-day use and movement of motor transport and heavy equipment. Its resource management module provides inventory, support requests, and task and dispatch management. It supports convoy management with an embarkation and marshaling module. It tracks critical events, including user time statistics. TC-AIMS interfaces with MDSS II. The integrated MAGTF II and LOGAIS software will enable an improved degree of integration between MDSS II and TCAIMS.

- Asset Tracking Logistics and Supply System (ATLASS) is another primary MAGTF II logistics automated information system. It provides automated support for ground-common supply and maintenance.

(5) Theater Medical Information Program. The Theater Medical Information Program (TMIP) provides a global capability that links medical information data bases to integration centers. These integration centers are accessible to Navy medical personnel and operate in support of Marine forces. The goal for TMIP is to provide theater medical integrated automated information by using the GCCS and the GCSS, which links all echelons of medical care in support of Marine Corps forces.

(6) Naval Tactical Command Support System. The Naval Tactical Command Support System (NTCSS) is used by the ACE. It provides status and ad hoc reports to the Battle Group Logistics Coordinated Support System (BGLCSS). The NTCSS is formulated around the Shipboard Nontactical Automated Data Processing Program III (SNAP III).

(7) Shipboard Nontactical Automated Data Processing Program III. The SNAP III began

the process of integrating shipboard computers by adopting the C2 systems architecture for command support applications. The MWSG and MALS use SNAP III hardware to provide automated information processing support for aviation-peculiar supply, finance, and organizational maintenance management.

(8) Naval Aviation Logistics Command Management Information System. MWSG, MALS, and organizational squadrons use the Naval Aviation Logistics Command Management Information System (NALCOMIS) software application to provide automated information processing support for maintenance of aviation equipment and spares to aviation units and selected base and garrison activities throughout the Marine Corps.

(9) Shipboard Uniform Automated Data Processing System. The Shipboard Uniform Automated Data Processing System (SUADPS) is the supply software application used by MALS to provide financial, inventory, and logistic management of aviation supply support for Marine Corps aircraft.

(10) Conventional Ammunition Integrated Management System. The Conventional Ammunition Integrated Management System (CAIMS) provides on-line inventory management data such as ammunition location, quantity, materiel condition, purpose code, and requisition status.

(11) Retail Ordnance Logistics Management System. The Retail Ordnance Logistics Management System (ROLMS) is a personal computer-based inventory management tool designed to provide automated ammunition requisitioning, status accounting, and inventory management capability at the MALS ammunition supply point level. In addition, ROLMS provides the capability to interface with CAIMS via naval message from remote sites. It is the principle system used to provide visibility of class V(A) and class V(W) at the user level, and is a feeder system to CAIMS. ROLMS is currently replacing the Fleet Optical Scanning Ammunition Management System for class V(A) and Ammunition Logistic System for class V(W).

d. Functional Managers

The MAGTF commander appoints a functional manager for each logistic information system. This individual coordinates processing support as well as data collection and distribution with the G-6/S-6. Functional manager(s) for—

- Supply, maintenance, and disbursing systems are in the CSSE.
- Manpower management systems is the manpower information systems support officer under the MAGTF manpower staff officer (G-1/S-1).
- Aviation maintenance and flight readiness systems are in the ACE.
- Embarkation systems is the MAGTF embarkation officer.

e. Data Communications

The MAGTF G-6 establishes a data communications network. Intratheater data communications is essential to support high-volume CSS information exchange requirements. Users not served by the data communications network must use nonelectronic methods (e.g., courier diskette) to transfer large volumes of logistic data. When electronic data communication means are available, nonelectronic backup methods should still be planned.

f. Information Systems Support Planning

Planning for information systems support must include identification of requirements, establishment of priorities, and allocation of resources. The G-6/S-6 in conjunction with the functional manager must identify the communications and information systems requirements for each major functional system. The information systems management officer then identifies processing priorities and allocates communications and system resources. The MAGTF OPORD must document the requirements, priorities, and allocations. Also, the OPORD must show the data flow within the MAGTF and between the MAGTF and the Defense Information Systems Network data entry point. In addition, the OPORD must depict information systems equipment distribution and maintenance procedures. Ideally, the OPORD references the MAGTF communications and information systems SOP and gives only that supplemental information needed for the specific operation.

3007. Liaison

Liaison is "that contact or intercommunication maintained between elements of military forces or other agencies to ensure mutual understanding and unity of purpose and action." (JP 1-02) Commanders at every level routinely establish contact with other units in their area. At the tactical-level, this contact or liaison is established for general operations and logistic support coordination. Logistic and CSS liaison improves a CSS organization's ability to support the supported unit's concept of operations. Staff liaison may include the temporary or permanent assignment of liaison elements to integrate, coordinate, and execute military operations.

a. Liaison Elements

The liaison element is the commander's personal representative to another command. These designated liaison elements improve the contact and communications essential to effective command.

(1) Liaison Officer. A liaison officer is the most commonly employed technique for establishing and maintaining close, continuous contact between commands. Use of a single individual with the proper rank and experience conserves manpower while guaranteeing contact.

(2) Liaison Team. A liaison team is assigned to the supported organization when the workload or the requirement for better coordination dictates. Liaison teams normally include a liaison officer, a liaison chief, clerical personnel and/or drivers, and communications personnel with their equipment.

(3) Courier. A courier is "a messenger responsible for the secure physical transmission and delivery of documents and material." (JP 1-02) The courier can function as a liaison element to another command. An experienced, mature courier can amplify information about the situation or issues of concern.

b. Liaison Element Selection Considerations

Although there are no firm rules for selecting liaison personnel, the commander should consider requirements of the task and the individual's—

- CSS expertise.
- Rank.
- Experience.
- Knowledge.
- Personal initiative.
- Judgment.
- Communications skills.

For CSS units, the requirement for liaison is part of the assigned mission. However, the formal mission does not specify the type of liaison element to assign in each case. Command liaison should be conducted in all but the most unusual circumstances. The following considerations provide some insights into determining the best type of liaison element to use.

(1) Available Personnel. The lack of qualified personnel may prevent assignment of dedicated liaison elements even where there is a recognized need. If a liaison officer or team is not available, the commander can use couriers. The commander should select only those who have demonstrated the necessary maturity to handle the duties. The overriding consideration is always responsiveness to the supported unit.

(2) Workload. Workload is a variable that influences the commander's decision to provide liaison, as well as the specific type of liaison element. It is a function of the CSS unit's scope of operations, personnel situation, priorities, and time. The workload varies with the size and mission of both the supporting and supported units and can change during the course of an operation. The commander should assign liaison elements to subordinate headquarters as a first priority, although liaison officers or couriers may be adequate at lower levels. In some situations, the workload may require little more than routine liaison between principal staff officers or their assistants.

(3) Proximity. When units are in proximity, the commander may rely on principal staff officers to maintain effective communications. Conversely, the workload may dictate the use of a dedicated liaison element despite the unit's location.

(4) Tactical Situation. The need for liaison increases as the pace of tactical operations increases. In a static situation, requirements and procedures are routine. As the tempo of operations increases, maintaining liaison becomes more difficult as well as more critical. Liaison is especially critical during offensive operations and periods of turbulence.

(5) Timeliness. To complement and enhance the desired effects of early CSS planning, liaison elements should be assigned at the first opportunity. Early coordination between combat and CSS units ensures the timely involvement of the CSS units in the planning process.

c. Exchange of Liaison Elements

Traditionally, commanders establish liaison from senior to subordinate, supporting to supported, and left to right. As with all rules, however, there are situations that dictate exceptions. For example, often situations dictate the exchange of liaison elements between units.

(1) Senior to Subordinate. The assignment of liaison elements within the same command is unusual. The senior headquarters would initiate such assignments. Headquarters must provide the liaison element, with associated support equipment, to the subordinate unit.

(2) Supporting to Supported. The inherent nature of the supporting role normally dictates that the supporting unit provides the liaison element to the supported unit. For task-organized CSS units, the availability of liaison elements depends on the identification of potential liaison requirements during the planning phase. Based on those requirements, the parent command should task-organize the CSS unit with the personnel and equipment to effect liaison.

(3) Reinforcing to Reinforced. Similar type units reinforce one another. The CSS unit assigned a reinforcing mission provides a liaison element to the reinforced CSS unit.

(4) Left to Right. Traditionally, units on the left flank are responsible for establishing liaison with units on their right. However, CSS units generally do not provide liaison elements to adjacent units. Liaison between the respective commanders and principal staff officers is the norm in such cases.

d. Liaison Element Duties and Responsibilities

Liaison duties and responsibilities closely correlate with those of the G-4/S-4 of the supported unit. The duties are separated into three broad categories.

(1) Advise and/or Assist. The liaison element advises both the supporting commander and the supported commander. It assists the supported unit to determine its requirements, to ascertain associated priorities, and to assign appropriate allocations. The liaison element advises the supported unit on the capabilities of the supporting unit. It assists the supported unit G-4/S-4 to identify those COAs that are most and least supportable from the CSS viewpoint.

(2) Monitor. The liaison element observes the operations of the supported unit and monitors the status of those functional areas in which the parent CSS organization has a concern. Simultaneously, it keeps abreast of the status of its parent organization's operations. Specifically, the element follows activities that affect the capability to provide continuous support.

(3) Coordinate. The liaison element coordinates and expedites the flow of support and information between the two organizations. In this regard, the liaison element serves as the conduit for two-way communications. It is not a substitute for direct coordination between commanders and principal staff officers; rather, it complements and augments such coordination.

e. Liaison Procedures

Initially, the commander of the supporting unit should accompany the selected liaison representative(s). This allows the commander to introduce the selected liaison element to the supported commander and staff. This gesture can have a significant long-term impact on the success of subsequent actions with the supported unit.

To effectively conduct liaison duties, the element must—

- Become familiar with the capabilities, limitations, and concept of operations of its parent organization before assuming its duties.
- Report to its assigned unit fully prepared to carry out its duties and responsibilities.
- Become familiar with the structure and functions of the supported unit.
- Know the supported unit's mission, concept of operations, and scheme of maneuver.

Chapter 4

Planning

This chapter describes the planning process and planning products for tactical logistics. In addition, it identifies key factors in each tactical logistic functional area for consideration to help ensure thorough and effective planning. Planning for tactical logistic is concurrent with the larger planning process that prepares the MAGTF for operations.

4001. Logistic Planning Concepts

The following basic concepts govern the planning of tactical logistics:

- Logistic planning should be concurrent with operations planning.
- Combat and combat support units should exploit their organic logistic capabilities before requesting assistance from combat service support sources.
- The impetus of logistics is from the rear, directly to the using unit.
- The logistic system must be responsive, effective, and efficient.

4002. Planning for Expeditionary Operations

Logistic self-sufficiency is a primary consideration when planning expeditionary operations because MAGTFs are organized to conduct operations in austere environments. Marine forces and MAGTF commanders provide the operational logistic capabilities necessary for conducting expeditionary operations, while tactical logistics are provided by MAGTF commanders and their subordinates. This expeditionary or temporary opera-

tions support will be withdrawn after the mission is accomplished. These missions may include—

- Providing humanitarian assistance.
- Establishing and keeping peace.
- Protecting U.S. citizens.
- Countering an act of aggression.
- Defeating an enemy in combat.

a. Phases of Action

Expeditionary operations involve five broad phases of action which have strategic, operational, and tactical considerations. See Marine Corps Doctrinal Publication (MCDP) 3, *Expeditionary Operations*, for additional information.

(1) Deployment. Deployment is the movement of forces to the area of operations. Deployment is initially a function of strategic mobility. Operational-level movement in theater completes deployment as forces are concentrated for tactical employment. Deployment support permits the MAGTF commanders to marshal, stage, embark, and deploy their commands. Although deployment is a strategic and operational-level concern, tactical-level CSS units (e.g., FSSG) may be required to assist the deployment.

(2) Entry. Entry is the introduction of forces onto foreign soil. Normally, entry is accomplished by sea or air, although in some cases forces may be introduced by ground movement from an expeditionary base in an adjacent country. Logistic capabilities are used in the entry phase to develop entry points (e.g., an airfield or port, an assailable coastline, a drop zone, an accessible frontier).

(3) Enabling Actions. These actions are preparatory actions taken by the expeditionary force to facilitate the eventual accomplishment of the mission. Enabling actions may include seizing a port, airfield, or other lodgment for the introduction of follow-on forces and the establishment of necessary logistic and support capabilities. In case of disaster or disruption, enabling actions may involve the initial restoration of order and stability. In open conflict, enabling actions may involve delaying an enemy advance, attacking certain enemy capabilities, or capturing key terrain that is necessary for the conduct of decisive actions.

(4) Decisive Actions. These actions are intended to create the conditions that will accomplish the mission. In disasters, decisive actions may include relief operations. In disruptions, they often include peacemaking and peacekeeping until local government control can be reestablished. In conflict, they usually involve military defeat of the adversary. Logistic organizations provide support across the spectrum of decisive actions.

(5) Departure or Transition. Because expeditions are by definition temporary, all expeditionary operations involve a departure of the expeditionary force or a transition to a permanent presence of some sort. Departure is not as simple as the tactical withdrawal of the expeditionary forces from the scene. It requires withdrawing the force in a way that maintains the desired situation while preserving the combat capabilities of the force. For example, care must be taken to reload the ships of an MPF or MEU to restore their sustainment capabilities because either force may be instantly ordered to undertake another expeditionary operation.

b. Forward-Deployed Logistic Capabilities

The Marine Corps maintains a war reserve program that allows MAGTFs to sustain themselves for a significant period of time during combat operations. Sustainment gives the MAGTFs the required endurance until theater-level supply is established. Sustainment resources that are forward deployed with MAGTFs are augmented and replenished with materiel managed in the war reserve, MPF, and land prepositioning programs. The resulting logistic self-sufficiency is a fundamental, defining characteristic of expeditionary MAGTFs.

(1) War Materiel Requirement. Normally, stocks are maintained to ensure that MAGTFs can deploy with sufficient ground-common equipment and supplies to support 60 days of contingency operations. The 60-day level provides reasonable assurance that the force can be self-sustaining until resupply channels are established. The MAGTF ACE can deploy with sufficient aviation-peculiar equipment and supplies for 90 days of contingency operations. Normally, class V(A) ammunition is not computed in the ACE 90-day sustainment figure due to the large lift requirement associated with class V(A).

(2) Maritime Prepositioning Force. The MPF is the combination of prepositioned materiel and airlifted elements with a sustainment capability of 30 days. Smaller MAGTFs may be sustained ashore for more or less time depending on the size of the force, the number of MPS in support of that force, and other variables such as inclusion of an aviation logistics support ship (TAVB).

(3) Land Prepositioned Programs. The Norway airlanded Marine expeditionary brigade (NALM) is the Marine Corps' only land prepositioned program. Agreements between the United States and Norway established the prepositioned NALM stocks which are used for regional contingencies. These stocks are maintained at the same levels as the MPF levels.

c. Marine Expeditionary Planning Organization

The plans and future operations sections prepare plans using the Marine Corps Planning Process (MCPP). See MCWP 5-1, *Marine Corps Planning Process*, for more detail. Future and current operations sections oversee the execution of those plans. Subordinate elements and smaller MAGTFs conduct the same planning, however, their greater focus on the current battle and smaller size may dictate modifications to the staff organization.

(1) Plans Section. Under the staff cognizance of the G-5, the plans section—

- Provides a link between higher headquarters planning sections and future operations section.
- Focuses on deliberate planning and follow-on phases of a campaign or operation.
- Develops branch plans and sequels.

(2) Future Operations Section. Under the cognizance of the G-3/S-3, the future operations section—

- Coordinates with the plans section and current operations sections to ensure integration of the next battle plan.
- Interacts with intelligence collection and the targeting process to shape the next battle.
- Manages the command's PDE&A cycle to match higher headquarters battle rhythms and to create the conditions for the success of current operations.

(3) Operational Planning Team. An OPT is a temporary organization formed around the plans or future operations section to conduct integrated planning. While the current operations section manages the execution of current operations, an OPT plans future operations and develops the OPLAN, OPORD, or fragmentary order. The OPT integrates the various staff sections, battlefield function representatives, and subordinate liaisons into the planning process.

(4) Current Operations Section. This section receives the OPORD from future operations and executes the OPORD from the combat operations center (COC). Under the cognizance of the G-3/S-3, current operations—

- Coordinates and executes the current order.
- Monitors operations of the MAGTF.
- Prepares fragmentary orders to modify the current OPORD.
- Assesses shaping actions and the progress toward the commander's decisive actions.
- Coordinates terrain management.
- Maintains essential maps and information.
- Provides plans and future operations with situational awareness.

- Provides transition officers to future operations.

4003. Types of Joint Planning

MAGTF planners must be familiar with JOPES because the Marine Corps continues to operate in a joint or combined environment. As described in JOPES, there are two primary methods of planning joint or combined operations: deliberate and crisis action planning. The distinction between the following methods is important because it reflects significant differences in the amount of time available for MAGTF planning:

- The deliberate or contingency projection planning process is a cyclic process for the development of OPLANs.
- Crisis action or time-sensitive planning involves emergencies with possible national security implications.

4004. Marine Corps Planning Process

The MCPP is the process operating forces' commanders and their staffs use to provide input to the joint planning process and to plan force organization and employment. Applicable across the range of military operations, the MCPP is designed for use at any echelon of command. It complements joint deliberate and crisis action planning procedures outlined in JOPES and provides Marine commanders with a tool for preparing plans and orders. Logisticians participate in all steps of the MCPP with the representatives of the other warfighting functions, staff sections, subject-matter experts, and command representatives. See MCWP 5-1 for a detailed discussion of the MCPP.

The MCPP establishes procedures for analyzing a mission, developing and analyzing COAs against the threat, comparing friendly COAs against the commander's criteria and each other, selecting a COA, and preparing an OPORD for execution. It organizes the planning process into six manageable, logical steps. See figure 4-1.

The MCPP provides commanders and their staffs with a means to organize their planning activities and transmit the plan to subordinates and subordinate commands. Through this process, all levels of command begin their planning effort with a common understanding of the mission and commander's guidance. Interactions among various planning steps allow a concurrent, coordinated effort that maintains flexibility, makes efficient use of time available, and facilitates continuous information sharing.

4005. Concept of Logistic Support

The concept of logistics and CSS is a broad statement of the essential logistic and CSS tasks involved in supporting the conduct of MAGTF operations. It gives an overall picture of CSS operations and addresses solutions to shortfalls cited in the CSS estimate. In addition, it is the foundation for subsequent development of detailed logistic and CSS plans and orders by the MAGTF elements.

The MAGTF commander's concept for logistics is contained in annex D of the MAGTF OPORD. It provides guidance for subordinate MAGTF elements and information required for coordination with logistic support agencies external to the MAGTF. The MAGTF G-4/S-4 prepares annex D, and subordinate G-4/S-4s conduct the detailed planning needed to accomplish the logistic and CSS tasks promulgated in the OPORD.

4006. Planning Elements

The following elements must be addressed in each phase and stage of logistic planning.

a. Mission

The MAGTF mission is paramount. The missions of subordinate elements must complement the MAGTF mission and may dictate additional parameters for tactical logistic planning.

b. Concept of Operations

Logistic personnel should fully understand the supported commander's concept of operations. This is vital if they are to anticipate the requirements of the supported organizations. Anticipa-

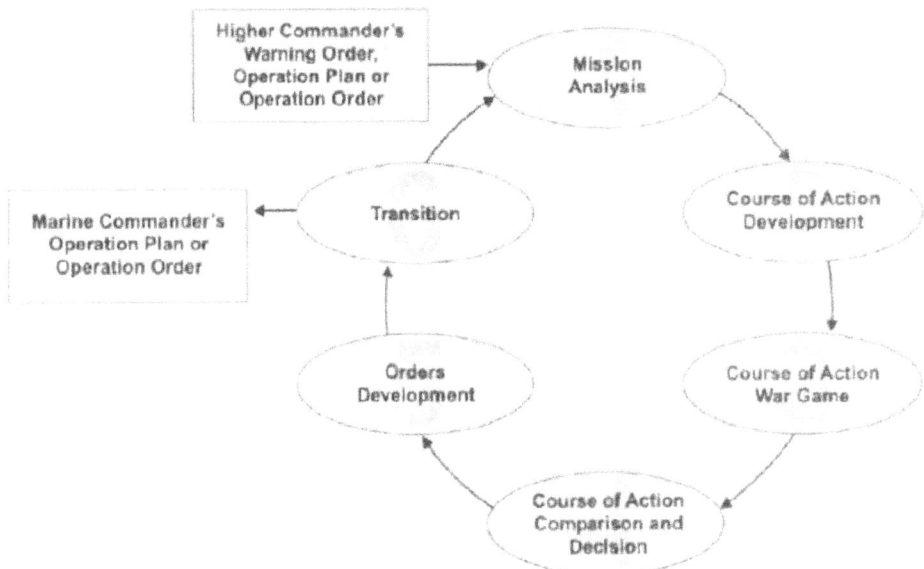

Figure 4-1. The Marine Corps Planning Process.

tion is key to the principles of responsiveness and flexibility.

c. Forces

Available forces and OPLANs dictate logistic requirements. The availability of support from other Services or host nations influences the concept of logistics and CSS. Similarly, enemy capabilities influence the selection of a concept of logistics and CSS in a given situation.

d. Theater Characteristics

Theater characteristics include the distance between the objective area and sources of supply. Also important is the turnaround time for airlift and sealift assets. Local populations and environmental conditions (e.g., facilities, road nets, weather, terrain) also effect support operations.

e. Intensity of Operations

The expected intensity of operations is a key planning factor for quantifying logistic and CSS requirements.

f. Timing and Duration

The anticipated timing and duration of operations influence planning and preparation, as the time available to complete plans or to procure and stage equipment and supplies may be limited.

4007. Planning Techniques

Limited information and limited time are characteristics of MAGTF planning. Upon receipt of the mission, the MAGTF staff reviews existing OPLANs, SOPs, and joint and Marine Corps lessons learned for related information. Staff members compare plans and SOPs to the assigned mission and to available information at each stage of the planning process. Operational planning often begins with a nucleus staff. During the initial phase, the MAGTF should place particular emphasis on the following techniques.

a. Flexible Approach

Planning is a continuous process that requires a flexible approach. Initial estimates are based on assumptions and minimal data. Commanders and staffs must continually evaluate previous decisions and guidance. New information can confirm or invalidate previous assumptions or data.

b. Timely Effort

Logistic planning must begin as early as possible at all levels of command. Early identification of requirements, capabilities, and special considerations accelerates coordination, timely guidance, and essential decisions. As the concept of operations becomes more specific, subordinate elements can begin preparation of more detailed logistic plans.

c. Coordinated Planning

To accomplish the MAGTF mission, every aspect of the operational concept requires coordination among the GCE, ACE, and CSSE. To achieve this, every element has certain responsibilities for logistic planning. This mutual dependence requires concurrent, parallel, and detailed staff planning between and among all elements. Simultaneously, the MAGTF headquarters must coordinate with higher, adjacent, and supporting commands and, possibly, with participating joint and combined staffs. This coordination is essential for integrating MAGTF logistic and CSS operations with those of other organizations.

d. Concurrent and Parallel Development

Based on both initial and revised guidance, the MAGTF and its elements develop their plans in a concurrent and parallel manner. Integrated planning shortens the planning cycle, enables early identification of potential problems, and improves anticipation of requirements. With proper coordination, concurrent efforts can prevent difficulties that might occur if planning is sequential or isolated. Logistic planning must parallel operational planning. Likewise, the MAGTF concept of operations cannot be developed without full consideration of the supporting concept of logistics and CSS.

4008. Deployment Planning Considerations

There are two tactical logistic support scenarios to consider when planning for deployment. Under either of the following options, the tactical logistic planner must consider MAGTF requirements in all six CSS functions and their subfunctions:

- The MAGTF can deploy to an area with an established logistic support base. This can be host nation support, inter-Service support, or a combination of the two. The logistic planner must plan for reliance on, or expansion of, the existing support base. In addition, the planner must consider an effective alternative to that support if it stops.

- The MAGTF can deploy to an area without an established logistic support base. In this scenario, the logistic planner must rely on inherent logistic resources to support the MAGTF.

4009. Commander's Intent

Planners cannot foresee every eventuality, and even if they could, plans cannot practically address every possible situation. Commander's intent is the commander's personal expression of the purpose of the operation. Commander's intent helps subordinates understand the larger context of their actions and guides them in the absence of orders. It allows subordinates to exercise judgment and initiative, in a way that is consistent with the higher commander's aims, when the unforeseen occurs. Regardless of the form that it takes, the commander's intent must—

- Be clear, concise, and easy to understand.
- Support the higher, supported commander's intent.

- Include how the commander envisions achieving a decision.
- Provide an end state or conditions that, when satisfied, accomplish the purpose.

4010. Operational Planning Considerations

Logistic planning focuses on satisfying the logistic requirements generated by the supported force. This planning addresses the estimation of materiel and functional support requirements as well as the organization and employment of organic and supporting tactical logistic organizations. Materiel and functional support requirements are calculated based on experience, assigned missions and tasks, as well as operational factors (e.g., such as time available, weather, enemy).

MAGTF commanders and staff officers should consider the following examples when planning. These examples provide insights for developing and maintaining throughput systems and sustainment capabilities for the execution of logistic support of MAGTF tactical operations.

a. Supply

(1) Ground. Commanders should optimize the basic load for all supplies, including class IX repair parts. The unit's basic load should not exceed the commander's anticipated requirements, even if the unit can carry additional quantities.

(2) Aviation. The squadron maintenance staffs should ensure that their pre-expended bins have been replenished by the supporting MALS. Aviation staffs must cordinate with the supporting MALS, MWSS, and MAG headquarters for aviation-peculiar logistic support en route and within the theater.

b. Maintenance

Each MAGTF element should make maximum use of organic maintenance contact teams and CSSE maintenance support teams. Repair and return of equipment as far forward as possible speeds return of equipment to the user. It also reduces the burden on both transportation and control capabilities.

c. Transportation

Because transportation is the most limited and limiting logistic capability in the MAGTF, it requires close management. Improper management of transportation assets may degrade combat operations. Supplies should be moved only as needed.

d. External Support

MAGTF plans should make maximum use of host nation and inter-Service support available within the theater of operations. Plans should include, but not be limited to, use of facilities, supplies, utilities, captured materiel, and civilian labor. The CSSE commander should keep the number of CSS installations to a minimum and ensure dispersion of installations and capabilities.

e. Forward Support

The farther forward the CSS unit, the less responsibility it should have for routine support tasks. CSSDs should be responsible only for those supplies and services that are critical to combat operations.

f. Air Support

In planning for sustained operations, the MAGTF should expect to receive critical items primarily by air; however, this does not preclude thorough planning for surface lift.

g. Alternate Supply Routes

Transportation planning at every echelon should include the development of alternate supply routes. Use of a single supply route increases the chances that enemy action could severely disrupt or prevent movement.

h. Security

The CSSE commander is inherently responsible for the organization's security. While continuing to provide support, the CSSE commander must employ both active and passive measures to defend against attempts to disrupt support operations.

4011. Functional Area Planning Considerations

a. Supply

Compromises that are acceptable in peacetime to improve economy and enhance accountability may not be appropriate in a combat situation. For example, storage of a commodity in a single dump site may be appropriate in peacetime. Centralization in wartime may be unresponsive and reduce survivability. Therefore, the CSSE commander may establish multiple CSSAs. Their capacities and locations vary based on the tactical situation, the concept of operations, and the scheme of maneuver.

(1) **Supply Cycle.** The supply process is a cycle that involves procurement, use, and replenishment of supply items. The cycle period for each supply item varies based on usage rate, storage and transport capacity, and procurement lead time. Normally, the shorter the cycle, the more intensive the management and transportation effort becomes. Conversely, items with longer cycles require forward planning and more storage.

(2) **Phases of Supply Support.** The CSSE and ACE perform the tactical supply that affects the sustainability of the MAGTF. Tactical supply extends from receipt of finished supplies through issue for use or consumption by the user. The CSSE and ACE control the supply process through forecasting, requisitioning, receiving, storing, stock controlling, shipping, disposition, identifying, and accounting procedures established in directives. Ideally, the procedures used in peacetime are the same as those used in wartime. Combat requirements often necessitate rapid processing of requests submitted by unusual methods.

b. Maintenance

Ideally, maintenance procedures should be the same in peacetime and combat but peacetime or garrison maintenance procedures and techniques may not work effectively in combat or field conditions. Maintenance support for Marine aviation has been developed under the Marine aviation logistics support program (MALSP). MALSP operations are described in chapter 5. Logisticians must consider the following factors when planning maintenance systems and procedures:

- Maintenance activities must operate in harsh conditions during tactical operations.

- Limited resources may require around-the-clock work schedules.

- Contamination in the battlespace may further complicate and delay repair of equipment.

- Units must minimize the time required to repair combat essential items. To minimize repair time, units should—

  - Perform only mission essential maintenance during combat. Units must recover, evacuate, and repair equipment as far forward as possible. The lowest level maintenance activity with the proper capability should make the repairs. Repairing equipment as far forward as possible reduces transportation requirements and increases equipment availability.

  - Evacuate inoperable equipment only if they cannot repair it forward or if the repairs will take excessive time. The MAGTF must have a well-defined and understood recovery and evacuation process. In combat, recovery and evacuation may be the most difficult maintenance function. However, this function may also be the most important to sustain the MAGTF's combat power.

  - Make critical repair parts available as far forward as practical. Combat may even require positioning critical parts at the using-unit level. Combat may also dictate greater reliance on selective interchange.

c. Transportation

Transportation planning is throughput planning. It involves the determination of throughput requirements: what, where, when, and how personnel and materiel must move to sustain the force.

The transportation planning process is the same regardless of mode, distance, or locale. The operational commander provides requirements and establishes priorities based on the concept of operations. The transportation planner sequences movement requirements in the following order:

- Determine the desired arrival time at destination.
- Select mode of transportation.
- Determine load and pickup points, intermediate and transfer points (as required), as well as offload and drop points.
- Apply time-distance factors.
- Reconcile conflicting requirements for limited transportation assets (including MHE) and support facilities.
- Test movement plan for feasibility.

(1) Planning Elements. The following main elements must be considered when planning transportation:

- **Requirements List.** The requirements list identifies what personnel, supplies, and equipment the planner must move. The planner integrates data from all sources, sequencing it by required delivery date and by priority within the required delivery date. He further sorts it by destination and compiles a single time-phased listing.
- **Lift Mode.** The selected lift mode identifies what transportation means move the personnel or cargo between the point of origin and destination.
- **Routing.** Routing moves from load and pickup points to intermediate and transfer locations to offload and drop points.
- **Timing.** Timely arrival of personnel, supplies, and equipment at the intended destination(s) is the goal of transportation planning. The key to

transportation scheduling is flexibility. Timing of the beginning and end of each leg of a movement increases flexibility. Basic limitations to timeliness include—

- Required delivery date at the destination.
- Time when personnel, supplies, and equipment are available for movement from their points of origin.
- Time and/or distance factors.
- Throughput capacities of support facilities.
- Capacity and security of staging bases and supply depots.
- Special requirements caused by terrain, climate, and environment.

(2) Planning Process. The transportation planner follows the listed steps when planning for transportation:

- **Determining Requirements.** Each requirement for personnel, equipment, or supplies generates a corresponding requirement for transportation. Transportation planners express initial requirements in terms of tonnage and square footage or the number of personnel and the distance. The planner estimates requirements based on the supplies needed to support the MAGTF and the average distances during each phase of the operation.
- **Determining Resources.** The transportation planner must consider—
  - Type of transportation units available.
  - Characteristics and capabilities of each mode of transportation.
  - Capabilities of available civilian transportation. (The estimate is based on a survey of facilities, inspection of equipment, and agreements negotiated with civilian transportation operators.)
  - Availability of indigenous labor or prisoners of war to supplement personnel resources.
  - Capabilities of available host nation transportation, both civilian and military.
- **Balancing Requirements and Resources.** The balancing process determines whether transportation capabilities are adequate to support the operation. It establishes the workload for each

transportation mode. This step is the most time-consuming portion of the transportation planning process. Planning must include more than just gross quantities of cargo and transportation resources. It must include planning for C2 and for transportation unit support.

- **Determining Critical Points.** On completing the preliminary plan, the planner has enough information to analyze the transportation system. The planner can identify critical points where bottlenecks can delay throughput. The bottlenecks may occur as a result of shortfalls in either personnel, equipment, or facilities. The planner should also identify critical time periods. Development and analysis of alternative schedules, modes, or routes can alleviate bottlenecks and increase flexibility.
- **Coordinating.** Complete coordination is mandatory for integrated transportation support. Original guidance is seldom valid throughout the planning process. Constant coordination is necessary if transportation plans are to change as the commander's concepts, requirements, priorities, and allocations change.

d. General Engineering

The MAGTF engineer assigns and integrates construction tasks and priorities for both Marine and naval construction force (NCF) engineer components assigned to the MAGTF. The NCF headquarters assists the MAGTF engineer in planning and coordinating construction requirements to best use the unique capabilities of the NCF. Continuous liaison is vital during the planning, deployment, and execution phases of MAGTF operations. The following engineer support planning areas require special consideration:

- **Heavy Equipment.** Most construction equipment is heavy and slow moving. It offers little protection for operators. Though able to negotiate rough terrain, its speed is such that it cannot keep up with the supported maneuver forces and must be transported by other assets.
- **Transportation.** Engineer units do not have enough transportation assets to move themselves. When moving a large volume of

equipment rapidly or over extended distances, augmentation is necessary.

- **Construction Materials.** Many CSS engineering tasks require large amounts of construction materials. The time, manpower, equipment, and fuel required to assemble and use these supplies are often significant. Careful planning will minimize multiple handling during movement of these items to the construction site. Movement directly from the source of supply to the job site is optimal.

- **Supply, Maintenance, and Ordnance Support.** Supply, maintenance, and ordnance support for engineer operations is extensive. Engineer units have many low-density items of equipment requiring special maintenance to keep them operational. Low-density items range from mine detectors to stationary pumps and generators to mobile construction equipment. Unique ordnance items include explosive line charges and cratering charges.

- **Utilities Support.** Water purification, fuel distribution, and power generating equipment require significant motor transport, MHE, manpower, and fuel. Space requirements are normally large, and camouflage is difficult. Utilities installations also generate large amounts of heat and noise.

e. Health Service

Commanders are responsible for the health and welfare of their troops. The MAGTF medical units have extensive, cumbersome equipment that requires external transportation, fuel, and utilities support. In addition, medical units' footprint creates significant real estate management challenges. Although HSS staffs conduct medical planning within the MAGTF, logistic planners should ensure—

- Complimentary equipment and associated consumables kits (authorized medical allowance lists [AMALs] and authorized dental allowance lists [ADALs]) are in sufficient quantities to support the force.

- Narcotics handling and security procedures are established.

- Medical regulating channels and procedures for the movement and tracking of casualties between and within the levels of care are established.

- The mix of dedicated versus opportune lift for casualty evacuation is decided based on the concept of operations, casualty estimates, and METT-T.

- MAGTF level II and level III treatment facilities are identified and medical evacuation policies are established.

- Preventive medicine requirements and preventive medicine technicians for insect control and redeployment agriculture inspections are identified.

- Mass casualty procedures are established.

- Primary and secondary casualty receiving and treatment ships (CRTS) are identified for amphibious operations.

- Medical requirements for the area of operations (e.g., immunizations, anti-venom, and antimalarial medication) are identified.

Additional guidance can be found in the Chairman of the Joint Chiefs of Staff Manual (CJCSM) 3122.03, *Joint Operation Planning and Execution System, Volume II, Planning Formats and Guidance*, sets forth administrative instructions and formats to develop OPLANs. Guidance for medical services is located in annex Q of the CJCSM 3122.03.

f. Services

Planning considerations for services vary for each particular services function and the operational situation. The following factors are common to all services functions:

- **Responsibility.** Units are responsible for executing command services functions consistent with the organic capabilities specified in their table of organization (T/O) mission statement. Equipping and manning of detachments should be consistent with this specification. Higher echelon organizations are responsible for augmenting or reinforcing subordinate unit capabilities. The CSSE provides CSS services functions to the MAGTF elements as directed by the MAGTF commander.

- **Chain of Command.** Combat service support services functions are typically implemented in operational chains of command. In contrast, most command services functions normally operate in administrative chains of command in garrison and may continue to do so even after deployment. Element commanders must consider problems that deployments might pose for continuing administrative support when preparing plans for command services functions. When appropriate, specific guidance should be issued for shifting command services functions to the operational chain of command and processing these functions via staff cognizance of the MAGTF CE.

4012. Coordinating Support

Effective logistic planning requires a coordinated effort between the supported force and the supporting organizations. Both supported and supporting organizations make planning and subsequent support operations more efficient through careful calculation of requirements over specified periods of time while coordinating to reconcile potential shortages or excesses. Ground-common and aviation-peculiar logistic support must be provided in the right quantity, at the right time, and in the right place. Providing too much materiel or too robust a service at one location may disrupt operations of the supported unit or deprive other supported units of what they need when they need it. Effective planning can minimize the occurrence of shortages or excesses.

Supported organizations must—

- Calculate their requirements as precisely as possible.
- Factor organic or attached and/or direct support cargo and personnel transportation capacity into the requirements calculation.
- Prioritize requirements.
- Integrate requirements with expected schedule and duration of the operation.
- Verify critical materiel or services allocations made by higher authority when determining requirements for tactical missions.

Supporting organizations must—

- Provide the support required.
- Review with the supported organization the support requirements as they are developed.
- Coordinate with the supported organization to refine the requirements based on the supported organization's competing requirements.
- Procure materiel and task-organize internally to provide support efficiently.
- Plan support distribution by anticipating demand.

4013. Intelligence Support

Intelligence information is essential for planning tactical logistic operations. Logistic intelligence is specific intelligence information that assists logistic organizations in accomplishing their assigned missions. It focuses on the infrastructure in the area of interest and on how the weather, enemy, and terrain would affect tactical logistic operations. Logistic intelligence is a product of the MAGTF's intelligence cycle and intelligence preparation of the battlespace (IPB) functions. The following IPB products are typically of interest to logisticians:

- Lines of communications and route studies.
- Port and harbor studies.
- Airfield studies.
- Drop zone and helicopter landing area studies.
- Bridge and inland waterway studies.
- Key facilities and targets overlays.
- Specialized weather and terrain studies.
- Modified combined obstacle overlay (MCOO).

4014. Host Nation Support

When feasible, MAGTF plans should make maximum use of host nation support available within the theater of operations. Host nation support can augment MAGTF capabilities. Bilateral (between the United States and a single country) and multilateral (among members of a coalition such as the North Atlantic Treaty Organization [NATO]) host nation support agreements can be an integral part of sustainability planning. MAGTFs use host nation support to enhance their sustainability and capabilities. However, host nation support is not a substitute for essential MAGTF organic tactical logistic and CSS capabilities. Normally, host nation support agreements are prepared at the strategic level. Implementation of existing agreements and/or preparation of new agreements must be coordinated between the MAGTF CE and the appropriate higher authority in the United States chain of command. Plans should include, but not be limited to, use of facilities, supplies, utilities, captured materiel, and civilian labor.

4015. Planning Documents

The logistics/CSS estimate, annex D of the OPORD (concept of logistics and CSS), and the CSSE OPORD are the primary MAGTF tactical logistic planning documents. Table 4-1 summarizes the standard logistic planning documents and identifies the preparer.

Table 4-1. Logistic and CSS Planning Documents.

Document	Prepared By
Logistic/Combat Service Support Estimate	GE, GCE, ACE, CSSE down to battalion and squadron level
Annex D (Logistics/Combat Service Support) to OPORD	GE, GCE, ACE, CSSE down to battalion and squadron level
CSSE Operation Order	CSSE

a. Logistics/Combat Service Support Estimate

The estimate is a rapid assessment by the G-4/S-4 of logistic capabilities and limitations for each proposed COA. It analyzes the COAs under consideration to provide the logistic aspects of relative combat power. The estimate helps determine the most desirable and most supportable COA from the CSS standpoint. Additionally, this document provides the basis for later planning. See appendix B of this publication for a sample of the logistic/CSS estimate.

The commander decides which COA will be used to accomplish the assigned mission. As an advisor, the G-4/S-4 provides the commander with information and makes recommendations based on the logistics/CSS estimate.

The logistic/CSS estimate is the result of an examination of the logistic factors which influence contemplated COAs and an appraisal of the degree and manner of that influence. The estimate looks at the six tactical logistic functional areas. The estimate compares requirements, available assets, problems, limitations, advantages, and disadvantages for each COA. The logistic/CSS estimate assesses the limitations of each COA. It also determines what actions are necessary to overcome any problems or limitations. If any COA is not supportable, the estimate specifically states this. It gives the commander enough information to make a decision based on the suitability, feasibility, acceptability, and relative merit of each COA from a logistic standpoint.

b. Annex D to the Marine Air-Ground Task Force Operation Order

Annex D reflects the commanders' plans, guidance, and directions for employment of logistic capabilities. This annex complements the concept of operations and amplifies paragraph 4 of the OPORD (Administration and Logistics). Annex D begins with the concept of operations and the supporting concept of logistics. It assigns tasks and responsibilities for logistics and CSS among the elements in each functional area. It also identifies support required from external agencies. Finally, it provides guidance and information (such as priorities and allocations) for planning, coordinating, and executing MAGTF logistic operations. See appendix C of this publication for a sample Annex D (Logistics/Combat Service Support).

(1) Commander's Guidance. Annex D promulgates the commander's overall plan and guidance for the provision of logistic support to the MAGTF during each phase of the operation. This annex specifies those requirements, priorities, and allocations that are necessary for the integration of the logistic effort in support of the MAGTF. It includes deployment, employment, sustainment, and redeployment planning matters. It includes external support coordination requirements and internal employment directives to present a single, unified plan for logistic support.

(2) Concept of Logistics and Combat Service Support. The concept of logistics and CSS (paragraph 3a of annex D) is a broad statement of the essential logistic and CSS tasks involved in supporting the concept of operations. It is the basic unifying foundation for subsequent development of detailed logistic and CSS plans and orders by the MAGTF elements.

(3) Staff Responsibility. The MAGTF G-4/S-4, in coordination with other staff sections and the subordinate S-4s, prepares annex D. This document also contains the specific requirements, priorities, and allocations for logistics and CSS to support the concept of operations and scheme of maneuver. Each subordinate organization down to the battalion and squadron level publishes an annex D. Optionally, they may use paragraph 4 of the OPORD to provide logistic guidance to subordinate units. Use of and reference to local SOPs contribute to sound plans and help avoid unnecessarily lengthy and detailed OPORDs.

(4) Concept of Aviation Logistic Support. Aviation logistic support is addressed in the aviation estimate of supportability and Appendix 10 (Aviation Logistic Support) to annex D to the OPORD.

c. Combat Service Support Element Operation Order

The CSSE OPORD states the mission of the CSSE, establishes task organizations, and assigns missions to each subordinate unit. It also states the CSSE commander's requirements, priorities, and allocations for accomplishing the mission.

The CSSE OPORD amplifies information normally contained in SOPs concerning CSS provided to other MAGTF elements. Primarily, the OPORD provides specific guidance and direction to subordinate CSS units regarding their tasks and missions. The CSSE G-3/S-3 is responsible for preparing the CSSE OPORD. The CSSE G-4/S-4 prepares annex D to the CSSE OPORD.

d. Standing Operating Procedures

SOPs are a set of operating instructions that can be standardized. These standardized procedures are applicable unless ordered otherwise. SOPs are general orders that deal with tactical and administrative procedures not covered by regulatory or doctrinal publications.

The recurrent nature of logistic functions lends them to procedural standardization. SOPs contribute to simplicity, clarity, and brevity. Reliance on SOPs in the various CSS planning documents simplifies and shortens those documents. It is not necessary to list SOPs as references; however, the order should cite the SOPs in the body of the document.

In addition to their advantages in the preparation of planning documents and orders, SOPs improve support by promoting familiarity and mutual confidence between supported and supporting units and personnel. They also reduce the confusion often associated with combat conditions.

e. Other Planning Documents

The G-4/S-4 has staff cognizance for major input to other documents. Many of these documents are unique to landing force operations.

Other doctrinal publications, such as JP 3-02.1, *Joint Doctrine for Landing Force Operations*, and NWP 3-02.1, *Ship-to-Shore Movement*, discuss the following documents in detail:

- Embarkation plan.

- Plan for landing supplies.

- Landing plan (appendix 3 to annex R of the OPORD prepared by the G-3/S-3).

- Organization for embarkation and assignment to shipping tables.

Chapter 5

Logistic Functional Area Support Operations

This chapter discusses the tactics, techniques, and procedures for each of the tactical-level logistic functional areas. To support tactical-level operations, logisticians commonly discuss support requirements in terms of functional areas and develop systems and plans for each area. Although logisticians develop separate systems and plans for each functional area, all functions must be integrated into the overall logistic support effort.

Section I. Supply

The process of providing materials and items used to equip, support, and maintain a military force are part of the supply cycle. The supply cycle is divided into the production and the consumption phases. Production extends from determination of procurement schedules to acceptance of finished supplies by the military Services. Consumption extends from receipt of finished supplies by the military Services through issue for use. This section addresses the various supply classes and subfunctions available to support tactical-level operations. The CSS organizations identified as sources of supply during the various stages of amphibious operations and sustained operations ashore are the same for requesting other CSS.

5101. Combat Service Support Element Supply Support Operations

The CSSE commander's primary concern is providing the MAGTF commander with a supply capability and resupply when required.

a. Landing Force Supplies

Landing force supplies are the supplies and equipment in the assault echelon and the assault follow-on echelon (AFOE) of the ATF. They sustain the landing force until a distribution pipeline is established from the supporting establishment to the theater of operations. Predeployment planning determines the type and quantity of landing force supplies. The categories of landing force supplies are the basic load, prepositioned emergency supplies, and remaining supplies.

(1) **Basic Load.** A basic load consists of the types and quantities of supplies that assault forces carry to a specific mission, including the supplies carried by individuals. Usually, basic loads are expressed either as days of supply or days of ammunition. The basic load may change as the tactical situation dictates. There may be a basic load for landing and a different basic load for operations ashore. The basic loads for surface and helicopter-borne forces may be different. The basic load should not exceed the capabilities of a unit's organic transportation or the commander's estimate of supply requirements for combat.

(2) **Prepositioned Emergency Supplies.** The commander uses prepositioned emergency supplies for replenishment early in the ship-to-shore movement. These supplies are available on call for immediate delivery to units ashore and are categorized as either floating dumps or prestaged helicopter-lifted supplies.

(a) Floating Dumps. Floating dumps consist of selected prepackaged class I, III, V, and VIII supplies. On-call floating dumps support surface assault elements and are staged aboard landing craft or assault amphibious vehicles for immediate delivery to units ashore. The primary control officer dispatches floating dumps to the beach in response to requests by the supported commander ashore, via the tactical-logistical group

(TACLOG). Ashore, landing craft and/or assault amphibious vehicles are unloaded to expand the size of supply dumps in the beach support area (BSA). The commander terminates the use of floating dumps when the level of supplies ashore is sufficient to meet critical needs.

(b) Prestaged Helicopter-Lifted Supplies. The commander prestages helicopter-lifted supplies to support helicopterborne units but, if required, can use the supplies to support surface assault units. Prestaged helicopter-lifted supplies are prepackaged, high-priority supplies positioned aboard helicopter transport ships. Like floating dumps, these supplies are available on call for units ashore. Requests for this category of supplies are made by the unit to the TACLOG. After the initial stages of the assault, remaining supplies are used to expand supply dumps ashore. Both prestaged helicopter-lifted supplies and floating dumps may be assigned landing serial numbers to help identify and deliver specific materiel.

(3) **Remaining Supplies.** Excepting supplies issued for basic loads and prepositioned emergency supplies, the remaining are MAGTF supplies. They constitute the major portion of the supplies transported to the operational area in the assault echelon and the AFOE. When transitioning from operational maneuver from the sea to sustained operations ashore, the commander uses these supplies to build dumps ashore. The CSSE unloads the bulk of remaining supplies during general unloading.

b. Sustainment

Sustainment involves those supplies provided to the landing force other than landing force supplies. Sustainment sources include—

- Host nation and inter-Service support.

- Supplies aboard other ships or aircraft not in the ATF.

- CINC-directed cross-servicing or common servicing.

c. Ground Supply Operations During the Amphibious Assault

Figure 5-1 depicts the management and execution of ground supply operations during the amphibious assault.

(1) **Landing Force Support Party.** The LFSP is the forward echelon of the CSSE formed to facilitate the ship-to-shore movement. The LFSP provides CSS, to include supply support, to the assault elements of the GCE during the early stages of the amphibious assault. The LFSP coordinates the combined CSS efforts of the shore party teams on the beaches and helicopter support teams in helicopter landing zones. It establishes contact with the landing force TACLOG. See chapter 6 for further discussion of the LFSP.

(2) **Tactical-Logistical Group.** The TACLOG is a temporary landing force organization that is established at each level of the Navy ship-to-shore control organization. The TACLOG advises the Navy control groups of landing force requirements for the waterborne and helicopterborne ship-to-shore movements. The TACLOG monitors ship-to-shore movement and helps the Navy control the movements of scheduled waves, on-call waves, and nonscheduled serials. See chapter 6 for further discussion of the TACLOG.

(3) **Supply During the Assault.** Initial assault units will request supplies directly from the TACLOG until a short party or HST is established ashore. At that point, assault units submit CSS requests for supplies to either the shore party or HSTs. The teams either fill or relay requests to the TACLOG. In an emergency or when communications fail, the assault element may pass requests directly to the TACLOG.

(4) **Shore Party Supply Operations.** After the shore party group lands, it establishes inland dump sites. It controls the receipt of selective unloading. Shore party group and HST supply personnel unload, sort, store, safeguard, and issue supplies. Shore party teams and HSTs distribute supplies directly to the consumer by using the fastest available means. The emphasis is on re-

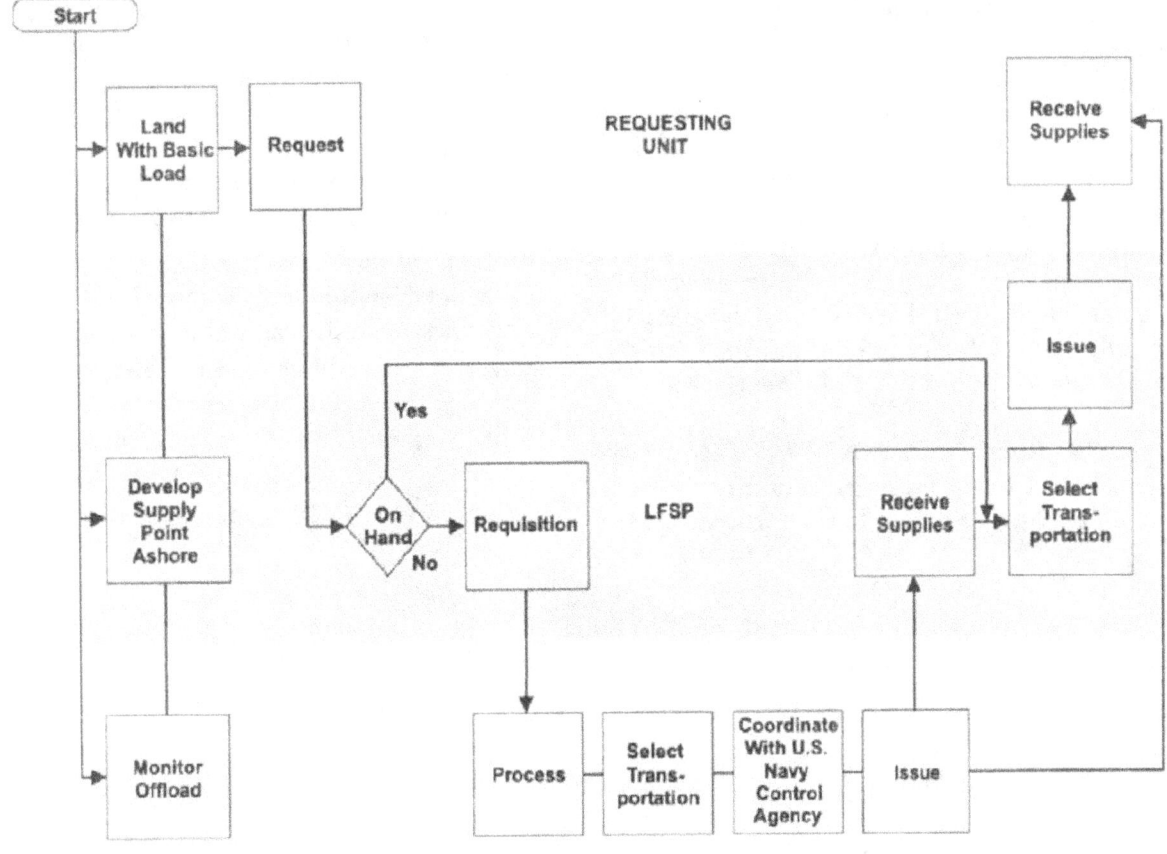

Figure 5-1. Ground Supply Operations During the Amphibious Assault.

sponsiveness, even at the expense of economy and accountability.

(5) Critical Items. If a critical item is not on hand, the shore party or HST notifies the TACLOG. The TACLOG locates the item and coordinates transportation from the Navy control organization.

(6) Prioritization. Before the Navy assigns transportation to move unscheduled supplies ashore, the TACLOG must determine the impact on the tactical situation. It must assess the priority against the priority for landing scheduled and on-call serials.

(7) Helicopter Delivery. The shore party team or HST receives supplies and distributes them to the user. Delivery can be directly from the ship by helicopter to the user.

d. Ground Supply Operations During Subsequent Operations

Battalions and air groups have organic supply capability. Marine Corps and/or Navy directives and local operating procedures dictate the procedures that units with organic supply capabilities use to request replenishment in combat. Figure 5-2, on page 5-4, depicts management and execution of ground supply operations after the CSSE is ashore and functioning.

(1) User Requests Support. Simple, locally established manual procedures are the norm for initial requests from users. On receipt of user requests, the supporting CSSE determines whether the item is on hand. If it is available, the CSSE transports it to users on unit distribution. Consumers on supply point distribution are notified where and when they can pick up the item. If the item is not on hand, the CSSE passes the requisition to the next higher level. The CSSE will keep the requesting unit informed about the status of the pending requisition until distribution is made.

(2) CSSE Support. The CSSE receives requisitions from a subordinate CSSD or directly from the user. The CSSE uses formal procedures for both stock replenishment and passing unfilled user requests to other logistics support organizations. Where possible, CSSEs use automated systems to pass and track both requisitions and reports. During the early stages of an operation before automated systems are established, the CSSE use manual requisition procedures.

(3) Unfilled Requisitions Support. The CSSE in theater passes unfilled requisitions to an in-theater source, if available, or to the FSSG or Marine Corps supporting establishment in the continental United States (CONUS). Marine Corps user manuals and MAGTF OPORDs establish specific supply procedures for CSSEs during operations.

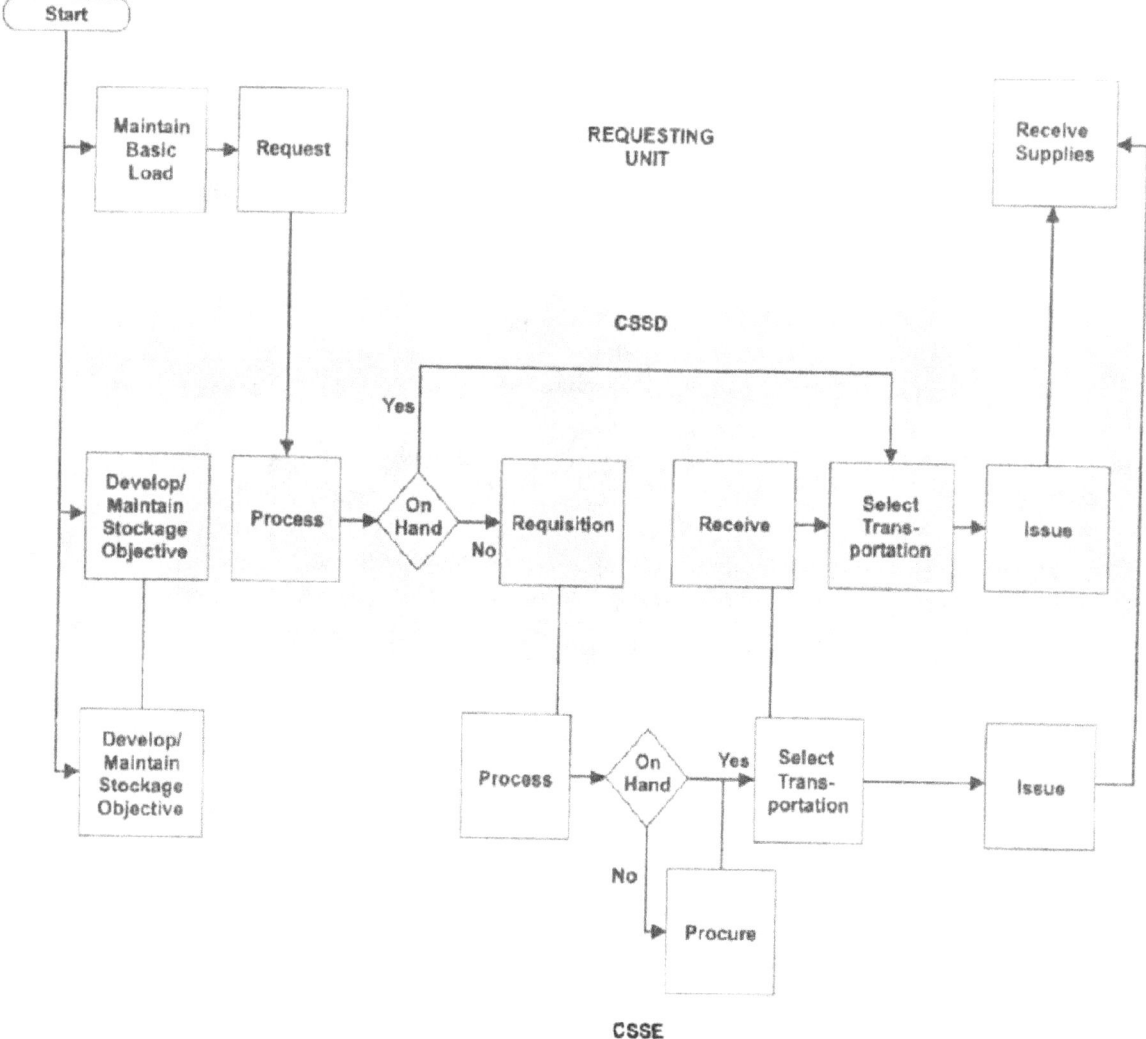

Figure 5-2. Ground Supply Operations During Subsequent Operations.

(4) Mode of Transportation. The CSSE normally provides and selects the mode of transportation to deliver supplies and equipment to subordinate CSSDs or directly to the user. Usually, surface transportation is used but water and air transportation are good alternatives. Although the CSSE selects the mode of transportation, the consumer influences the decision by providing information that might help the CSSE make the decision. For example, a request for a rapid ammunition resupply from a unit preparing to repel an imminent attack would probably justify the use of helicopters.

(5) Delivery Method. Direct shipment to the consumer is the best method of delivery. Bypassing intermediate installations reduces handling. Sometimes supplies must be delivered to the supporting CSSD. This method achieves transportation economies when moving large bulk quantities by taking advantage of lifts of opportunity. Rather than hauling a partial load, trucks can carry noncritical supplies to the CSSD for later forwarding to the consumer.

(6) Distribution Method. The MAGTF G-4/S-4 and CSS commander, in coordination with the supported units, select the method of distribution. Conflicts will be resolved by the MAGTF commander. Normally, CSSEs support committed infantry units by unit distribution and support other units by supply point distribution.

5102. Ground Combat Element Supply Support Operations

Figure 5-3, page 5-6 depicts a tactical situation in which a CSSE is in direct support of GCE units. In this example, infantry battalions are on unit distribution and artillery and armor units are on supply point distribution. The CSSD establishes liaison with the infantry regiment. Requests from the battalions go directly to the CSSD, which issues supplies based on the supported commander's priorities and allocations.

a. Commander's Flexibility

The supported commander organizes in a variety of ways to accomplish the mission. For example, the commander may divide CEs into A and B command groups and/or position the organic logistics differently than previously described. The commander should position organic logistics forward of the supporting CSS installation. The ground unit supply train is a means of internally task-organizing and employing the logistic assets of tactical units.

When employing combat trains, some of the GCE unit's organic logistic capabilities are forward. Maintenance contact team repairmen, ammunition technicians, and supply personnel are with the combat trains to provide front-line support. Routinely, the unit establishes a main echelon with essential elements that support tactical operations. The commander locates most of the unit's logistic capability with the unit or field train. Often the commander locates these trains with the supporting CSSE.

Finally, all units have administrative elements located behind the GCE rear boundary. In the administrative rear, supply and warehousing personnel distribute individual equipment and care for tentage, personal effects, and other equipment not required to sustain combat operations. Table 5-1, on page 5-6, shows breakdowns of a typical battalion in combat.

b. Supply Trains

Trains serve as the link between forward tactical elements and the supporting CSSE. The use of trains enables logistics to be performed as far forward as the tactical situations permit. Depending on the situation, trains may provide logistics to the battalion's organic and attached units. Trains may be fully mobile. However, trains are usually movable rather than mobile. In the Marine Corps, this concept applies to unit, battalion, and regimental trains.

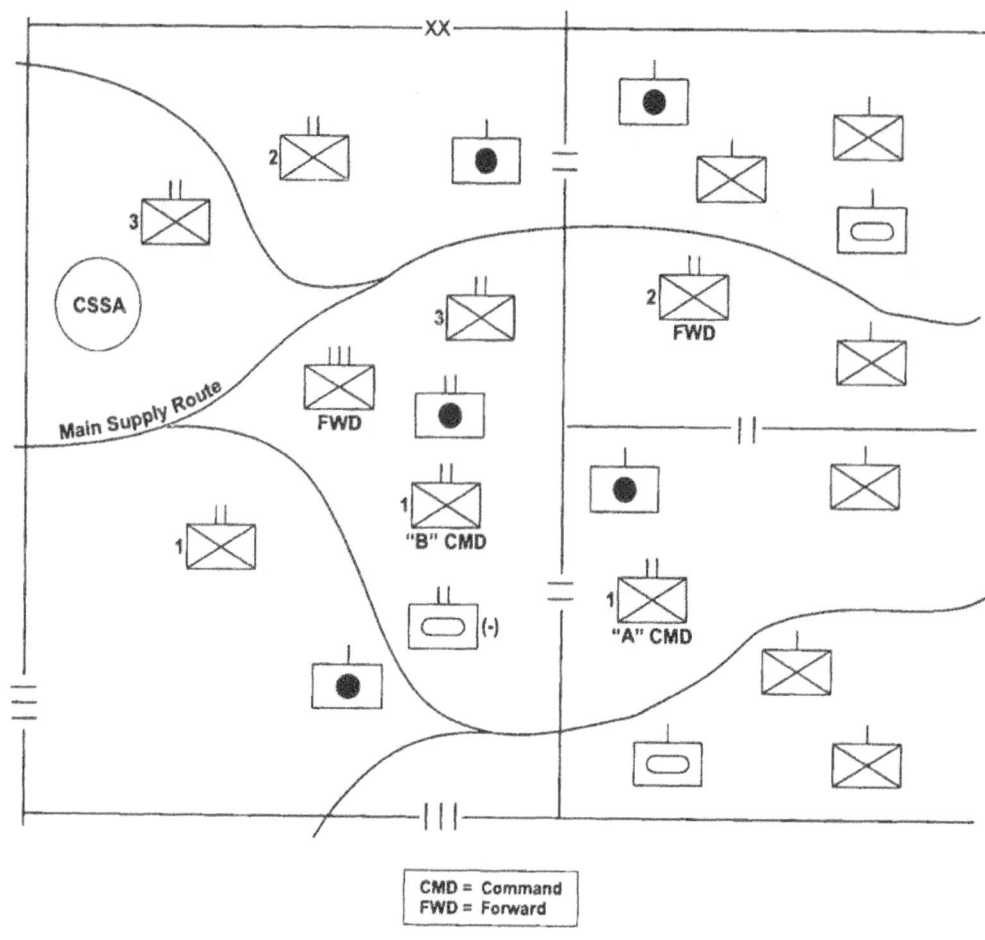

CMD = Command
FWD = Forward

Figure 5-3. Supply Distribution for Ground Combat Element Units.

Table 5-1. Battalion Task Organization for Combat.

Rear	Main Command Post	Forward Command Post
S-1/adjutant	executive officer	commanding officer
supply chief	headquarters commandant	S-2
administrative		S-3
supply clerks	S-4A/S-4 chief	fire support coordinator
replacements	motor transport officer	
casuals		S-4
	ordnance officer	communications officer
	supply officer	
	organic logistics	organic logistics

(1) Unit Trains. Unit trains centralize the units' organic logistic assets. These trains are most appropriate in defensive, slow-moving, or static situations. The commander uses this option when a tactical situation dictates self-contained train operations for centralization and control. For example, during the early phases of an amphibious operation the battalion must locate its logistics capability in the BSA or landing zone. The use of unit trains in this situation provides simplicity, economy, and survivability against ground attack.

(2) Battalion Trains. Normally, to improve responsiveness, flexibility, and survivability against air attack, trains supporting battalion-sized units are echeloned into combat trains and field trains.

(a) Combat Trains. Combat trains are organic elements that provide critical logistics in forward areas. Mobility is the key for combat trains, which are kept as small as possible to move with the supported forces. A combat train's survivability depends on its small size and its own firepower. Usually, a combat train—

- Transports some battalion corpsmen with limited medical supplies.
- Carries maintenance contact teams.
- Hauls rations, fuel, ammunition, and critical spare parts.

(b) Field Trains. Field trains consist of the battalion's remaining logistic assets and are located farther to the rear than the combat trains. Field trains may carry the battalion aid station, the mess section, and the supply section.

(3) Regimental Train. The regimental train consists of the logistics assets required to sustain the regimental headquarters and attached units under the direct control of the regiment. Logistics needed by combat units should be allocated to battalion trains, and logistics that are not time-critical can be consolidated in the regimental train.

(4) Positioning Considerations. Logistic principles of responsiveness and survivability should be the main considerations when selecting a train site. In general, trains should be located—

- On defensible terrain to allow the best use of limited personnel assets.
- In an area with enough space to permit dispersion.
- In an area that provides concealment.
- On firm ground to support heavy vehicle traffic.
- Near a suitable helicopter landing site.
- Close to main supply routes.
- In an area that allows good communications.

(5) Positioning Responsibility. The S-4 coordinates with the executive officer, headquarters commandant, and S-3 in selecting train locations. When the train collocates with another element, such as the supporting CSSD, the S-4 must also coordinate with that element. This option improves coordination and security. Turnaround time, communications requirements, or other mis-

sion-related considerations may necessitate locating the trains elsewhere.

(6) Train Displacement. Proper positioning of trains minimizes displacements and increases the quantity and quality of support. When displacing trains, the S-4 selects the technique that best complements the battalion's tactical operations. Trains may be displaced concurrently with the displacement of the tactical elements or by echelon. Echeloned displacement enhances continuity of logistic support.

(7) CSS Trains. Trains are employed in numerous ways by CSS units in the resupply process. Figure 5-4, on page 5-8, illustrates train techniques that are commonly used during resupply operations. The distances provided in figure 5-4 would be reduced for close terrain (e.g., urban or jungle) or expanded for high enemy threat. The CSSDs may move forward to resupply unit trains, which resupply the using units. The CSSDs are positioned where most responsive, yet survivable.

(8) Replenishment Methods. The service station and tailgate issue methods are the two most common methods used to replenish unit trains.

(a) Service Station. The service station method (figure 5-5 on page 5-9) involves vehicles leaving their tactical positions and entering an established resupply area. The number of vehicles being resupplied at one time depends on the enemy situation and resupply capabilities. The resupply area is designated as a series of resupply points for vehicles. Traffic flow through the resupply area is one way to enhance efficiency. After completing resupply, the vehicles move to the holding area for a precombat inspection, if time permits.

(b) Tailgate Issue. The tailgate issue method is normally conducted in an assembly area. This method involves resupply while combatants remain in their positions. Vehicles stocked with petroleum, oils, lubricants, and ammunition stop at each individual vehicle position to conduct resupply services. This method places the resupply vehicles at greater risk, but maintains tactical positioning and reduces traffic flow. If the tailgate issue method is used in forward positions, then re-supply must be masked by the terrain. See figure 5-6, page 5-10.

5103. Aviation-Peculiar Supply Support Operations

The Navy provides supply support for aircraft and aviation support equipment (ASE) in the ACE. The Marine Corps supply system provides ground supply support to aviation elements. For aircraft ammunition, the source of supply is either the Navy or a theater activity. The CSSE distributes aircraft fuel to the MWSS operating the fuel dispensing system at an airfield. The CSSE distributes class V(A) to the MALS, which operates the aviation ammunition supply point.

a. Marine Aviation Logistics Squadron

When a MAG deploys, the MALS is the focal point for aviation supply and maintenance. Fig-ure 5-7, on page 5-11, depicts these aviation-related supply relationships. The MALS supply and maintenance departments manage aircraft consumable and reparable parts and supplies. The MALS supply department receives requisitions from the intermediate and organizational mainte-nance activities. It also receives requisitions from elements of the MWSS (i.e., expeditionary air-field). If the item is not in stock, the MALS passes the requisition to the naval supply activity in the theater support area, which either fills the request or forwards it to the appropriate source in CONUS.

b. Replacement Aircraft

The squadron requests replacement aircraft and depot-level repair of aircraft. It passes the request for replacement aircraft to the aircraft group, which passes it to the ACE. The ACE passes the request to the type commanders (FMF Atlantic and/or Pacific and Naval Air Force Atlantic and/or Pacific). The MALS, MAG, ACE, and type commanders coordinate placement of aircraft into

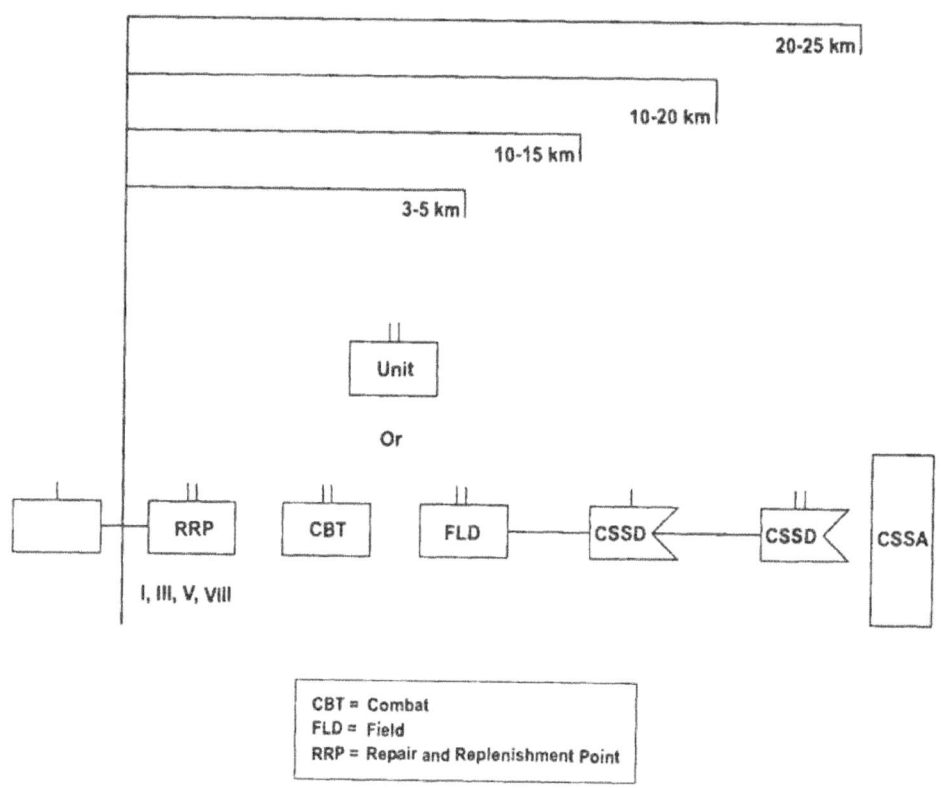

Figure 5-4. Train Techniques Commonly Used During Supply Operations.

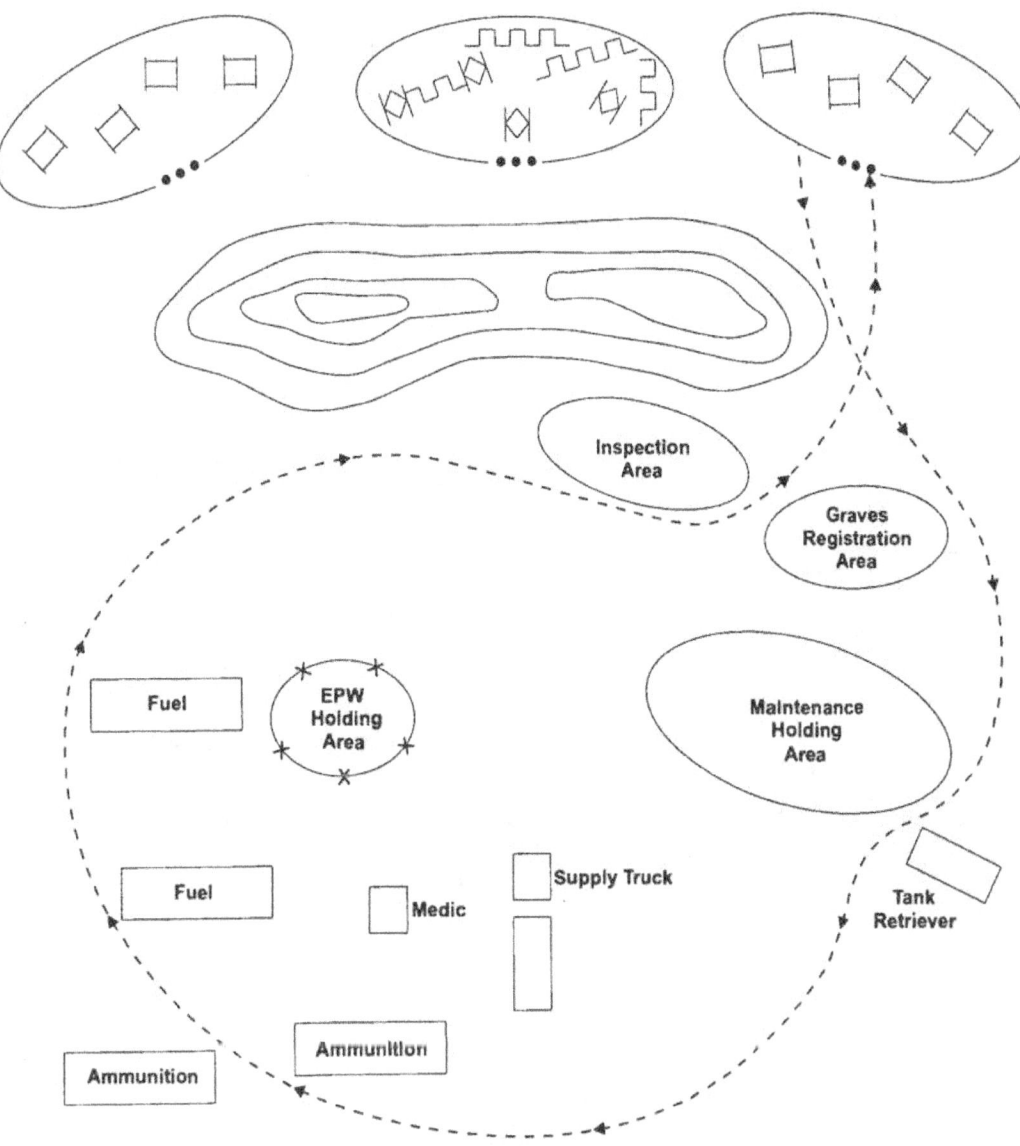

Figure 5-5. Service Station.

depot maintenance. The transferring activity is responsible for flying replacement aircraft directly to the receiving squadron or to an airfield near the receiving squadron. The receiving squadron accepts the aircraft and reports the aircraft's status to the ACE.

c. Aircraft Fuel and Ammunition

The CSSE normally establishes a fuel depot ashore, from which it draws fuel to deliver to the MWSS which, in turn, dispenses fuel to aircraft. Similarly, the CSSE normally establishes one or more centralized ammunition supply points (ASPs) for the purpose of receiving, accounting, storing, and issuing of class V material. Central ASPs are generally supported by ammunition technicians provided by the FSSG, along with a small cadre of aviation ordnance technicians who assist in the throughput of class V(A) to outlying satellite ACE ASPs. (Satellite ASPs are generally established for both air and ground units in an

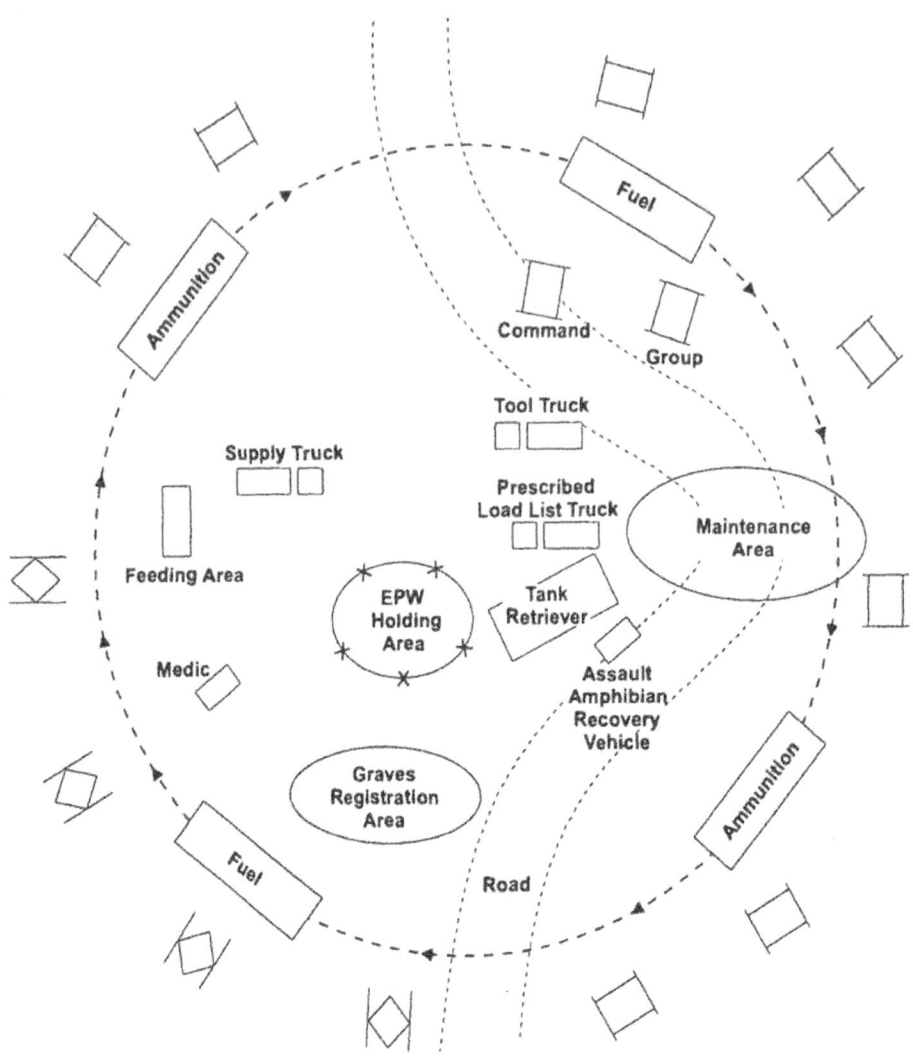

Figure 5-6. Tailgate Issue.

effort to minimize the effects of time and distance on the efficient delivery of munitions to the end user.)

Satellite ASPs used to support the ACE should be collocated with the airfield. The ACE (MALS) aviation ordnance department is staffed for and fully capable of all functions similar to those performed by a central ASP. The MALS aviation ordnance department is responsible for establishing, operating, and maintaining ACE satellite ASPs. Class V material arriving at the airfield is received and stored under the direction of the ACE aviation ordnance department unless accompanying documentation specifies further transportation to either a centralized ASP or another satellite ASP.

Aviation ordnance personnel augment CSSE ammunition company on a contingency basis. The augmentees should be knowledgeable of aviation ordnance peculiarities and different inventory reporting requirements that exist for Navy-owned ammunition. These personnel are assigned to the

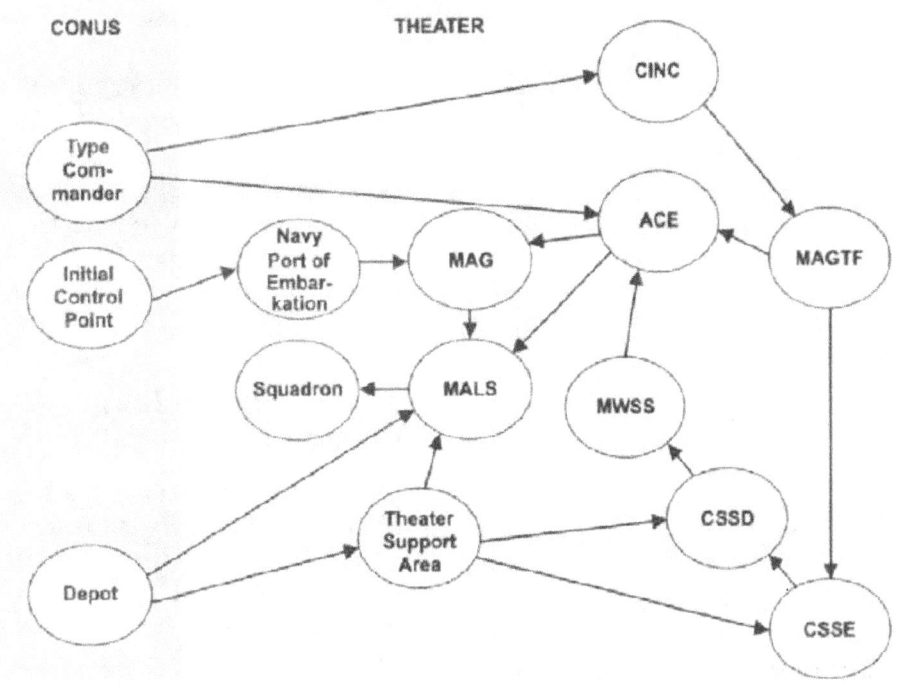

Figure 5-7. Aviation-Related Supply When Deployed.

ASP nearest the SPOE responsible for storing and distributing class V(A) and (W) ammunition arriving in-theater. They assist in the receipt, segregation, storage, and distribution of class V(A) within the theater of operations. Lessons learned reports from Desert Shield/Storm and Restore Hope highlighted the need for this augmentation.

d. Relationship Between Combat Service Support Element and Aviation Units

Figure 5-8 shows the relationship between aviation units and the CSSE for ground supply support and for aircraft fuel and ammunition support.

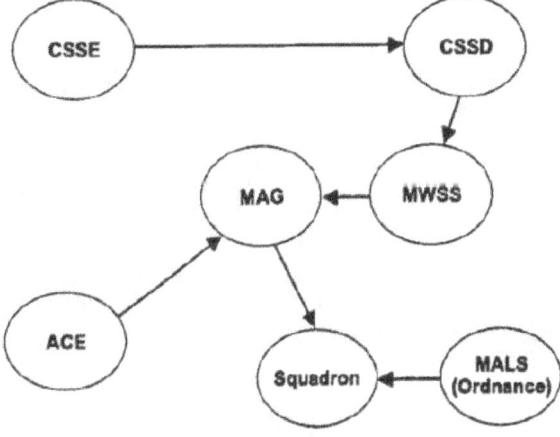

Figure 5-8. Ground Supply When Deployed.

Section II. Maintenance

Maintenance involves those actions taken to retain materiel or restore it to serviceable condition. While the purpose and functions of equipment maintenance are universally applicable, the Marine Corps has developed applications for the support of ground-common and aviation-unique equipment. This section describes maintenance support for the levels, echelons, and subfunctions described in chapter 1.

5201. Ground Maintenance Support Operations

This section discusses the maintenance tactics, techniques, and procedures; intermediate and organizational maintenance operations; and the recovery, evacuation, and repair cycle for ground maintenance support. The maintenance process is followed during the amphibious assault, transition period, and subsequent operations ashore. See figure 5-9, page 5-14.

a. Maintenance During Amphibious Assault

Assault force elements land with a few organizational maintenance personnel. The majority of the organizational maintenance capability lands in nonscheduled waves. Once the first assault waves are ashore, the LFSP provides the only significant maintenance capability.

Although the LFSP has limited recovery, evacuation, and repair capabilities, it has a small block of critical repair parts tailored to match the quantity and type of equipment in the assault waves. The LFSP replaces components and assemblies rather than repairing them. It uses selective interchange to offset the limited depth and breadth of repair parts. One of the first tasks of the LFSP maintenance detachment is to establish maintenance and salvage collection points.

The LFSP must develop an aggressive recovery and evacuation plan because extensively damaged items may provide repair parts for other essential items. Damaged equipment should be placed on resupply vehicles returning to the LFSP. Assault elements should abandon equipment only when the tactical situation prevents recovery. When unable to recover equipment, units should report the location of the item to the LFSP for later recovery and evacuation.

b. Maintenance During Transition Periods

When the tactical situation ashore stabilizes, the MAGTF commander lands nonscheduled units such as unit trains with the organizational maintenance elements. As the assault units' organizational maintenance capability expands, the LFSP shifts its efforts to intermediate maintenance. Assault units normally position their trains near the LFSP to permit mutual support, to avoid duplication of facilities, and to reduce the transportation burden.

c. Maintenance During Subsequent Operations

When appropriate, the MAGTF commander lands the additional CSSE units. Once the CSSE is established ashore, the MAGTF commander disestablishes the LFSP. After the AFOE arrives, the CSSE commander reaches full maintenance capability. When the maintenance unit cannot repair an item, it evacuates the item to the next higher level.

d. Organizational Maintenance

Units owning equipment have organizational maintenance responsibilities. Proper maintenance is essential to sustain combat operations. The maintenance contact team is the centerpiece of organizational maintenance.

(1) Maintenance Contact Team Capabilities. The maintenance contact team consists of organizational maintenance repairmen with tools, test equipment, and critical, high-usage repair parts. These repairmen inspect, diagnose, classify, and repair equipment at forward sites. In addition, the maintenance contact team may include communications, engineer, motor transport, or ordnance repair personnel. The logistics officer determines the exact number of Marines and mix of skills in maintenance contact teams and positions them in the appropriate train. When using combat trains, maintenance contact teams are forward where they are more responsive to the tactical unit. If deployed with a unit train, maintenance contact teams are farther to the rear.

(2) Maintenance Contact Team Operations. Maintenance contact teams (MCTs) conduct recovery, evacuation, and repair. They determine whether an item is reparable at the recovery site. The MCT either fixes the item, requests parts and an intermediate level maintenance support team (MST) from the CSSE, or supervises the item evacuation. Figure 5-9 shows relationships between various maintenance agencies. The GCE collection points represent the battalion and regimental trains.

e. Intermediate Maintenance

The three elements of an intermediate maintenance concept are the MST, the CSSE forward maintenance detachment, and the FSSG intermediate maintenance activity (IMA).

(1) Maintenance Support Team. The MST is an intermediate maintenance version of the MCT. The MST has intermediate maintenance repairmen with tools, test equipment, repair parts, and likely a wrecker or maintenance vehicle. These repairmen inspect, diagnose, classify, and repair equipment at forward sites. The CSSE operations officer determines the number of Marines and mix of skills per team. Normally, MSTs move forward to repair a specific item of equipment. This technique allows the MST to draw the needed parts and tools before moving based on input from the MCT.

(2) CSSE Forward Maintenance Detachment. The CSSE forward maintenance detachment is the element of a CSSD that operates the mainte-

nance facilities and collection points far forward. The forward support maintenance detachment—

- Evacuates inoperable equipment from supported units' collection points.
- Performs intermediate maintenance within its capabilities.
- Provides repairmen, tools, and test equipment to maintenance support teams.

(3) FSSG IMA. The FSSG IMA provides robust principal end item repair and component rebuild support to the MEF. The FSSG commander establishes a centralized IMA in the force combat service support area (FCSSA) to perform complex, time-consuming maintenance activities during sustained operations ashore, such as Desert Shield/Desert Storm. The CSSE commander forms multiple on-call MSTs and, during surge periods, sends them forward either to assist MCTs or to augment the CSSE forward maintenance detachments.

f. Recovery, Evacuation, and Repair Cycle

These capabilities differ during the various phases of combat operations and increase as more of the MAGTF lands. See appendix D for a depiction of the maintenance recovery, evacuation, and repair cycle during combat.

(1) Recovery Responsibility. As much as capability and the tactical situation allows, the owning units are responsible for retrieving immobile, inoperative, or abandoned materiel. They move recovered equipment to a maintenance collection point or a main supply route.

(2) Evacuation. If neither the owning unit nor the CSSE can repair a recovered item, the CSSE evacuates it. If the MAGTF commander authorizes selective interchange, the CSSE may remove and use parts before evacuating an item. The CSSE evacuates recovered equipment directly to a designated repair or disposal agency.

(3) Nonreparable Equipment. If materiel is in danger of capture, the owning unit should recover

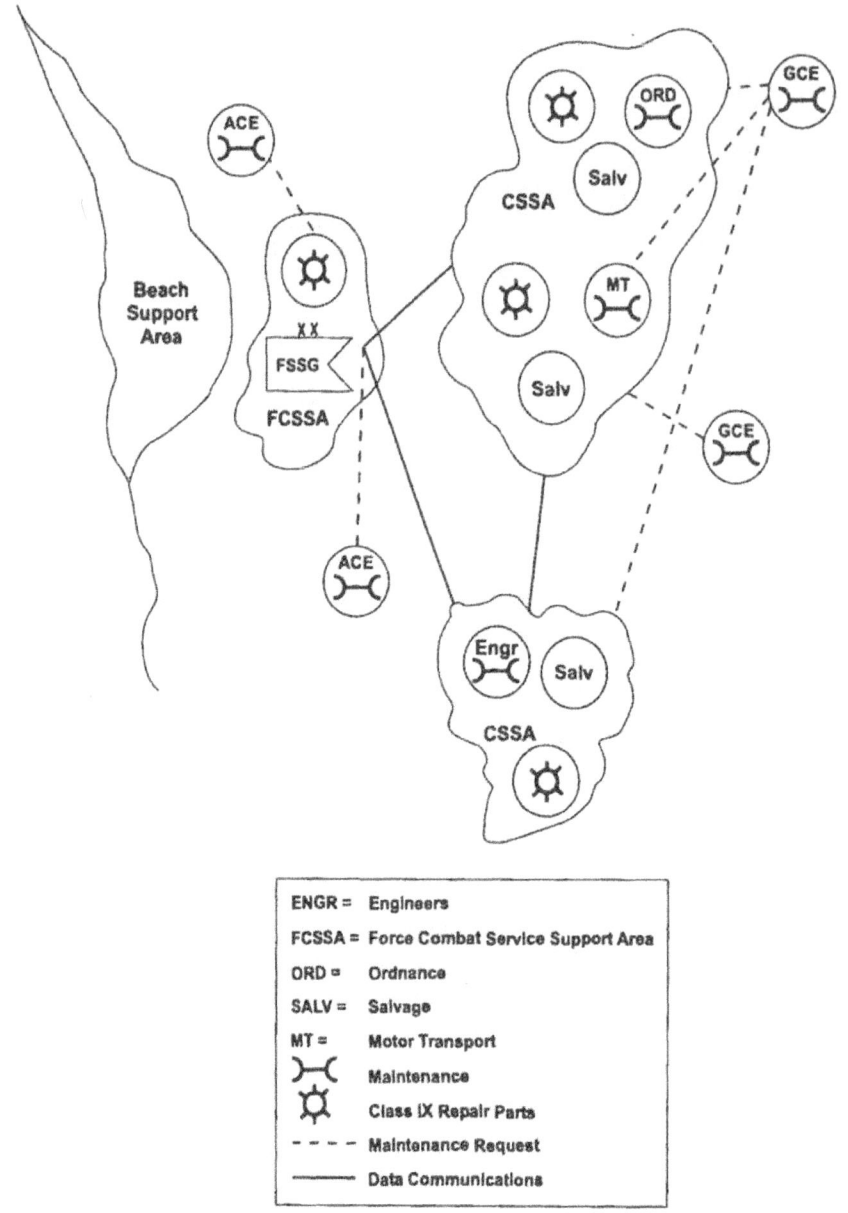

Figure 5-9. Ground Equipment Maintenance Process in Combat.

all salvageable parts and components and destroy the remaining equipment.

(4) Recovery Considerations. Commanders should closely monitor and control recovery and evacuation operations. Logistics officers must establish recovery and evacuation priorities and carefully allocate personnel and equipment to these operations. For example, combat vehicles, weapons, and weapons' platforms often have a higher recovery priority than other items. Also, the extent of damage affects recovery priority. When the unit must recover two or more of the same item, the item requiring the least repairs should be recovered first. The following is a suggested recovery priorities list:

- Items immobilized by terrain.
- Items with failed or damaged components that require little repair.

- Damaged items that require significant expenditure of recovery and repair effort to return them to operation.
- Contaminated items that require significant recovery, repair, and decontamination effort.
- Salvageable items.
- Enemy materiel.

(5) Positioning. Combat and combat support unit commanders should position their recovery capability forward. As a rule, the recovery capability consists of personnel and equipment organized in maintenance contact teams. The CSSE commanders distribute maintenance assets to achieve a balance between economy and responsiveness.

5202. Aviation-Peculiar Maintenance Support Operations

The Marine aviation logistics support program (MALSP) and the MPF program (including aviation logistic support ships) provide aircraft support personnel with the ability to sustain all aircraft types that comprise a MAGTF ACE. Specifically, these programs enable aviation logisticians to identify and integrate the people, aircraft support equipment, mobile facilities and/or shelters, as well as spares and/or repair parts needed to support a MAGTF ACE.

a. Marine Aviation Logistics Support Program

Most Navy-funded logistic support for aviation units is provided under MALSP. The primary objective of MALSP is to expedite the delivery of required aviation-peculiar logistics to support any contingency. MALSP and MPF provide a building block method of quickly task-organizing, deploying, and sustaining ACE aviation peculiar assets by structuring aviation logistic support into contingency packages that can be phased into an operating area.

(1) Support Packages. MALSP provides comprehensive and replenishable sustainment packages while reducing lift requirements and force closure time. These support packages are used as building blocks to keep aircraft operational during every phase of an operation.

(a) Fly-In. Fly-in support packages (FISPs) can be viewed as enabling packages. They provide the organizational-level spare parts support that allows Marine aircraft to commence flight operations immediately on arrival in theater. The FISPs are airlifted to the operating site as part of the fly-in echelon (FIE). They are combined with the organizational-level and/or limited intermediate-level aircraft support equipment transported aboard MPF ships. This combination of assets is capable of providing critical aviation support for 30 days of combat flying. If flight operations require more than 30 days of spare parts support, then contingency support packages (CSPs) are provided to augment the FISP.

(b) Contingency. The CSPs augment the FISPs by adding common maintenance support items which are used by more than one Marine aviation unit and peculiar maintenance support items used for a specific aircraft or support equipment application. These packages support both organizational- and intermediate-level maintenance. The CSPs integrate the maintenance equipment, mobile facilities, spare parts, and personnel to support and sustain each type of deployed tactical Marine aircraft. Rapidly deployable organizational-level individual material, mobile facilities allowances, and personnel allocations are identified in master allowance documents for each aviation element. The master allowance documents consist of T/Os, individual material readiness lists (IMRLs), tables of basic allowance (TBA), aviation consolidated allowance list (AVCAL), and coordinated ship-station allowance list (COSAL). The CSP allowances are computed at the combat flying-hour rate for a 90-day endurance period and are supplemental allowances to those identified in AVCAL, COSAL, IMRL, and TBA. The CSP allowances, which are derived from the master allowance documents, are separated into the following subcategories:

- **Common Allowances.** Common CSP allowances consist of those Marine common assets that the rotary- or fixed-wing MALS of an ACE provide to support the majority of assigned aircraft. A fixed-wing Marine common item is one that has application to at least the F/A-18 and AV-8B aircraft which are part of an ACE. A rotary-wing common item is one that has application to at least the CH-53E, CH-46E, and AH-1W aircraft which are a part of an ACE. Weight, cube, cost, reliability, and supportability are the primary considerations in determining what parts are included in the CSP. For planning purposes, it is assumed that the fixed- and rotary-wing MALS will be geographically separated.

- **Peculiar Allowances.** Peculiar CSP allowances consist of those maintenance items required for intermediate-level support of a specific type/model/series (T/M/S) aircraft and of associated support equipment that a MAG provides to a MAGTF ACE.

(c) Follow-On. Follow-on support packages (FOSPs) represent the final MALSP building block. The introduction of the FOSP would, in essence, provide ACE aircraft with the same support received in garrison.

(2) Reconfiguration for Deployment Support. Marine aircraft squadrons of a particular T/M/S aircraft are generally consolidated and attached to only two or three MAGs. To form an ACE, one or more fixed- and rotary-wing MAGs reconfigure into a task-organized fighting unit by retaining or attaching only mission-essential aircraft, aircrew, and operations support personnel and equipment. Under MALSP, aviation logisticians identify people, IMRL items, TBA, and AVCAL and/or COSAL allowances that are needed to support the quantities of each T/M/S of aircraft being detached and attached to ensure that reconfigured MAGs include the necessary MALSP resources.

(3) Support Personnel Requirements. Staffing and organization are two personnel considerations in support of the MALSP.

(a) Staffing. Without adequate staffing of qualified maintenance, supply, and administrative personnel, this program would not succeed. The

MALS and supported squadrons' T/Os should provide the right quantity of skilled personnel to support a task-organized ACE.

(b) Organization. Each MALS is organized to provide a core intermediate-level capability of supervisory and common support personnel necessary to maintain fixed- or rotary-wing aircraft that join an ACE. The MALS T/O contains the personnel component of a common CSP, which forms the nucleus of an ACE allowance list (fixed- or rotary-wing). Each tactical aircraft squadron T/O has a separate listing of intermediate-level billets that consist of military occupational specialty (MOS) skills that are peculiar to that squadron's T/M/S aircraft. The MALS provides the MAGTF commander with the capability to support the peculiar requirements of the T/M/S aircraft assigned to that ACE. Whenever the MAG detaches aircraft and sends them to an ACE, a unit deployment, or an exercise, the MALS uses the intermediate maintenance portion of aircraft squadron T/Os and produces a complete CSP (i.e., IMRL, AVCAL, COSAL, TBA) for the receiving MALS.

b. Aviation Logistics Support Ship

The aviation logistics support ship (TAVB) concept was developed to transport critical intermediate-level maintenance and supply assets to a forward operating area in support of deployed Marine aircraft. The primary mission of the TAVB is to provide dedicated sealift for movement of intermediate-level logistic support for use in the rapid deployment of a MAGTF ACE. A secondary mission—to serve as a national asset dedicated to strategic sealift—can be exercised if the embarked MALS is phased ashore. To enhance responsiveness, one ship is berthed on the east coast and another on the west coast of the United States. Both ships can be configured to allow for tailored intermediate-level repair capability while underway, in stream, or pierside.

(1) Manning and Communications. When activated, the MSC operates the TAVBs with civilian manning. The TAVB carries a Navy communications van to support its tactical missions and to provide interoperability with naval groups and task forces.

(2) Marine Aviation Logistics Squadron Operations. MALS operations aboard TAVBs are subdivided into the activation and operational modes.

(a) Partial In-Transit Activation. The MALS can be partially activated during ship transit. Before embarkation, the mission-essential weapon replacement assembly (WRA) and system replacement assembly (SRA) support required during transit must be determined. During partial MALS operations, some inoperable WRAs and/or SRAs can be repaired en route, thereby reducing the requirement for the procurement of spare reparable components; however, component repair capability is driven by the availability of support in the MAG at the time the TAVB is loaded. In the operational mode, mobile facilities are designated as either functional or nonfunctional. A functional mobile facility requires some degree of service from the ship (such as power, low-pressure air, or water). During the ship's transit, functional mobile facilities must be either accessible or manned. On the other hand, nonfunctional mobile facilities are not critical to mission support while aboard the TAVB and are therefore neither operated, manned, nor accessible.

(b) Operational Mode. The TAVB in the MALS operational mode can accommodate approximately 300 mobile facilities, of which 186 are functional and 114 (30 maintenance and 84 supply) are nonfunctional. Functional mobile facilities are stowed on the main and second decks in single or double tiers. Double-tiered units are in clusters of four or eight. Access to upper-tier mobile facilities on the main and second decks is provided by ladders and scaffolding systems called access modules. Access to nonfunctional mobile facilities stowed below the second deck is by end-connected access modules. Remaining nonfunctional mobile facilities stowed below the second deck or deep stowed are not accessible while the TAVB is underway.

(3) Operational Concepts. There are five conceptual TAVB operational considerations.

(a) Primary Operational Concept. The primary TAVB operational concept is to transport an intermediate-level capability, with spare parts and aircraft support equipment to support an ACE deployed in support of a MAGTF.

(b) Deployment. On notification of movement, the TAVB is expected to arrive in the objective area within 15 to 20 days to unite with aircraft, personnel, and maintenance support prepositioned by the fixed-wing flight ferry and the FIE units.

(c) Entry. If conditions permit, transfer of the MALS ashore begins when the TAVB docks.

(d) Enabling Actions. MALS operations can be sustained in the objective area if rapid movement ashore is not possible. Under these conditions, the TAVB prioritizes its workload in support of flight-line maintenance requirements to ensure that mission essential WRA and SRA support is provided.

(e) Amphibious Landing. Although the TAVB is designed primarily to support MPF and an air contingency MAGTF, it could be tasked to support an amphibious operation. In all cases, the TAVB requires an unopposed entry into an objective area before offloading.

c. Maritime Prepositioning Ships

The MPF program provides fleet commanders with deployment flexibility by including organizational-level and limited intermediate-level aviation support equipment and class V(A) in each MPF squadron.

Maritime prepositioning ships are roll-on and roll-off, civilian-crewed, Military Sealift Command-chartered ships that are organized into three MPS squadrons (MPSRONs). In peacetime operations, they are usually forward deployed in strategic locations worldwide. Currently, MPSRON-1 and MPSRON-3 are composed of four ships each and MPSRON-2 is composed of five ships.

(1) Capabilities. Each MPSRON has a fixed set of embarked equipment and supplies. Generally, this set contains sufficient quantities of supplies (except classes VI and X) to sustain a MEB for 30 days of combat operations. To support ACE operations, each MPSRON contains a tailored set of organizational-level aircraft support equipment for each T/M/S aircraft assigned to the supported ACE. Additionally, each MPSRON includes limited intermediate-level facilities equipment. This equipment is designed to provide common intermediate-level functions normally associated with the MALS (i.e., tire and wheel buildup, battery maintenance). On arrival at the port of debarkation, aircraft equipment will be off-loaded, and when combined with the equipment embarked aboard the FIE, T/M/S aircraft FISP allowances, and support personnel, the ACE will be capable of sustained combat flight operations for up to 30 days or, if augmented, until the arrival of the host MALS via the TAVB.

(2) Unique Features. The association of specific forces with their prepositioned materiel is a unique feature that sets apart the MPF program from other afloat prepositioned programs. This critical association facilitates the rapid employment of materiel in support of expeditionary operations. The strategic stationing of MPSRONs contributes to worldwide responsiveness and provides the ability to mass a large force at one point by using several squadrons and associated forces.

Section III. Transportation

Transportation is movement from one location to another by using highways, railroads, waterways, pipelines, oceans, and air. Transportation is needed to put combat power (personnel and materiel) in the correct locations at the proper times to start and maintain operations. Any major disruption of transportation support can adversely affect a MAGTF's capability to support and execute the assigned mission.

5301. Motor Transport Operations

Motor transport operations may be either combat support or CSS. The commander may attach motor transport units to supported units. The commander may also control allocated motor transport resources by assigning an appropriate mission. Successful motor transport operations require careful management.

Economical transportation operations dictate matching the number and type of vehicles to the task and reducing the turnaround time. Factors that affect turnaround time are distance, rate of march, and the time it takes to load and unload. The turnaround time can be delayed if shippers and receivers responsible for loading and unloading vehicles are slow or fail to release the vehicles after unloading.

a. Operational Techniques

The commander may increase the tonnage moved with a fixed number of trucks by adopting some or all of the following techniques:

- Loading each vehicle to its maximum allowable capacity.
- Increasing the authorized speed of the vehicles (existing traffic and weather conditions dictate a safe operating speed).
- Synchronize delivery and pickup schedules to various units.
- Reducing turnaround time.

b. Types of Haul

(1) **Local (Short) Hauls.** The ratio of running time to loading and unloading time is small for local hauls. Trucks running local hauls make several trips per day. The measure of effectiveness for evaluating local haul operations is the amount of tonnage moved during the operational period.

(2) **Line (Long) Hauls.** The ratio of running time to loading and unloading time is large for line hauls. Trucks running line hauls make only one trip or portion of a trip per operating shift. The measures of effectiveness for evaluating line haul operations are the time consumed, distance traveled, and tonnage hauled during the operational period. The transportation agency expresses this measure in either ton-miles or ton-kilometers.

(3) **Zonal Hauls.** Truck operations confined within the territorial boundaries of one command are intrazonal. Trucks crossing boundaries and operating under the area control of more than one command are interzonal. The MAGTF commander makes policies and maintains control over interzonal operations.

c. Hauling Methods

(1) **Direct Haul.** A direct haul completes a single transport mission in one trip. No transfer of supplies or exchange of equipment occurs. The commander uses direct haul to speed forward movements before establishing transfer or exchange points. This method is most common for local hauls because long distance direct hauls are hard on both the driver and equipment.

(2) **Shuttle.** A shuttle involves the same vehicles making repeated trips between two points. This method is most common for local hauls.

(3) **Relay.** Relay hauling is the continuous movement of supplies or troops over successive segments of a route without transferring the load. The motor transport unit does a relay by changing drivers, tractors, or both for each segment. This

method is most common for line hauls. The relay system, using tractor- or semi-trailer combinations, is the most efficient method of line-haul operations. This technique is best used when there is a well-developed road network that is not subject to interdiction. Relay is also the best method to use when the unit cannot complete a one-way haul in one day. Containerization increases the effectiveness of this system by making better use of the truck's tonnage capability. This system provides rapid throughput of cargo and guarantees adequate supervision and support along each segment of the route.

d. Cargo Clearance

Clearing cargo from a beach, port, railhead, or airfield permits continuous discharge of ships, trains, or aircraft. Terminal operation units are responsible for cargo clearance. The availability and proper use of motor transport and MHE are essential. The transportation support unit plans and sets up the circulation network and regulates the flow of vehicles throughout the terminal area. Beach clearance operations are especially difficult as a result of the generally poor road conditions and the temporary nature of the available support facilities. Air terminal clearance is easier because roads and facilities are often better. However, to unload the aircraft and clear the terminal rapidly, vehicles may not be loaded to maximum capacity.

e. Convoy Operations

Convoys are task-organized to meet the requirements of the assigned mission. A convoy may include a transport element, an escort or security element, a C2 element, and various support elements. Because units plan and execute their own convoy operations, the convoy commander is the direct representative of the commander initiating the operation and is responsible for the conduct, safety, security, and accomplishment of the convoy's mission. However, higher headquarters often establish control measures and regulations governing convoy operations on main supply routes. Commanders publish control measures and regulations in local SOPs and in their OPORDs. These control measures include start points, checkpoints, halts, and release points.

Commanders also classify routes in their area of operations.

f. Types of Routes

(1) Open Route. An open route has minimal control and does not require prior approval to use the route from the commander whose area the route crosses. The only supervision along the route is at critical intersections which are traffic controlled by military police who also enforce standard traffic laws.

(2) Supervised Route. The commander whose area the route crosses exercises limited control over a supervised route. Any column of 10 or more vehicles and any oversized or overweight vehicles require prior clearance. The commander may also limit access to the route. The military police establish traffic control posts and patrols.

(3) Dispatch Route. The commander whose area the route crosses exercises full control over a dispatch route and establishes priorities for its use. Any vehicle or group of vehicles requires prior approval to use the route.

(4) Reserve Route. The commander sets aside this type of route for the sole use of a specific unit, a special operation, or a certain traffic type. If the route is reserved for a specific unit, the commander of that unit determines the necessary control.

(5) Prohibited Route. Traffic is banned from this route.

5302. Port and Terminal Operations

a. Ship-to-Shore Movement

This type of movement is that portion of the amphibious operation assault phase that includes the deployment of the landing force from the ships to designated landing areas.

b. Shore-to-Shore Operation

This assault operation moves personnel and materiel directly from a shore staging area to the objective. It does not involve further transfers between types of craft or ships incident to the assault movement. Usually a single-Service operation, a shore-to-shore operation involves water crossings in assault craft or in assault craft and aircraft. The purpose of this operation is to establish a force on or withdraw it from the far shore.

c. Logistics Over-The-Shore Operations

Logistics over-the-shore (LOTS) operations are "the loading and unloading of ships without the benefit of fixed port facilities, in friendly or non-defended territory, and, in time of war, during phases of theater development in which there is no opposition by the enemy." (JP 1-02)

LOTS operations may be over unimproved shorelines, through partially destroyed ports, through shallow-draft ports, and through ports that are inadequate without LOTS capabilities. See JP 4-01.6, *Joint Tactics, Techniques, and Procedures for Joint Logistics Over the Shore (JLOTS)*, for a detailed discussion of LOTS operations. LOTS operations are used to load and unload—

- Break bulk ships.
- Roll-on and roll-off ships.
- Container ships.
- Bulk petroleum, oils, and lubricants ships.
- Water ships.
- Barges.

d. Joint Logistics Over-the-Shore

JLOTS operations may involve units and equipment from the Army, Navy, and Marine Corps and may follow amphibious assault operations. The transition from amphibious to JLOTS operations entails passing command of shore facilities to the Army once the amphibious operation ends. The JTF or unified commander directs such transitions. Amphibious operations and MPF operations use some of the same equipment and procedures as JLOTS operations.

e. Inland Waterway Operations

An inland waterway normally operates as a complete system. It involves—singly or in combination—rivers, lakes, canals, intracoastal waterways, and two or more water terminals. Inland waterways can relieve pressure on other modes of transportation. They are especially useful for moving a large volume of bulk supplies and heavy-outsize items that are not easily transported by other means. Although economical, inland waterways are relatively slow compared to other means of transportation. They are especially vulnerable to enemy action and climatic changes.

f. Inland Terminal Operations

Inland terminals serve air, rail, and motor transport operations. They provide cargo transfer facilities at interchange points. They form connecting links when terrain and operational requirements cause a change in carrier.

g. Staging Area Operations

MAGTF forces conduct staging area operations during amphibious and other types of movements. JP 1-02 gives two definitions for staging area. "1. Amphibious or Airborne—A general locality between the mounting area and the objective of an amphibious or airborne expedition, through which the expedition or parts thereof pass after mounting, for refueling, regrouping of ships, and/or exercise, inspection, and redistribution of troops. 2. Other Movements—A general locality established for the concentration of troop units and transient personnel between movements over the lines of communications."

5303. Air Delivery Operations

Air delivery offers the CSSE options for supply operations that present potential economies in terms of responsiveness, assets, and security. Air delivery lends itself to supply support operations in helicopterborne and subsequent operations ashore, especially for bulk items (e.g., classes I, III, and V). As the initial resupply effort in support of helicopterborne operations, coordinated air delivery operations can reduce ground transportation requirements while enhancing the sustainability and combat power of the supported force. As a means of sustainment in subsequent operations ashore, air delivery can reduce both the vulnerability of resupply convoys to enemy interdiction. In each case, economy of effort is achieved through the compensatory reduction of security requirements associated with air delivery.

5304. Deployment

MAGTFs deploy from permanent installations for forward deployments and combat operations. Regardless of the type of deploying force, designated transportation operating agencies control and coordinate the marshaling, embarkation, and movement of the forces.

a. Marine Corps Commands

The following Marine Corps commands may be involved with MAGTF deployments:

- HQMC.
- COMMARFORs.
- Deploying MEFs.
- Deploying MAGTF CE (if other than a MEF deployment).
- Divisions, MAWs, and FSSGs.
- Bases and air stations from which the forces deploy.
- Marine Corps logistics bases (Albany and Barstow).

b. External Transportation Agencies

The following commands external to the Marine Corps may be involved with MAGTF deployments:

- Supporting CINC.
- Supported CINC.
- Fleet commander.
- DLA (including remote storage activities).
- USTRANSCOM and its subordinate commands:

- MSC.
- AMC.
- MTMC.

c. Modes of Transportation

Transportation modes vary depending on the type of MAGTF, the purpose and duration of the deployment, and the anticipated employment. Deployments of larger MAGTFs require use of several transportation modes.

(1) **Amphibious.** Amphibious deployments require the following modes of transportation:

- Military or commercial trucks, buses, and rail from origins to POEs for all personnel, supplies, and equipment.
- Amphibious ships from SPOEs to the operating area.
- AMC or commercial charter airlift for AFOE and replacement personnel who cannot deploy by ship.
- Flight ferry of ACE aircraft that cannot deploy by amphibious ships.
- Commercial ships from SPOEs for the AFOE.

(2) **Maritime Prepositioning Force.** MPF deployments require the following modes of transportation:

- Military or commercial trucks and buses from origins to aerial SPOEs for personnel, supplies, and equipment in the FIE.
- Flight ferry of self-deploying ACE aircraft.
- MPF ships for deployment of maritime prepositioned supplies and equipment.
- AMC or commercial charter airlift for the FIE.

(3) **Marine Expeditionary Force.** The MEF deployments are the most complex deployments from a transportation perspective. The MEF elements deploy from different bases and stations that may be in widely separated geographic areas. A forward-deployed MAGTF may be on station and may serve as the MEF enabling force as additional MEF forces deploy.

(4) Forward-Deployed Marine Air-Ground Task Forces. Forward-deployed MAGTFs routinely deploy aboard amphibious ships or a combination of air and MPS ships for MPF operations. Transportation support planning frequently requires coordination with military detachments at foreign ports and airfields to arrange augmentation by foreign civilian transport and U.S. common-user land transportation agencies during scheduled port visits.

5305. Employment

Transportation available for employment in theater includes the organic assets of the MAGTF. It may also include transportation belonging to the joint force commander or to the host nation. Specific capabilities depend on the situation. Transportation assets may include airlift, rail, trucks, ships, boats, barges, and pipelines.

The MAGTF commander is responsible for movement control in the MAGTF operating area. Normally, the commander delegates this responsibility to subordinate commanders within whose zones of action or areas the movement takes place. Behind the GCE rear boundary, this normally is the CSSE commander.

When operating as part of a joint, allied, or coalition force, the MAGTF commander follows the traffic management and movement control regulations of that command. Normally, the higher commander establishes a movement control agency to provide movement management services and highway traffic regulation. This agency coordinates with allied and host nation movement control agencies. See FM 55-10, *Movement Control*, for a discussion of movement control in a theater of operations.

5306. Movement Control

Movement control combines the planning, routing, scheduling, and control of personnel and cargo movements over lines of communications to support the deployment of forces. This section discusses movement control techniques, management agencies, operating procedures, and host nation support.

a. Control Techniques

(1) Centralized Control. The MAGTF commander should centralize control of movements at the highest level. This function is normally controlled by the MEF's FMCC. The FMCC plan is executed by the LMCC under the control of the CSSE commander.

(2) Regulation. The MAGTF commander, through the FMCC, regulates and coordinates movements to prevent congestion and conflicting movements over lines of communications.

(3) Flexibility. The FMCC must be able to divert or reroute traffic to maintain continuous movement of personnel, supplies, and equipment. The transportation system must provide an uninterrupted flow of traffic and be able to adjust to changing situations. The MAGTF FMCC must use its limited transportation capabilities effectively.

(4) Maximum Use of Carrying Capacity. The LMCC must keep equipment loaded and moving. Transportation commanders should also allow for adequate vehicle maintenance and personnel rest while meeting the mission. This principle involves more than just loading each vehicle to its maximum carrying capacity. The MAGTF cannot store transportation capability that it does not use one day to increase capability on subsequent days. Idle, empty equipment is a waste of capacity. Similarly, fully loaded equipment sitting idle is as much a loss of capacity as partially loaded vehicles moving through the system. However, the tactical situation may not permit optimal use of transportation assets.

b. Control Agencies

Movement control agencies function the same during peacetime as they do during periods of conflict. Movement control agencies are either permanent or temporary. Every MAGTF should have a permanent transportation agency, though for smaller MAGTFs this may be no more than one or two individuals. Battalions and squadrons establish temporary unit movement control centers to manage a unit deployment.

c. Control During Deployments

(1) Movement Control Center. The movement control center is an agency that plans, routes, schedules, and controls personnel and supply movements over lines of communications. Every organization establishes and operates a movement control center for deployments.

(2) Local Standing Operating Procedures. Local SOPs establish the composition and procedures for movement control centers. Figure 5-10 depicts relationships between various commands, movement control agencies, and supporting organizations during deployment of a MAGTF.

(3) Marine Force Headquarters Movement Control Center. This center is primarily an information processing and advisory agency to keep COMMARFOR abreast of the status of subordinate unit deployments. This movement control center can coordinate with USTRANSCOM on transportation requirements, priorities, and allocations, as required.

(4) Force Movement Control Center. This is the MEF commander's agency to control and coordinate all deployment support activities. It also coordinates with the AMC, MSC, and MTMC.

(5) Logistic Movement Control Center. The CSSE or the supporting establishment organizes the LMCC to execute the FMCC transportation plan. Each marshaling base and/or station has an LMCC. The FMCC tasks the LMCCs to provide organic or commercial transportation, transportation scheduling, MHE, and other support as required.

(6) MAGTF/Division/Wing/FSSG Unit Movement Control Centers. The division, wing, and FSSG commanders provide forces to deploying MAGTFs. They control transportation and com-munications assets needed to execute deployments. On order, each command activates a UMCC to support the deployment. The FSSG establishes two subordinate agencies—departure airfield control group (DACG) at the aerial port of embarkation (APOE) and the POG at SPOEs. The DACG coordinates equipment turnover and aircraft loading with the airlift control element (ALCE) at the APOE.

(7) Organizational Unit Movement Control Centers. Every deploying unit down to battalion, squadron, and company level activates a UMCC to control and manage its marshaling and movement.

(8) Base Operations Support Group. Bases from which Marine forces deploy establish base operations support groups to coordinate supporting efforts with the deploying units.

(9) Station Operations Support Group. Air stations from which Marine forces deploy establish station operations support groups to coordinate their efforts with those of the deploying units.

(10) Flight Ferry Control Center. In addition to its movement control center, the aircraft wing establishes a flight ferry control center to control deploying aircraft. The flight ferry control center operates under the cognizance of the MAW G-3.

d. Control in Theater

(1) Movement Control Center. The movement control center is the primary agency in theater, as it is in CONUS. As during deployments, lower-level commands activate movement control centers only while they are conducting movements. The MAGTF and its major subordinate commands maintain active movement control centers at all times. These may be no more than the motor transport and embarkation staff officers. In joint and combined operations, the MAGTF movement control center establishes liaison and communications with the theater movement control center and other commands or host nations in whose areas it is operating.

(2) Local Standing Operating Procedures. Local SOPs establish the composition and procedures for movement control centers in theater. Figure 5-10 depicts relationships between various commands, movement control agencies, and supporting organizations after arrival in theater. Unit SOPs should be applicable during both deployment and employment. Modifications to meet specific theater requirements are in the transportation appendix to Annex D of the OPORD.

(3) Marine Air-Ground Task Force Control Agencies. Movement control agencies in theater are the same as in CONUS before deployment.

During amphibious operations, the MAGTF movement control center is the senior movement control agency. The MAGTF commander often delegates responsibility for routine day-to-day movement control to the CSSE. During joint and combined operations, the MAGTF movement control center is not the senior movement control agency.

e. Host Nation Support

The MAGTF should use host nation transportation support to augment its organic transportation capabilities. Upon arrival in theater, MAGTF civil affairs units should investigate the availability

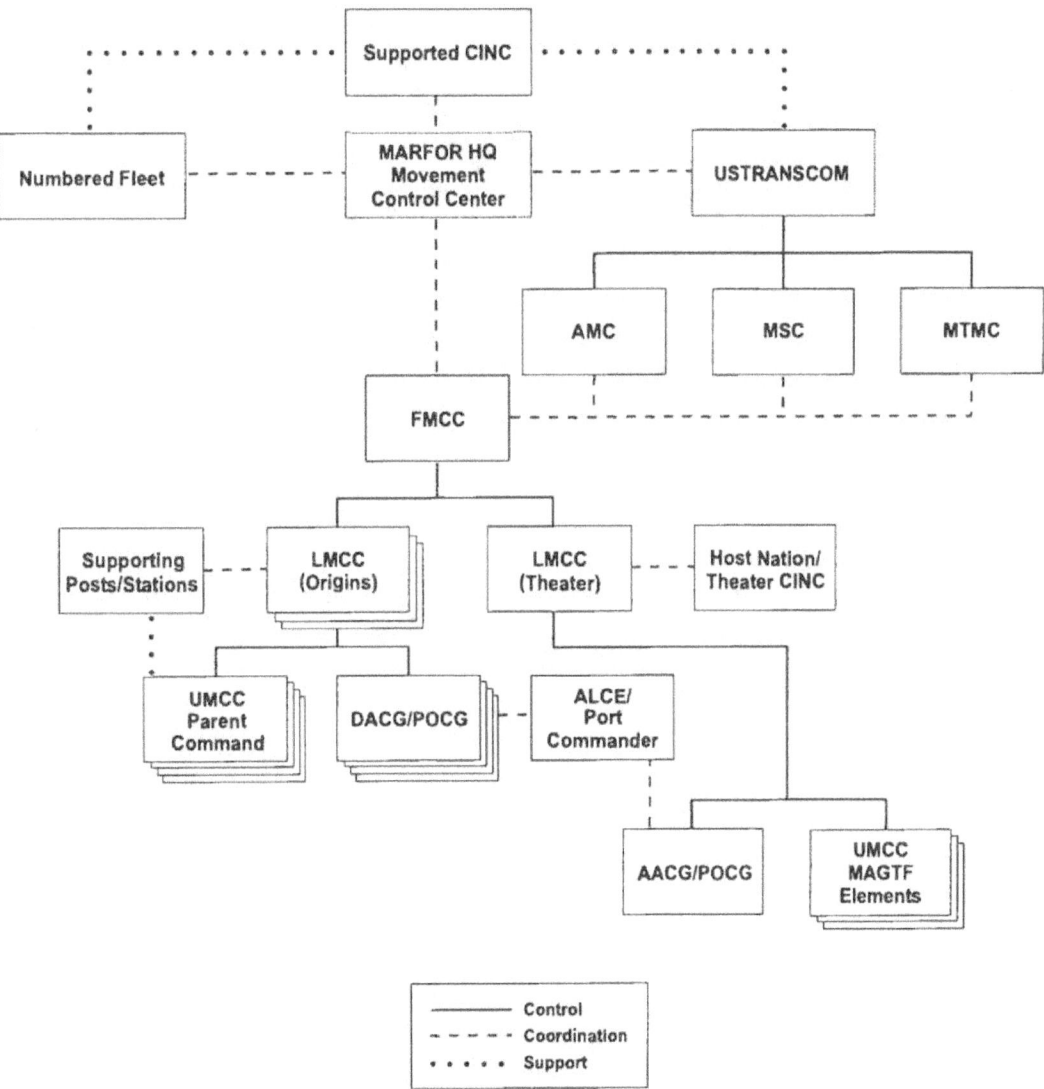

Figure 5-10. Movement Control Relationships during Deployment.

of such support. When operating in NATO or American, British, Canadian, Australian (ABCA) countries, the MAGTF is obligated to abide by certain agreements among the participating na-

tions. These agreements are called standardization agreements (STANAGs) in the NATO arena and quadripartite standardization agreements (QSTAGs) in the ABCA arena.

Section IV. General Engineering

General engineering supports the entire MAGTF and involves a wide range of tasks that sustain combat operations. Most general engineering support is provided by the engineer support battalion, while combat support engineering is provided by the combat engineer battalion. The MWSG and MWSS provide general engineering capabilities in support of aviation units. The MWSS has the engineering capabilities needed to construct expeditionary airfields and to conduct rapid runway repairs. For large-scale projects, the MWSS may be augmented by engineer support battalion and naval construction force (NCF) if construction needs exceed MAGTF capabilities.

commanders for the specific operation. The command relationships that they select determine who plans their transportation and provides other NCF support. When the NCF is under command of the MAGTF, the MAGTF is responsible for support of the NCF as established in appropriate doctrinal publications and/or other applicable agreements. If not under command of the MAGTF, the Navy commander is responsible for common-item support of the NCF. For additional details, see NWP 4-04.1, MCWP 4-11.5, *Seabee Operations in the MAGTF*, and NWP 3-02.14, *The Naval Beach Group.*

5401. Naval Construction Force

The NCF is a Navy engineer organization. It can construct, maintain, and/or operate shore, inshore, and/or deep ocean facilities that support Navy and Marine Corps units. NCF support can range from relatively short-lived support of amphibious operations to extended support of a land campaign.

Command relationships in amphibious operations are the joint responsibility of the senior Navy and Marine commanders. In supporting MAGTF and landing force operations, the NCF can be a separate component of a MAGTF or an ATF. Normally, elements of the NCF are placed under the command of the MAGTF. In such a case, the MAGTF commander may keep the NCF as a separate element, place it under either the CSSE or the ACE, or task-organize MAGTF engineer assets for coordination of effort. NCF units are not capable of providing most combat support functions associated with GCE operations and, therefore, would not normally be placed under the GCE.

The ultimate decisions on command relationships, missions, and tasks rest with the Navy and Marine

5402. Engineering Tasks

Engineering tasks range from support provided by Marine engineer organizations to external support provided by assigned forces such as the NCFs and civilian or host nation resources. The subfunctions of general engineering encompass several tasks, many of which might also be described as combat support tasks. Table 5-2, on page 5-28, shows a wide range of engineering tasks assigned to engineer organizations.

5403. Engineer Group Concept

Specific projects or conditions may arise that require the formation of an engineer group to support the MAGTF commander's concept of operations. This group will be composed of either two or more battalions or squadrons. Under the group concept, which specifically applies to combat support and CSS, the MAGTF commander task-organizes engineer assets as an engineer group. If external units are OPCON to the MAGTF, an engineer group can be task-organized from available NCF units, engineer attachments from other U.S. military forces, and/or host nation assets.

Table 5-2. Engineering Task Matrix.

Tasks	Organizations				
	Combat Engineer Battalion	Engineer Support Battalion	Marine Wing Support Squadron	Naval Construction Force	Civilian/ Host Nation Support
Beach improvements		X		X	
Camp construction, repair, and/or maintenance		X	X	X	X
Construction design		X		X	X
Demolition	X	X	X	X	
Engineer reconnaissance	X	X	X	X	X
Explosive ordnance disposal		X	X		
Field fortifications	X	X	X	X	X
Obstacle removal	X	X	X	X	X
Pioneer roads	X	X	X	X	
Planning and installation of obstacles and/or barriers	X	X	X	X	X
Pre-engineered structures		X	X	X	X
Rapid runway repair		X	X	X	
Tactical water and/ or hygiene service		X	X	X	
Tactical bulk fuel storage		X	X		
Tactical electrical supply		X	X	X	
Unpaved roads, airstrips, and/or marshaling areas		X	X	X	X
Vertical takeoff and landing and/or helicopter landing zone		X	X	X	X
War damage repair		X	X	X	X

Section V. Health Service Support

The focus of HSS emphasizes the provision of far-forward, mobile, medical and surgical support that is capable of stabilization and rapid evacuation of casualties who are unable to quickly return to duty. HSS is a process that delivers a healthy, fit, and medically ready force; counters the health threat to the deployed force; and provides critical care and management for combat casualties. See MCWP 4-11.1 for further guidance.

5501. Marine Air-Ground Task Force Capabilities

a. Command Element

The MEF CE is capable of providing routine and emergency treatment and preparation for evacuation by using its organic medical section.

b. Ground Combat Element

Injured and sick persons requiring hospitalization are readied and evacuated to the rear. Normally, a regimental or battalion aid station serves as the hub for medical support. Headquarters battalion, Marine division, medical section—

- Provides for emergency treatment and preparation for evacuation of all casualties.
- Treats minor illness and injuries.
- Supervises disease prevention and control measures.

Regimental and battalion infantry unit medical platoon or section provides—

- Preventive medicine.
- Treatment for minor illnesses and injuries.
- Emergency lifesaving for battle and non-battle casualties.

c. Aviation Combat Element

Health services personnel are assigned to the primary subordinate organizations in the MAW. The

MWSG and MWSS provide aid station capability for expeditionary airfield operations. MWSG and MWSS medical personnel—

- Provide for emergency treatment and preparation for evacuation of all casualties.
- Treat minor illness and injuries.
- Supervise disease prevention and control measures.

d. Combat Service Support Element

The medical battalion's primary mission is to perform those emergency medical and surgical procedures that, if not performed, could lead to death or loss of limb or body function. The battalion structure has 260 holding beds and 9 operating rooms. The medical battalion is made up of an H&S company and three surgical companies. The H&S company contains 8 shock-trauma platoons that have 10 patient-holding beds each. Each surgical company contains 60 beds and 3 operating rooms. The battalion's surgical companies provide the following support:

- Initial resuscitative surgical intervention.
- Temporary casualty holding.
- Ground evacuation support to forward medical elements.
- Preventive medical support.

The dental battalion task-organizes dental sections and detachments to HSS elements of the MAGTF. In an operational environment, the dental battalion's primary mission is to provide dental health maintenance with a focus on emergency care. In addition to medical support determined appropriate by medical battalion and surgical company commanders, dental detachment personnel may provide the following support:

- Postoperative.
- Ward.

- Central sterilization.

- Supply room.

5502. Capabilities External to the Marine Air-Ground Task Force

a. Casualty Receiving and Treatment Ships

The CRTSs have the largest medical capability of any amphibious ships in the ATF. For medical support capabilities of these vessels and their potential roles as CRTSs, see Fleet Marine Force Reference Publication (FMFRP) 1-18, *Amphibious Ships and Landing Craft Data.*

b. Fleet Hospitals

Fleet hospitals are transportable, medically and surgically intensive, and deployable in a variety of operational scenarios. See NWP 4-02.4, Part A, *Deployable Heath Service Support Platforms—Fleet Hospitals,* for more information.

c. Hospital Ship

The hospital ship (T-AH) is a floating surgical hospital. Its mission is to provide acute medical care in support of combat operations at sea and ashore.

5503. Patient Movement

Prompt movement of casualties through the evacuation system to treatment facilities is essential to decrease morbidity and mortality of battlefield casualties. A sound patient movement process ensures that patients move only as far rearward in the continuum of care as their needs dictate. This process also ensures the efficient and effective use of limited HSS assets. The NWP 4-02.2, Part A, provides a general summary of the HSS systems and specific tactics, techniques, and procedures for patient movement. For patient movement in joint operations, refer to JP 4-02.2. Patient movement is divided into two phases.

a. Evacuation

In the evacuation phase, patients are moved between point of injury or onset of disease to a facility that can provide the necessary treatment capability.

b. Medical Regulating

Medical regulating involves the actions and coordination necessary to arrange for the movement and tracking of patients through the levels of care. This process matches patients with a medical treatment facility which has the necessary HSS capabilities. It also ensures that bed space is available. In the medical regulating phase, destination MTFs are selected. These MTFs are equipped with the necessary HSS capabilities for patients being medically evacuated in, between, into, and out of different theaters of geographic combatant commands and CONUS.

Section VI. Services

The various nonmateriel and administrative support activities of the services functions are described in JP 4-0, *Doctrine for Logistic Support of Joint Operations*, Naval Doctrine Publication (NDP) 4, *Naval Logistics*, and MCDP 4, *Logistics*. As previously discussed in chapter 1, the Marine Corps categorizes services functions as being either combat service support services or command services.

5601. Combat Service Support Services

The CSSE is organized to provide CSS services for other MAGTF elements in operational chains of command.

a. Disbursing

Manpower restrictions and lack of mobility mandate that the committed MAGTF's disbursing support be located in the CSSE rear area. Geographical separation of the ACE, GCE, and CSS units necessitates collocating disbursing offices that are capable of providing the required disbursing services to both the ACE and the GCE. These offices respond to the taskings of their respective commanders but receive procedural direction from the MAGTF disbursing officer, who is solely responsible for all disbursing operations.

(1) Deployment Capability. Disbursing assets of the CSSE can be deployed to provide full-service disbursing support for all MAGTF organizations. Services for a MEF in theater are provided by the FSSG disbursing sections and platoons. This flexibility allows for the task-organizing of disbursing assets to meet the needs of the MAGTF commander.

(2) Phases of Support. Disbursing support meets two primary missions in theater—the payment of MAGTF obligations and pay-related support for deployed Marines and Sailors. Disbursing support is divided into three phases.

(a) Phase One. During the initial assault phase, when the force is establishing itself ashore, required disbursing services are minimal. Normally, the capability for payment of MAGTF obligations and/or individual emergency payments to Marines is available. During this phase, mission accomplishment and survival divert attention to the battlespace, and disbursing personnel may be committed to augmenting other CSS efforts. Therefore, a minimum of personal finance records maintenance and accounting requirements are met. When command attention turns to financial concerns, disbursing personnel ensure services are responsive and accurate.

(b) Phase Two. This phase begins when the need to establish an office to provide increased service is identified. In addition to phase one support, on-call, company-level check cashing is coordinated. The contact team approach is used to deliver support to MAGTF elements.

(c) Phase Three. The third phase is usually conducted during sustained operations ashore. In addition to disbursing tasks accomplished in phase two, phase three services include—

- Monthly on-call paydays to noncommitted forces.
- Guidance to the MAGTF commander on disbursing matters.
- Public voucher payment for assets purchased and services rendered.
- Civilian payroll support.
- Individual personal finance records maintenance.
- Data systems input for updating the central file, generating required reports, and submitting financial returns.
- Temporary additional duty and permanent change of station travel advances and settlements.
- Cash depository for the Marine Corps exchange, postal service, and clubs.
- Personal and U.S. Treasury check cashing.

- Currency conversion.
- Cross-Service support as required.

b. Postal

Postal assets are task-organized to provide postal support for the MAGTF and attachments. These assets include a mobile main post office and 12 mobile unit post offices. The main post office coordinates all postal functions and locations. Each unit post office is capable of providing full postal support to a reinforced regiment. Smaller detachments can be task-organized to support various sized MAGTFs.

(1) Support. The bulk of postal support is located throughout the MAGTF rear area. Unit post offices provide postal support to various CSSAs. On request from the GCE, mobile unit post offices may be located in the GCE rear area. The ACE may also request mobile unit post offices. These mobile units can provide full or partial postal services. In the event that postal services are not requested by the GCE or ACE, the mail delivery for GCE rear and ACE personnel is accomplished through resupply channels. All postal units respond to the taskings of their respective CSSE commanders but receive procedural direction from the MAGTF postal officer, who is solely responsible for all postal operations.

(2) Phases of Support. During amphibious operations, postal support is divided into three phases.

(a) Phase One. During the assault phase, postal services generally are not available.

(b) Phase Two. This phase begins when the need to establish a postal unit is identified. In addition to processing incoming and outgoing personal and official mail, unit post offices provide all postal services that are normally available in garrison. Mail delivery to units is accomplished by unit mail clerks and orderlies.

(c) Phase Three. The third phase begins when sufficient forces are ashore to establish a rear ar-

ea. In this phase, postal assets are committed in support of the MAGTF mission and perform the following functions:

- Advise the MAGTF commander on postal matters.
- Route mail to and from the battle area.
- Sell stamps and money orders.
- Accept letters and packages for mailing.
- Deliver and dispatch official and personal mail.
- Establish a casualty mail section.
- Coordinate the resupply of unit postal offices operating throughout the area. (Unit post offices are stocked with the supplies and equipment to support regimental-sized organizations for a period of 60 days without resupply.)
- Coordinate cross-Service support as required.

c. Exchange Services

A tactical field exchange is established when no other source of class VI support is available. The MAGTF commander determines when to establish a tactical field exchange, but the CSSE commander designates the site for the exchange. When needed, mobile exchanges are sent to MAGTF maneuver elements. Following the MAGTF commander's established guidance, the CSSE commander is directly responsible for the establishment of tactical field exchange location and mobile exchange operations.

(1) Tactical Field Exchange Operations. A deployed tactical field exchange activity is operated as a branch of the parent Marine Corps exchange from which the unit is deployed. All internal supplies, resale goods, and any resupply items are provided from that parent exchange. In the event of an extended deployment and/or employment or an extensive mobilization, exchange services will be provided by using morale, welfare, and recreation nonappropriated funds. Funding for equipment, supplies, and resale goods will be provided from mobilization contingency funds. Requirements for this type of support must be referred to Morale, Welfare, and Recreation Division, Headquarters, Marine Corps, (MW).

(2) Concept of Organization. Support is provided in the form of a branch store with a mobile operation of the parent Marine Corps exchange. The field exchange is provided by the CSSE. (Only class VI supplies required to stock the field exchange are provided by the parent Marine Corps exchange.)

(3) Resupply. The CSSE field exchange officer initiates resupply of class VI supplies for short-term support. Resupply class VI supply items are coordinated and shipped in the same manner as other supply blocks for deploying units. Under normal circumstances, resupply should not be necessary during operations that last 30 days or less. If resupply is needed, planning factors to be considered include troop strength, mission completion date, and the time it takes to resupply.

(4) Guidance. Marine Corps Order P1700.27, *Marine Corps Morale, Welfare and Recreation Policy Manual,* is the basic instructional document for Marine Corps exchange services.

(5) CSSE Functions. The CSSE provides exchange support for the MAGTF by—

- Providing CSSE Marines holding military occupational specialty (MOS) 4130 or 4131 to make up the exchange platoon.

- Ensuring exchange platoon personnel bring with them all supplies and equipment necessary to support the MAGTF for a period of 30 days without resupply. (The stock assortment is reviewed by the MAGTF commander before deployment.)

- Resupplying when necessary using the parent exchange or Marine Corps supply system. (Resupply is dependent on availability of air and sea transportation.) Acquisition cross-Service agreements can be used to arrange resupply from other military exchange organizations in theater, if available.

- Determining the number and exact location of tactical field exchange facilities (dependent on the tactical situation).

d. Security Support

Successful enemy action against command and control facilities and CSS installations can make it impossible for the MAGTF commander to accomplish the assigned mission. Enemy threat, however indirect, may be posed by conventional and/or unconventional forces. Consequently, combat support and CSS installations to the rear of the GCE should be considered high-priority, lucrative targets. The CSSE commanders are responsible for the security and survivability of their own units.

(1) Security Measures. All commanders must take both passive and active measures to provide security and to ensure the continuation of their units' missions despite the threat or the initiation of enemy action. These measures are listed in chapter 6 of this publication.

(2) Role of the Military Police. Security support is provided by the military police units in the FSSG and MWSG. These units, however, are insufficient to provide all security support functions simultaneously. A military police unit is an economy-of-force unit that must be used wisely. Support is based on the concept of operations and a clear understanding of priorities as established by higher headquarters. In support of the MAGTF, the military police functions include—

- Antiterrorism and force protection.
- Maneuver and mobility support operations.
- Area security operations.
- Law and order operations.
- Internment operations.

e. Legal Services

The FSSG, H&S battalion, legal services support section is the command entity that provides legal services support for the MAGTF. In support of a MAGTF, legal services support tasks are normally performed by the CSSE through one or more legal services support teams.

(1) Legal Services Support Section and Legal Services Support Teams. These teams are employed at appropriate times and places in support of major MAGTF personnel concentrations in the area of operations. Legal services support teams vary in number, size, and composition depending on the—

- Mission, size, and composition of the MAGTF.
- Expected duration of the operation.
- Scheme of maneuver and topography involved in the operation.

(2) MAGTF Support. Most legal services work in support of MAGTF operations involves—

- Injury, death, claims, and supply investigations.
- Legal review of OPLANs.
- Law of war training.
- Legal assistance.
- Nonjudicial punishment.
- Summary and special courts-martial.

(3) Marine Expeditionary Force Support. The MEF operations may involve the deployment of all available legal services personnel. Each major subordinate command has an organic staff judge advocate section to ensure the coordination of legal services support for the command and its subordinate organizations. The staff judge advocate provides legal advice to the commander.

f. Civil Affairs Support

Civil affairs is a command responsibility involving those activities between MAGTF elements, civil authorities, and local civilians in the area of operations. Whether assigned or task-organized, civil affairs units are normally assigned to the MAGTF CE and function under the staff cognizance of the MAGTF G-3/S-3. They assist in planning and conducting MAGTF civil affairs operations to implement MAGTF civil affairs missions and goals within the MAGTF area of responsibility. For MAGTF operations, civil affairs responsibilities are normally confined to periods of limited duration between the arrival of the first tactical units and the termination of operations or the transfer of responsibility to Army

civil affairs units. MAGTF civil affairs activities are normally limited to those minimum essential civil-military functions that are necessary for the accomplishment of the primary mission. Refer to JP 3-57, *Doctrine for Joint Civil Affairs*, for detailed guidance on civil affairs.

Civil affairs support is provided by all individuals and elements of the MAGTF to achieve the established civil affairs goals of the command. As a subfunction of services, civil affairs support is included in the six functional areas of CSS. Civil affairs support tasks are largely logistical in nature and generally involve population and resource control assistance in support of MAGTF operations; however, the capability to perform those tasks is not unique to the CSSE. Supported units also possess civil affairs support capabilities, and the CSSE provides support beyond the supported units' organic capabilities. Marine Corps civil affairs assets are MAGTF assets. Current Marine Corps civil affairs units reside in the Reserve establishment.

In the operating forces, designated personnel from the legal services support section provide a limited civil affairs capability to the MAGTF commander when civil affairs assets resident in the Reserve establishment are not available. When tasked, legal services support section personnel augment Reserve civil affairs units or, in the absence of Reserve units, form the MAGTF civil affairs unit. When so tasked and employed, legal services support section personnel are normally assigned to the MAGTF CE.

The civil affairs function is conducted in all phases and in every geographic zone of the operation.

g. Graves Registration

Graves registration and mortuary services are necessary functions in support of military operations. The G-1/S-1 is the cognizant staff officer. Mortuary services require specialized capabilities beyond those of the CSSE and the MAGTF. These services are provided by the Army for the Department of Defense.

Graves registration operations consist of search, recovery, and identification of deceased personnel and the final disposition of their personal property. Responsibility for the full and proper execution of graves registration operations is a leadership responsibility from the smallest unit to the largest. Individual actions in the recovery and accountability of fallen Marines and Sailors are the basis of the Marine Corps graves registration effort. Within the Marine Corps and for MAGTF operations, graves registration operations are separate from health services operations.

Inherently, every small-unit leader and commander bears responsibility for providing graves registration services. Graves registration procedures begin at the point where a Marine or Sailor dies. Formal chains of evacuation and accountability begin at the unit level. Each battalion should establish casualty collection teams and collection points, which are normally collocated with aid stations, to ensure that this function is addressed. JP 4-06, *Joint Tactics, Techniques, and Procedures for Mortuary Affairs in Joint Operations*, provides detailed information on this function.

5602. Command Services

Each MAGTF element is responsible for conducting the following command services.

a. Personnel Administration

Personnel administration is an important command service conducted at all major levels of the MAGTF. While providing personnel administration is a responsibility of the commander, this function is typically executed under the cognizance of the unit adjutant (G-1/S-1). The G-1/S-1 takes the lead in coordinating action between other staff functions (e.g., G-2/S-2, G-3/S-3, G-4/S-4). It is also responsible for all unit personnel matters to include the following personnel-related functions:

- Graves registration.
- EPWs handling procedures.

- Civilian personnel matters (e.g., contractors, civilian employees, refugees).
- Interior management.
- Discipline, law, and order.

The G-1/S-1 is responsible for preparing annex E to the MAGTF OPORD which sets forth the personnel requirements for the MAGTF. This document provides higher and subordinate headquarters with a general understanding of how personnel support will be provided for the MAGTF. Normally, annex E is prepared only at the MAGTF and higher headquarters level.

Annex E should address coordination and support with agencies external to the MAGTF. It should also address any inter-Service support or host country agreements. The following areas should be addressed in annex E:

- Relationships with the International Red Cross.
- Arrangements for transfer of prisoners of war between Services or acceptance of prisoners of war from Allied forces.
- Reports of law of war violations.
- Currency and credit controls.
- Use of U.S. citizen civilian personnel.
- Procurement and administration of non-U.S. citizen labor.
- Joint replacement depots.
- Joint, centralized graves registration procedures.
- Provision of common-user morale, welfare, and recreation services and facilities.
- Provision of postal and courier services.

b. Religious Ministries Support

Religious ministries support performs ecclesiastic functions and provides both faith-based and non-denominational counseling and guidance for all personnel. It is a significant factor in building and maintaining morale. Chaplains (ordained or accredited priests, ministers, and rabbis) are assigned throughout the MAGTF at the organizational level and higher. Chaplains normally report directly to the commander. Fleet Marine Force

Manual (FMFM) 3-61, *Ministry in Combat*, addresses religious ministries support in detail.

c. Financial Management

The Marine Corps founded its philosophy of financial management on the principle that financial management is inseparable from command.

(1) Responsibilities. The commander must make vital fiscal decisions and keep financial management in proper perspective as a part of balanced staff action. In this regard, the commander should recognize that financial management has no bearing on the determination of mission, but rather is a primary consideration in determining both the means and the time-phasing of mission accomplishment. The commander has two types of financial responsibility—command and legal.

(a) Command. Command financial responsibility parallels the commander's other responsibilities. The commander is tasked with controlling and administering of funds granted to perform the mission.

(b) Legal. When in receipt of an allotment or operating budget, the commander is legally responsible for the proper receipt and obligation of those appropriated funds.

(2) Management Operations. Financial management operations within the operating forces are divided into four fundamental areas—budgeting, accounting, disbursing, and auditing. To assist the commander in the accomplishment of these functions a general staff-level financial organization, the comptroller, is established at each major command. Commanders at lower echelons normally assign the additional duty of fiscal officer to a special staff officer (e.g., the supply officer) or an organizational staff officer (e.g., the S-4). The comptroller (or fiscal officer) acts as the principal financial advisor to the commander.

d. Communications and Information Systems

Communications and information systems collect, process, or exchange information. Under the cognizance of each element or subordinate organization G-6/S-6, these systems play an essential role in supporting command and control of the MAGTF.

In the past, communications and data processing were separate functional activities. The MAGTF CSSE played a significant role in MAGTF communications and data processing by providing garrison and forward-deployed centralized mainframe support of MAGTF automated information systems. However, network-based, functional area data processing applications on individual desktop computers throughout the MAGTF are becoming the norm. As a consequence, the communications and data processing support functions have been merged. In addition, MAGTF staff and functional area managers—including the logisticians—are becoming responsible for effectively using their computers and coordinating with their organizational G-6/S-6 for computer equipment maintenance and connectivity. See MCWP 6-22, *Communications and Information Systems*, for a comprehensive discussion of this topic.

e. Billeting

Billeting provides safe and sanitary living quarters for assigned personnel and billet assignments are based on the operational circumstances. Commanders exercise their billeting responsibility through subordinate unit leaders. The commander's logistics officer (G-4/S-4) normally has staff cognizance of billeting facilities support. Billeting options include—

- Family housing in garrison.
- Bachelor quarters in garrison.
- Berthing compartments on ships.
- Tents in the field.
- Rough bunkers in combat.
- Fighting holes in combat.

f. Messing

Food service is a function of command. Commanders with a food service T/O and T/E provide food service support designated by the unit mission statement. The CSSE is responsible for supplying class I (subsistence). Organizational food service responsibilities include—

- Accounting for all subsistence received from the CSSE.
- Storing properly all semiperishable and perishable supplies.
- Ensuring sanitation of the messhall.
- Preparing quality meals.
- Accounting of personnel fed.
- Filing reports.

(1) Messhalls. In combat operations, field messhalls are normally established at the battalion level. A large messhall (seating in excess of 2,000 personnel) is not recommended because it can be targeted easily by the enemy. There is a higher risk of food poisoning when operating under field conditions. GCE, CSSE, and ACE food service officers—

- Provide recommended sites.
- Determine sizes of the facilities.
- Designate which units to support.

(2) Field Feeding. The following rations are used to feed Marines in the field:

- Packaged operational rations (POR) include—
  - Meal, ready-to-eat (MRE).
  - Ration, cold weather (RCW).
  - Bread, shelf-stable (BSS).
- Unitized B-rations (UBRs) are semiperishable items packaged in 100-man modules that are individually palletized. UBRs require food service personnel and equipment to prepare the meals.
- Meal module tray pack (MMTP) is a complete meal for 18 persons. MMTPs are served by unit food service personnel using the tray ration heating system. This feeding method is em-

ployed for mobile unit personnel who cannot access hot UBR meals from the messhall. Without MMTPs, maneuver element personnel would be required to subsist on MRE's for extended periods of time.

(3) Coordination of Resources. The selection of food service resources depends on the operational situation. The family of rations (POR, UBR, and MMTP) were developed for any situation. Detailed food service resources planning is conducted at the G-4/S-4 level in close coordination with food service officers, commanders, messhall managers, and the CSSE.

(4) Personnel Requirements. Food service personnel requirements are based on the type of ration being used and the number of persons being served (see table 5-3)..

Table 5-3. Food Service Personnel Requirements.

Ration Type	Ratio of Cooks	Ratio of Messmen
UBR	1 cook per 75	1 per 50
MMTP	2 cooks per 250*	as needed
MRE/POR	not required	not required
*Using the tray ration heating system.		

g. Band

Traditionally, band members are trained in combat arms and may be used in a variety of roles, such as augmenting the headquarters defense in a combat environment. Designated major commands employ a military band to—

- Render honors.
- Provide military pomp at ceremonies.
- Perform on other occasions to raise or sustain morale.

h. Morale, Welfare, and Recreation

Activities, such as movies, special live-entertainment shows, and unit-level parties, are morale, welfare, and recreation (MWR) opportunities used to relieve the stress and tedium of military operations. MWR is managed through command channels, with access to funds and support starting at the unit level. Although MWR activities are desirable, they should not interfere with mission accomplishment.

Appendix A

Logistic and Combat Service Support Task-Organization Guide

Function	Capabilities			
	CE	ACE	GCE	CSSE
Supply Requirements Procurement Storage Distribution Salvage	Capable of internal ground supply tasks.	Group/squadrons capable of internal ground supply tasks. MALS performs aviation supply tasks.	Regimental headquarters, battalions, and separate companies capable of internal ground supply tasks.	Battalions capable of internal ground supply tasks. Supply battalion provides ground supply support for the MAGTF.
Maintenance Inspection and classification Service, adjustment, tuning Testing and calibration Repair Modification Rebuilding and overhaul Reclamation Recovery and evacuation	Capable of authorized maintenance tasks, first through limited third echelon, on assigned ground equipment.	Groups/squadrons capable of authorized maintenance tasks, first through limited third echelon, on assigned ground equipment. Squadrons perform organizational maintenance on assigned aircraft. MALS performs intermediate and limited dopot maintenance on supported aircraft.	Organizations capable of authorized maintenance tasks, first through limited third echelon, on assigned ground equipment.	Battalions capable of authorized maintenance tasks, first through limited third echelon, on assigned ground equipment. Maintenance battalion provides third and limited fourth echelon maintenance support for designated MAGTF ground equipment, as well as second and third echelon maintenance services to supported MAGTF organizations whose requirements exceed organic capabilities. Medical battalion performs maintenance on MAGTF class VIII (medical) materiel.

Function	Capabilities			
	CE	ACE	GCE	CSSE
Transportation Embarkation Landing support Port and terminal operations Motor transport Air delivery Freight/passenger transportation MHE	Capable of preparing assigned personnel, equipment, and supplies for air and/or surface embarkation; limited capability for ground transport using organic light and medium trucks.	General capability for preparing assigned personnel, equipment, and supplies for air or surface embarkation. Capable of managing terminal operations and providing air transport for selected passengers and cargo. Most organic ground transport centralized in the MWSSs.	Capable of preparing assigned personnel, equipment, and supplies for air and/or surface embarkation. Limited capability for ground transport using organizational light and medium trucks, reinforced as necessary with medium trucks from the truck company of the H&S battalion.	Capable of preparing assigned personnel, equipment, and supplies for air and/or surface embarkation. Support battalion provides landing support, air delivery, port and terminal operations, medium- and heavy-truck transportation of freight and passengers, and MHE.
General Engineering Engineer reconnaissance Construction Facilities maintenance Demolition/obstacle removal EOD	Limited organic capability, focused on establishing and running field command posts.	ACE capability for general engineering tasks is centralized in the MWSSs and focused on support of airfield operations.	Limited organic engineering capability for combat support tasks is centralized in the combat engineer battalion.	Engineer support battalion provides MAGTF capabilities for general engineering tasks and can also reinforce MWSSs and the combat engineer battalion if necessary.
Health Services Health maintenance Casualty collection Casualty treatment Temporary casualty holding Casualty evacuation	Limited organic capability for health care and unit-level casualty care and evacuation.	Organic capability for health care and unit-level casualty care and evacuation in separate squadrons and groups. Aviation medical services available in aircraft groups.	Organic capability for health maintenance and unit-level casualty care and evacuation in regimental headquarters, battalions, and separate companies.	Organic capability for health maintenance and unit-level casualty care and evacuation in all battalions. Medical battalion provides shock-trauma and surgical support to the MAGTF. Dental battalion provides dental services for the MAGTF.

Function	Capabilities			
	CE	ACE	GCE	CSSE
Services *CSS* Disbursing Postal services Exchange services Security support Legal services support Civil affairs support Graves registration	Limited organic capabilities for postal, security, and legal services.	Appropriate organic capabilities for disbursing, postal, security, and legal services; civil affairs; and graves registration in separate squadrons and groups.	Appropriate organic capabilities for disbursing, postal, security, and legal services, and graves registration in regimental headquarters and battalions.	Appropriate organic capabilities for disbursing, postal, security, and legal services; civil affairs; and graves registration in all battalions. H&S battalion provides additional support in all services to the MAGTF.
Command Personnel administration Religious ministries Financial management Information services Communications Billeting Messing Band Morale, welfare, and recreation	Capable of organic command support functions for assigned personnel and organizations; at the MEF level the CE may be required to organize, train, and equip a band.	Capable of organic command support functions for assigned personnel and organizations; at the MAW level the ACE may be required to organize, train, and equip a band.	Capable of organic command support functions for assigned personnel and organizations; at the division level the GCE may be required to organize, train, and equip a band.	Capable of organic command support functions for assigned personnel and organizations; normally the FSSG will not be tasked with organizing, training, and equipping a band.

1. The CE and the GCE contain organic capabilities for internal ground logistic functions per applicable T/Os and T/Es.

2. The ACE contains organic capabilities for internal ground-common and aviation-peculiar logistic functions per applicable T/Os and T/Es.

3. The CSSE contains organic capabilities for both internal and external (i.e., MAGTF support) ground logistic functions in accordance with the applicable T/Os and T/Es.

Appendix B

Sample Format of a
Logistic/Combat Service Support Estimate

Copy no. _____ of _____ copies
OFFICIAL DESIGNATION OF COMMAND
PLACE OF ISSUE
Date/time group
Message reference number

LOGISTIC/COMBAT SERVICE SUPPORT ESTIMATE (U)

(U) REFERENCES: As appropriate to the preparation of the estimate.

1. (U) Mission

    a. (U) Basic Mission. State the mission of the command as a whole.

    b. (U) Purpose of the Estimate

        (1) (U) Determine if combat service support (CSS) capabilities are sufficient to support proposed courses of action (COAs).

        (2) (U) Determine which COA is most desirable from a logistic and/ or CSS standpoint.

        (3) (U) Determine what measures must be taken by the commander to overcome logistic and/or CSS problems and/or limiting factors in supporting each COA.

2. (U) Situations and Considerations

    a. (U) Enemy Forces

        (1) (U) Present Disposition of Major Elements. Refer to the Intelligence Estimate.

        (2) (U) Major Capabilities. List enemy capabilities that are likely to affect friendly logistic and/or CSS matters.

CLASSIFICATION

(3) (U) <u>Other Capabilities and/or Limitations</u>. List enemy capabilities and/or weaknesses that are likely to affect the logistic and/or CSS or tactical situation.

b. (U) <u>Own Forces</u>

(1) (U) <u>Present Disposition of Major Combat and Combat Support Elements</u>. May be shown as a situation map or an overlay appended as an annex with reference to the Aviation Combat Element (ACE) Logistic/CSS Estimate by including the statement "See also Aviation Combat Element Logistic/CSS Estimate."

(2) (U) <u>COAs</u>. State the tactical COAs that are under consideration.

c. (U) <u>Characteristics of the Area</u>. List those characteristics that are likely to affect the logistic and/or CSS situation such as weather, terrain, hydrography, communications routes, and local resources.

d. (U) <u>Current Logistic and/or CSS Status</u>. Give a brief description of the current logistic and/or CSS status, including any planned or known changes before and during the period covered by the estimate. The following subparagraphs address typical CSS areas of concern. If possible, state specific quantities.

(1) (U) <u>CSS Organizations and Task Organizations</u>. Each organic CSS organization or task organization is described using the following format:

(a) (U) <u>Locations</u>. May be an overlay.

(b) (U) <u>Missions and/or Tasks</u>

(c) (U) <u>Task Organizations and Command Relationships</u>

(d) (U) <u>General Capabilities and Status</u>. Capabilities and status are described in terms of task organization using the applicable categories listed in paragraphs (2) through (13) below.

(e) (U) <u>Tactical Responsibilities</u>. List if any.

(f) (U) <u>Communications and Automated Data Processing Systems Support Arrangements</u>

(page number)

CLASSIFICATION

CLASSIFICATION

(2)   (U) Personnel

    (a) (U) Strengths. Identify strengths of each major subordinate unit.

    (b) (U) Replacements. Identify replacements on hand, replacements to be received, and the quality of the replacements.

    (c) (U) Morale. Determine the level of fighting spirit, significant factors affecting current morale, religious and welfare matters, and awards.

    (d) (U) Personal Services Support. Identify the required exchange, postal, recreational, and special services support.

    (e) (U) Military Justice. Identify court martial and correction facilities.

    (f) (U) Personnel Procedures. List significant items, if any.

(3)   (U) Supply. Identify procurement, storage, distribution, and salvage methods.

(4)   (U) Maintenance. Determine management, operations, and workload.

(5)   (U) Transportation. Identify motor transport, helicopters, amphibious vehicles, and cargo aircraft; motor transport convoy control; and main supply routes.

(6)   (U) Engineer Support. Identify construction and maintenance of roads, bridges, airfields, helicopter landing sites, bulk fuel sites and pipelines, camps, and utilities (including bath, fumigation, laundry, electrical power, and water points).

(7)   (U) Landing Support. Identify beach, landing zone, and air delivery support operations.

(8)   (U) Medical and/or Dental. Identify preventive medicine, graves registration and casualty collection, evacuation (including evacuation policy), and hospitalization support.

(page number)

CLASSIFICATION

CLASSIFICATION

(9) (U) Military Police. Identify the number on hand and evacuation procedures for prisoners of war, the straggler rates and control, and the traffic control methods.

(10) (U) Civilian Employees. Identify the number, restrictions on use, and organization of civilian employees.

(11) (U) Civil Affairs Support. Identify CSS of the civil affairs effort.

(12) (U) Automated Data Processing Systems. Identify management, operations, and support of command automated data processing systems support.

(13) (U) Miscellaneous. Identify food services, material handling equipment, and financial management (disbursing, budgeting, and accounting) methods.

e. (U) Assumptions. State those assumptions made for the preparation of this estimate. An example of the critical assumption is the estimation of the length of time for the entire operation and for each COA (if different).

f. (U) Special Factors. List items not covered elsewhere, such as state of training of CSS personnel or task organizations.

3. (U) Analysis. Under each of the following categories, analyze each COA that is under consideration in light of all significant factors to determine problems that may arise, measures necessary to resolve those problems, and any limiting factors that may exist.

a. (U) Course of Action #1

(1) (U) Logistic and/or CSS Organizations and Task Organizations. Describe each organic logistic and/or CSS organization or task organization using the following format.

(a) (U) Locations. May be an overlay.

(b) (U) Missions and/or Tasks

(c) (U) Task Organizations and Command Relationships

(page number)

CLASSIFICATION

CLASSIFICATION

(d) (U) <u>General Capabilities and Status</u>. Describe capabilities and status in terms of task organization using the applicable categories listed in paragraphs (2) through (13) below.

(e) (U) <u>Tactical Responsibilities</u>. If any.

(f) (U) <u>Communications and Automated Data Processing Systems Support Arrangements</u>

(2) (U) <u>Personnel</u>

(a) (U) <u>Strengths</u>. Identify the strengths of each major subordinate unit.

(b) (U) <u>Casualties</u>. Determine expected casualties for this COA.

(c) (U) <u>Replacements</u>. Identify replacements on hand, replacements to be received, and the quality of the replacements.

(d) (U) <u>Morale</u>. Identify significant factors affecting current morale, religious and welfare matters, and awards.

(e) (U) <u>Personal Services Support</u>. Identify exchange, postal, and recreation and/or special services support.

(f) (U) <u>Personnel Procedures</u>. List significant items, if any.

(3) (U) <u>Supply</u>. Identify procurement, storage, distribution, and salvage methods.

(4) (U) <u>Maintenance</u>. Identify management, operations, and workload.

(5) (U) <u>Transportation</u>. List motor transport, helicopters, amphibious vehicles, and cargo aircraft; motor transport convoy control; and main supply routes.

(6) (U) <u>Engineer Support</u>. Identify construction and maintenance of roads, bridges, airfields, helicopter landing sites, bulk fuel sites and pipelines, camps, and utilities (including bath, fumigation, laundry, electrical power, and water points.)

(page number)

CLASSIFICATION

CLASSIFICATION

(7) (U) Landing Support. Identify beach, landing zone, and air delivery support operations.

(8) (U) Medical and/or Dental. Identify preventive medicine, graves registration, casualty collection, evacuation (including evacuation policy), and hospitalization support.

(9) (U) Military Police. Identify the number on hand and evacuation procedures for prisoners of war, the straggler rates and control, and the traffic control methods.

(10) (U) Civilian Employees. Identify the number, restrictions on use, and organization of civilian employees.

(11) (U) Civil Affairs Support. Identify the CSS of the civil affairs effort.

(12) (U) Automated Data Processing Systems. Identify management, operations, and command automated data processing systems support.

(13) (U) Miscellaneous. Identify food services, material handling equipment, and financial management (disbursing, budgeting, and accounting) methods.

b. (U) Course of Action #2. Same subparagraphs as shown for COA #1.

c. (U) Course of Action #3. Same subparagraphs as shown for COA #1.

4. (U) Evaluation. Based on the foregoing analyses, summarize and compare the advantages and disadvantages of each COA under consideration from a logistic and/or CSS standpoint.

5. (U) Conclusion

a. (U) Preferred Course of Action. State which COA, if any, can best be supported from a logistic and/or CSS standpoint.

b. (U) Major Disadvantages of Other Courses of Action. State whether any or all of the remaining COAs can be supported from a logistic and/or CSS standpoint, citing the disadvantages that render them less desirable.

(page number)

CLASSIFICATION

CLASSIFICATION

c. (U) <u>Logistic and/or CSS Problems and Limitations</u>. Cite any significant logistic and/or CSS problems to be resolved and any limitations to be considered in each COA.

d. (U) <u>Decision or Action</u>. State those measures that are necessary to resolve those logistic and/or CSS problems cited above.

/s/ _____
_____

ANNEXES: (As required)

(page number)

CLASSIFICATION

(reverse blank)

Appendix C

Sample Format of Annex D
(Logistics/Combat Service Support)

Copy no. ____ of ____ copies
OFFICIAL DESIGNATION OF COMMAND
PLACE OF ISSUE
Date/time group
Message reference number

ANNEX D TO OPERATION ORDER OR PLAN (NUMBER) (OPERATION CODEWORD) (U)
LOGISTICS/COMBAT SERVICE SUPPORT (U)

(U) REFERENCES: Cite references necessary for a complete understanding of this annex.

1. (U) Situation

   a. (U) Enemy. Refer to Annex B (Intelligence). Provide available information on enemy actions or intent to conduct actions to disrupt or degrade envisioned friendly logistic and combat service support (CSS) operations. Include information on enemy capabilities or assets that can augment friendly logistic and CSS operations.

   b. (U) Friendly. List supporting logistic or CSS organizations not subordinate to the force and the specific missions and tasks assigned to each.

   c. (U) Infrastructure. Refer to Annex B (Intelligence). Provide information on existing infrastructure, such as ports, factories, fuel and water sources, and lines of communications that can be used to support friendly logistic and CSS operations.

   d. (U) Attachments and Detachments. Refer to Annex A (Task Organization). List other Service and nation logistic and CSS units attached to the force. List all Marine Corps logistic and CSS units detached to support other friendly forces.

CLASSIFICATION

e. (U) Assumptions. State realistic assumptions and consider the effect of current operations on logistic capabilities.

f. (U) Resource Availability. Identify significant competing demands for logistic resources where expected requirements may exceed resources. Include recommended solutions within resource levels available for planning, if any, and reasonably assured host nation support.

g. (U) Planning Factors. Refer to and use approved planning factors and formulas, except when experience or local conditions dictate otherwise. When deviating from planning factors, identify the factors and the reason.

2. (U) Mission. State in a clear and concise manner the mission of the logistic and CSS forces and the logistic objectives that support accomplishment of the command's purpose and tasks.

3. (U) Execution

a. (U) Concept of Logistics and Combat Service Support. State the concept for logistic and CSS operations necessary to implement the order or plan. Describe how the logistic and CSS assets will be organized and positioned to execute the mission. The concept may include planned employment of other Service and nation logistic and CSS forces, host nation support logistic capabilities, or operation of the lines of communications.

b. (U) Tasks

(1) (U) Assign logistic and CSS responsibilities to subordinate logistic organizations.

(2) (U) Identify and assign responsibility for logistics and CSS required from other commands, Services, or nations.

(3) (U) Identify and assign responsibility for logistics and CSS required for forces assigned or attached from other commands, Services, or nations.

(4) (U) Identify and assign responsibility for logistics and CSS required for Marine Corps forces assigned or attached to other commands, Services, or nations.

CLASSIFICATION

CLASSIFICATION

(5) (U) Assign responsibilities to support joint boards and committees, such as transportation and procurement, and other Services or nations providing services.

4. (U) <u>Administration and Logistics</u>

a. (U) <u>Logistics and Combat Service Support</u>

(1) (U) <u>Supply</u>. Refer to Appendix 7 (Supply). Summarize the following, in coordination with supporting commanders and Service component commanders, if different from standard planning factors. Place detailed discussions in appendices and listings of supply depots, terminals, and lines of communications in tabs or the appropriate appendixes.

(a) (U) <u>Distribution and Allocation</u>

<u>1</u> (U) Purpose, location, and projected displacement of main and alternate supply depots or points and supporting terminals and ports to be used or considered.

<u>2</u> (U) Prepositioned logistic resource allocation.

<u>3</u> (U) Existing terminals and lines of communications and the known or estimated throughput capability. Indicate the time-phased expansion necessary to support the plan.

<u>4</u> (U) Indicate anticipated shortfalls.

<u>5</u> (U) Indicate common user logistic supply support responsibilities and arrangements.

(b) (U) <u>Level of Supply</u>

<u>1</u> (U) Indicate the time-phased operating and safety levels required to support the plan.

<u>2</u> (U) Indicate the prepositioned war reserve materiel requirements to support the time-phased deployments pending resupply.

<u>3</u> (U) Specify significant special arrangements required for materiel support beyond normal supply procedures.

(page number)

CLASSIFICATION

CLASSIFICATION

<u>4</u> (U) Indicate anticipated shortfalls.

<u>5</u> (U) Indicate common user logistic supply support responsibilities and arrangements.

(c) (U) <u>Salvage</u>. Provide instructions for, and identify the logistic impact of collection, classification, and disposition of salvage.

(d) (U) <u>Captured Enemy Materiel</u>. Provide instructions for the collection, classification, and disposition of enemy materiel. See Annex B (Intelligence) for further guidance. See Appendix 10 to Annex B (Intelligence) for specific instructions for the disposition of captured enemy cryptographic equipment.

(e) (U) <u>Local Acquisition of Supplies and Services</u>. See JP 4-01 and the current version of DOD Instruction 3020.37, *Continuation of Essential DOD Contractor Services During Crisis*.

<u>1</u> (U) Identify acquisition of goods and services in the following categories:

<u>a</u> (U) The general categories of materiel and services that are available and contemplated as a supplement to regular sources.

<u>b</u> (U) Those that may be used as emergency acquisition sources.

<u>2</u> (U) Make a statement concerning the dependability of the local acquisition or labor source in each of the above categories and the joint or Service element that will obtain or manage these resources.

<u>3</u> (U) State that all essential contractor services, to include new and existing contracts, have been reviewed to determine which services will be essential to OPLAN execution. Make a statement concerning the existence of contingency plans to ensure the continuation of these essential services.

(f) (U) <u>Petroleum, Oils, and Lubricants</u>. Refer to Appendix 1 (Petroleum, Oils, and Lubricants Supply).

(page number)

CLASSIFICATION

CLASSIFICATION

(2)   (U)   <u>External Support</u>. Refer to Appendix 11 (External Support). Provide the required planning information including type and quantity of support and instructions where inter-Service and cross-Service arrangements for common supply and service support are appropriate.

    (a)   (U)   Summarize major support arrangements that are presently in effect or that will be executed in support of the plan.

    (b)   (U)   Include significant inter-Service and cross-Service support arrangements. Refer to appropriate annexes or appendixes.

    (c)   (U)   Include foreign and host nation support.

(3)   (U)   <u>Maintenance</u>

    (a)   (U)   <u>General</u>. Refer to Appendix 12 (Maintenance).

    (b)   (U)   <u>Specific Guidance</u>

        <u>1</u>   (U)   Include sufficient detail to determine the requirements for maintenance facilities needed to support the plan.

        <u>2</u>   (U)   Indicate the level of maintenance to be performed and where it is to occur, including host nation or contractor facilities, if applicable.

(4)   (U)   <u>Transportation</u>

    (a)   (U)   <u>General</u>. Refer to Appendix 4 (Mobility and Transportation). Provide general planning or execution guidance to subordinate and supporting organizations to facilitate transportation of the force and its sustainment. This can include movement and use priorities.

    (b)   (U)   <u>Mobility Support Force and Movement Feasibility Analysis</u>. Provide an estimate of the mobility support and movement feasibility of the plan. Include in the analysis any appropriate remarks affecting mobility and transportation tasks. Consider the availability of adequate lift resources for movements of personnel and equipment, airfield reception capabilities, seaport and aerial port terminal capabilities, and port throughput capabilities. Also, consider any features that will adversely affect movement operations, such as the effect of deployment or employment of forces

(page number)

CLASSIFICATION

CLASSIFICATION

and materiel on airfield ramp space (to include possible host nation support).

(5)   (U) <u>General Engineering Support Plan</u>. Refer to Appendix 13 (General Engineering). State the rationale if Appendix 5 (Civil Engineering Support Plan) is not prepared. Indicate the general engineering support activities applicable to the basic operation order or plan and the policies for providing these services.

(6)   (U) <u>Health Services</u>. Refer to Appendix 9 (Health Services).

(7)   (U) <u>Services</u>. Refer to Appendix 8 (Services).

(8)   (U) <u>Mortuary Affairs</u>. Refer to Appendix 2 (Mortuary Affairs) or, if not used, indicate the mortuary affairs activities applicable to the OPORD or OPLAN and policy for providing these affairs.

(9)   (U) <u>Ammunition</u>. Refer to Appendix 6 (Nonnuclear Ammunition) or if not used, discuss any critical ammunition issues that may affect the ability of the force to accomplish the mission.

(10) (U) <u>Aviation Logistic Support</u>. Refer to Appendix 10 (Aviation Logistic Support) or Annex D (Logistics/Combat Service Support) of the aviation combat element OPORD or OPLAN. Critical aviation logistic and CSS support issues may be discussed if they affect the ability of the force to accomplish the mission.

(11) (U) <u>Operations Security Planning Guidance for Logistics</u>. Refer to Tab C (Operations Security) to Appendix 3 (Information Operations/ Command and Control Warfare) to Annex C (Operations). Provide comprehensive operations security planning guidance for planning, preparing, and executing logistic and CSS activities. At a minimum, address base, facility, installation, logistic stocks, physical, and lines of communications security. Provide guidance to ensure that logistic and CSS activities promote essential secrecy for operational intentions, capabilities that will be committed to specific missions, and current preparatory operational activities.

b. (U) <u>Administration</u>. Include general administrative guidance to support logistic and CSS operations for the basic operation order or plan. If reports are required, specify formats for preparation, time, methods, and classification of submission.

(page number)

CLASSIFICATION

CLASSIFICATION

5. (U) <u>Command and Signal</u>

    a. (U) <u>Command Relationships</u>. Refer to Annex J (Command Relation-ships) for command relationships external to logistic units. Provide support relationships.

    b. (U) <u>Communications and Information Systems</u>. Refer to Annex K (Combat Information System) for detailed communications and information systems requirements. Provide a general statement of the scope and type of communications required.

ACKNOWLEDGE RECEIPT

Name
Rank and Service
Title

APPENDIXES

1 - Petroleum, Oils, and Lubricants Supply
2 - Mortuary Affairs
3 - Sustainability Analysis
4 - Mobility and Transportation
5 - Civil Engineering Support Plan
6 - Nonnuclear Ammunition
7 - Supply
8 - Services
9 - Health Services
10 - Aviation Logistic Support (Normally provided in the aviation combat element plan or order.)
11 - External Support
12 - Maintenance
13 - General Engineering

OFFICIAL:
s/
Name
Rank and Service
Title

(reverse blank)

Appendix D

Maintenance Recovery, Evacuation, and Repair Cycle Flowchart

The flowchart on the following pages summarizes the maintenance recovery, evacuation, and repair cycle during combat.

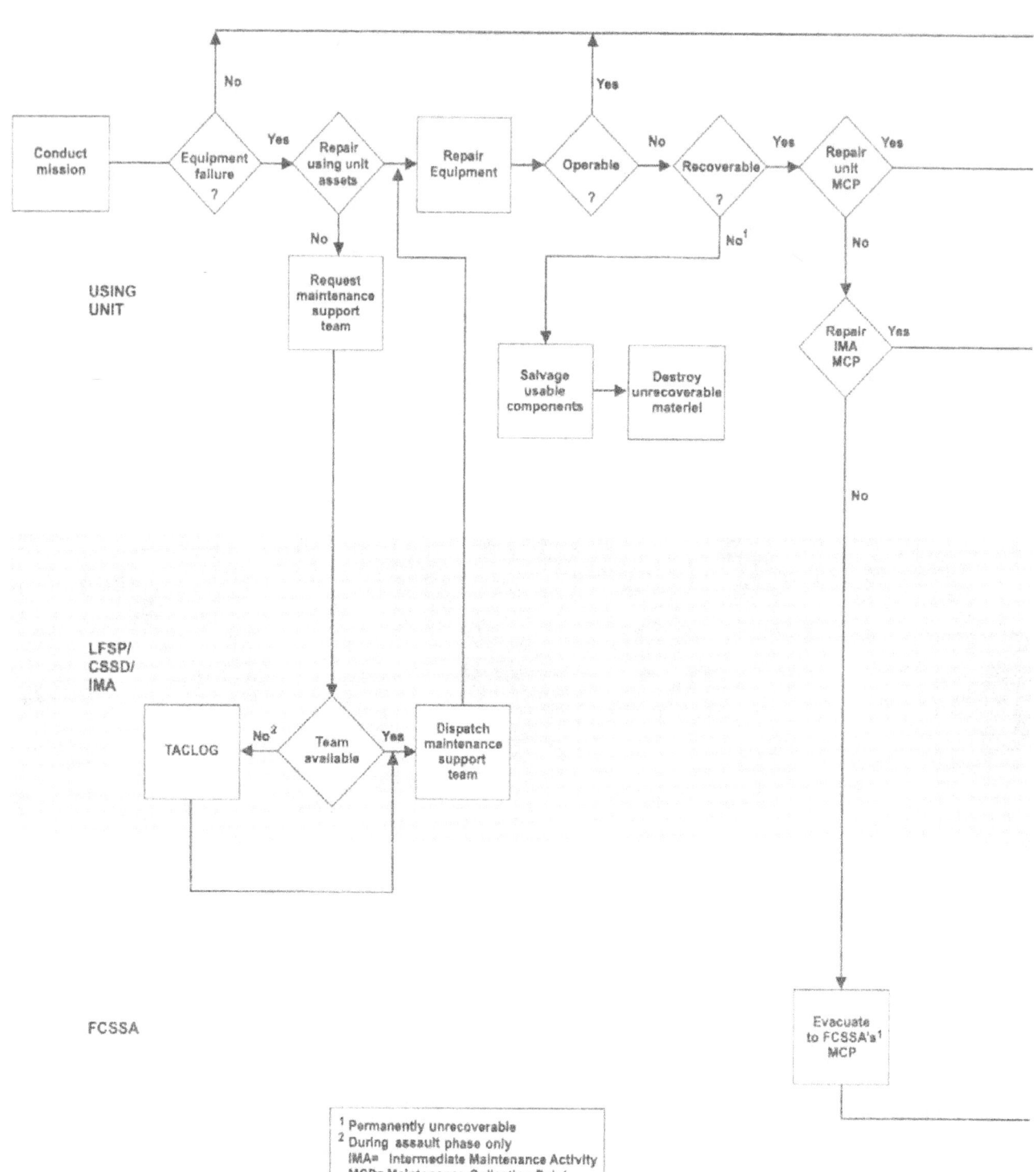

USING
UNIT

LFSP/
CSSD/
IMA

FCSSA

¹ Permanently unrecoverable
² During assault phase only
  IMA= Intermediate Maintenance Activity
  MCP= Maintenance Collection Point
  MSR= Main Supply Route

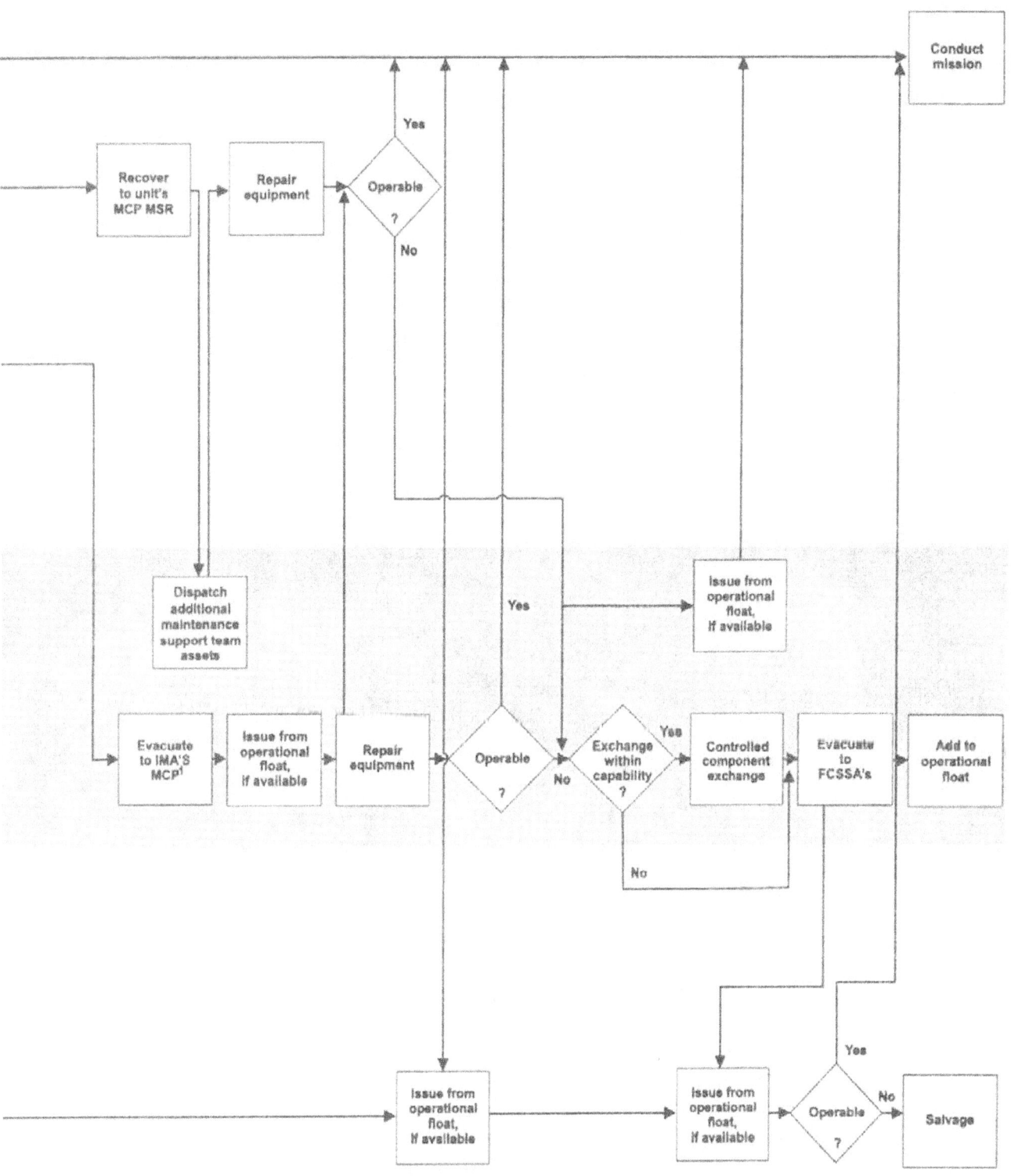

Appendix E

Glossary

Section I. Abbreviations and Acronyms

AAA............................ arrival and assembly area
AACG ....arrival airfield control group
AAOG...... arrival and assembly operations group
ABCA .... American, British, Canadian, Australian
ACE .... aviation combat element
ADAL ....authorized dental allowance list
AFOE......................... assault follow-on echelon
AIMD............ aviation intermediate maintenance department
AIS ....automated information system
ALCE..............................airlift control element
ALD .... aviation logistics department
AMAL............authorized medical allowance list
AMC ....Air Mobility Command
AMMOLOGS ....Ammunition Logistics System
AOA.........................amphibious objective area
AOR ....area of responsibility
APOD.....................aerial port of debarkation
APOE.........................aerial port of embarkation
ASC(A) ....assault support coordinator (airborne)
ASE..........................aviation support equipment
ASP .... ammunition supply point
ATF.......................... amphibious task force
ATLASS .... Asset Tracking Logistics and Supply System
AVCAL........ aviation consolidated allowance list

BGLCSS ...... Battle Group Logistics Coordinated Support System
BLT.............................battalion landing team
BOG ....beach operations group
BSA............................beach support area
BSS .... bread, shelf-stable
BSSG ....brigade service support group

C2............................command and control
C4I ....command, control, communications, computers, and intelligence

CAIMS...... Conventional Ammunition Integrated Management System
CCIR ....commander's critical information requirements
CE ....command element
CINC....................commander in chief
CJCSM....... Chairman of the Joint Chiefs of Staff manual
CLZ.............................craft landing zone
COA ....course of action
COC .... combat operations center
COMMARFOR ....Commander, Marine Corps Forces
COMMARFORLANT......... Commander, Marine Corps Forces, Atlantic
COMMARFORPAC............ Commander, Marine Corps Forces, Pacific Reserve
COMNAVAIRLANT ......Commander, Naval Air Force, Atlantic
COMNAVAIRPAC ....Commander, Naval Air Force, Pacific
COMNAVAIRRESFOR........ Commander, Naval Air Force Reserve
CONUS .... continental United States
COSAL .... coordinated ship-station allowance list
CRTS .... casualty receiving and treatment ship
CSP ....contingency support package
CSS .... combat service support
CSSA ....combat service support area
CSSD ....combat service support detachment
CSSE.................combat service support element
CSSG .... combat service support group
CSSOC............................. combat service support operations center

DACG .... departure airfield control group
DLA .... Defense Logistics Agency
DOD.................................. Department of Defense

EOD .... explosive ordnance disposal
EPW .... enemy prisoner of war

FARP .... forward arming and refueling point
FCSSA ....force combat service support area
FIE .... fly-in echelon
FISP ....fly-in support package
FLOT ....forward line of own troops
FM................................U.S. Army Field Manual
FMCC .... force movement control center
FMF ....Fleet Marine Force
FMFM .... Fleet Marine Force manual
FMFRP....................Fleet Marine Force reference
                                                             publication
FOSP ....follow-on support package
FSSG ....force service support group

G-1/S-1 ....manpower or personnel staff officer
G-2/S-2............................. intelligence staff officer
G-3/S-3............................. operations staff officer
G-4/S-4................................. logistics staff officer
G-6/S-6............. communications and information
                                                    systems officer
GCCS .... Global Command and Control System
GCE ....ground combat element
GCSS ....Global Combat Support System
GPMRC ....Global Patient Movement Require
GSORTS .... Global Status of Resources and
                                                Training System

H&S .... headquarters and service
HA.................................... humanitarian assistance
HDC ....helicopter direction center
HLSC .... helicopter logistics support center
HLZ.................................helicopter landing zone
HMMWV ....high mobility, multipurpose
                                                        wheeled vehicle
HQMC .... Headquarters Marine Corps
HSS .... health service support
HST ....helicopter support team

IMA................. intermediate maintenance activity
IMRL .... individual material readiness list
IPB ......intelligence preparation of the battlespace
ISSA................... inter-Service support agreement

JCS .... Joint Chiefs of Staff
JFC ....joint force commander

JOPES ....Joint Operation Planning and
                                                Execution System
JP... joint publication
JTF ....joint task force

LAR ....light armored reconnaissance
LCAC.......................landing craft air cushion
LFOC ....landing force operations center
LFSP ....landing force support party
LMCC ....logistic movement control center
LOGAIS...........Logistics Automated Information
                                                                    System
LOTS ....logistics over the shore
LSE ....landing support equipment

MACCS .... Marine air command and control
                                                                    system
MACG .... Marine air control group
MAG ....Marine aircraft group
MAGTF ....Marine air-ground task force
MALS .... Marine aviation logistics squadron
MALSP ....Marine aviation logistics support
                                                                    program
MARFORLANT................. Marine Corps Forces,
                                                                Atlantic
MARFORPAC........Marine Corps Forces, Pacific
MARFORRES ....Marine Corps Forces Reserve
MAW ....Marine aircraft wing
MCC.............................movement control center
MCDP .... Marine Corps doctrinal publication
MCOO .... modified combined obstacle overlay
MCPP.................Marine Corps Planning Process
MCRP ....Marine Corps reference publication
MCSSD............... mobile combat service support
                                                                detachment
MCT...........................maintenance contact team
MCTEEP..........Marine Corps Training, Exercise,
                                            and Employment Program
MCWP ......Marine Corps warfighting publication
MDSS II................. MAGTF Deployment Support
                                                                System II
MEB.......................Marine expeditionary brigade
MEF ....Marine expeditionary force
MEU............................Marine expeditionary unit
MEU(SOC) ..... MEU (special operations capable)
MHE......................materials handling equipment
MIMMS .... Marine Integrated Maintenance
                                                Management System
MLC...........................Marine logistics command

MLSE........multinational logistic support element
MMTP.............................meal module tray pack
MOOTW.........military operations other than war
MOS......................military occupational specialty
MPF ....maritime prepositioning force
MPS ....maritime prepositioning ships
MPSRON.............. maritime prepositioning ships squadron
MRE............................. meal, ready-to-eat
MSC............................ Military Sealift Command
MSSG.....................MEU service support group
MST ....maintenance support team
MTF .... medical treatment facility
MTMC .... Military Traffic Management Command
MWHS.........Marine wing headquarters squadron
MWR ....morale, welfare, and recreation
MWSG ....Marine wing support group
MWSS.................. Marine wing support squadron
MWSS(FW) ....MWSS (fixed-wing)
MWSS(RW).........................MWSS (rotary-wing)

NALCOMIS.................. Naval Aviation Logistics Command Management Information System
NALM.......................... Norway airlanded Marine expeditionary brigade
NATO ....North Atlantic Treaty Organization
NBC ....nuclear, biological, and chemical
NCF.................................naval construction force
NCR ....naval construction regiment
NDP ....naval doctrine publication
NSE.....................................Navy support element
NTCSS........... Naval Tactical Command Support System
NWP.................................naval warfare publication

OPLAN ....operation plan
OPORD...operation order
OPP ....offload preparation party
OPT....................operational planning team

PDE&A...........planning, decision, execution, and assessment
PMSP ....provisional mobile security platoon
POE...port of embarkation
POG .... port operations group
POR.........................packaged operational rations

QSTG .....quadripartite standardization agreement

RAOC .... rear area operations center
RAS.................................rear area security
RCW ....ration cold weather
rein ....reinforcing
ROLMS.........................Retail Ordnance Logistics Management System
RSSP ....ration supplement sundries pack

SASSY .... Supported Activities Supply System
SE..support element
SEAL ....sea-air-land
SELF............strategic expeditionary landing field
SLRP ....survey, liaison, and reconnaissance party
SNAP III .... Shipboard Nontactical Automated Data Processing Program III
SOP ....standing operating procedure
SPMAGTF.....................special purpose MAGTF
SPOE...............................seaport of embarkation
SRA..........................system replacement assembly
STANAG ....standardization agreement
SUADPS ..... Shipboard Uniform Automated Data Processing System

TACC.................tactical air control center (USN)
TACLOG ....tactical-logistical group
TADC...................tactical air direction center
T-AH.. hospital ship
TAVB.....................aviation logistics support ship
TBA.................................tables of basic allowance
TC AIMS .... Transportation Coordinator's Automated Information for Movement System
T/E ....table of equipment
TMIP........ Theater Medical Information Program
T/M/S .... type/model/series
T/O .... table of organization
TOW ....tube-launched, optically tracked, wire-missile command link guided
TSO................................ tactical security officer

UMCC.................... unit movement control center
URB ....unitized B-rations
USMC.......................United States Marine Corps
USN .... United States Navy
USTRANSCOM ....................U.S. Transportation Command

VIP .... very important person

WRA.....................weapon replacement assembly

Section II. Definitions

A

air delivery—Also called air drop. The unloading of personnel or materiel from aircraft in flight. (JP 1-02) It can be effected from either a fixed-wing aircraft or a helicopter, and it may be a low-velocity drop (less than 30 feet per second), high-velocity drop (greater than 30 feet per second), or free drop. Used to its full potential, air delivery offers the commander a degree of versatility that can greatly enhance his tactical and sustainability capabilities.

airfield—An area prepared for the accommodation (including any buildings, installations, and equipment), landing and takeoff of aircraft. (JP 1-02)

amphibious assault—The principal type of amphibious operation that involves establishing a force on a hostile or potentially hostile shore. (JP 1-02)

amphibious operation—An attack launched from the sea by naval and landing forces, embarked in ships or craft involving a landing on a hostile or potentially hostile shore. As an entity, the amphibious operation includes the following phases: **a.** planning—The period extending from issuance of the initiating directive to embarkation. **b.** embarkation—The period during which the forces, with their equipment and supplies, are embarked in the assigned shipping. **c.** rehearsal—The period during which the prospective operation is rehearsed for the purpose of: (1) testing adequacy of plans, the timing of detailed operations, and the combat readiness of participating forces; (2) ensuring that all echelons are familiar with plans; and (3) testing communications. **d.** movement—The period during which various components of the amphibious task force move from points of embarkation to the objective area. **e.** assault—The period between the arrival of the major assault forces of the amphibious task force in the objective area and the accomplishment of the amphibious task force mission. (JP 1-02)

assault support coordinator (airborne) (ASC(A))—An aviator who coordinates, from an aircraft, the movement of aviation assets during assault support operations. (MCRP 5-12C)

assign—**1.** To place units or personnel in an organization where such placement is relatively permanent, and/or where such organization controls and administers the units or personnel for the primary function, or greater portion of the functions, of the unit or personnel. **2.** To detail individuals to specific duties or functions where such duties or functions are primary and/or relatively permanent. (JP 1-02)

aviation logistics support ship (TAVB)—Operated by the Military Sealift Command, this ship provides dedicated sealift for movement of an intermediate maintenance capability to support the rapid deployment of Marine Corps fixed- and rotary-wing aircraft units in support of the MAGTF aviation combat element. It can also be used for resupply in a conventional container or roll-on/roll-off configuration.

B

bare base expeditionary airfield—Bare base expeditionary airfields provide the capability for using an existing airfield or road network to establish an expeditionary airfield. A bare base expeditionary airfield is established in place of a full expeditionary airfield because of the extensive embarkation and/or construction requirements associated with the full expeditionary airfield, and the associated airfield matting required. The bare base expeditionary airfield concept calls for the use of available concrete and/or asphalt-surfaced facilities. It involves embarking only those assets necessary for conducting air operations (e.g., airfield lighting and/or marking, landing aids, arresting gear). Bare base kits have been established to support all expeditionary airfields.

basic load—The quantity of supplies required to be on hand within, and which can be moved by, a unit or formation. It is expressed according to the wartime organization of the unit or formation and maintained at the prescribed levels. (JP 1-02) Basic loads are the types and quantities of supplies that the commander directs a unit to carry for a specific operation. The basic load is the initial source of supply support. Subordinate commanders must maintain these levels. The basic load should not exceed what the unit can carry on organic transportation, nor should it exceed what the commander thinks is needed to continue combat operations until replenishment becomes available.

battle—A single, hostile engagement between operating forces of opposing nations.

beach party—The naval component of the shore party. (JP 1-02)

beach support area—In amphibious operations, the area to the rear of a landing force or elements thereof, established and operated by shore party units, which contains the facilities for the unloading of troops and materiel and the support of the forces ashore; it includes facilities for the evacuation of wounded, enemy prisoners of war, and captured materiel. (JP 1-02) The beach support area is one of the first combat service support (CSS) installations established ashore during an amphibious operation. Established by the shore party group and/or team, the CSS element commander may eventually disestablish it, retain it, or consolidate it as part of the force CSS area. In some situations, the beach support area may be the only CSS installation ashore. In other situations, it may be one of several CSS installations.

C

campaign—A series of related military operations aimed at accomplishing a strategic or operational objective within a given time and space. (JP 1-02)

casualty—Any person who is lost to the organization by having been declared dead, duty status-whereabouts unknown, missing, ill, or injured. (JP 1-02)

casualty collection—The assembly of casualties at collection and treatment sites. It includes protection from further injury while awaiting evacuation to the next level of care. Planning for casualty collection points must include site selection and manning.

casualty evacuation—The movement of the sick, wounded, or injured. It begins at the point of injury or the onset of disease. It includes movement both to and between medical treatment facilities. All units have an evacuation capability. They may use any vehicle to evacuate casualties. If they do not use a medical vehicle, they should replace the vehicle that they use with a medical vehicle at the first opportunity. Similarly, aeromedical evacuation should replace surface evacuation at the first opportunity.

casualty treatment—Triage and all levels of care from self-aid or buddy aid through resuscitative care.

classes of supplies—All items necessary for the equipping, maintenance, and operation of a military command, including food, clothing, equipment, arms, ammunition, fuel, materials, and machinery of all kinds. For planning, management, and administrative purposes, supplies are divided into 10 classes:

- **Class I.** Subsistence, including gratuitous health and welfare items.
- **Class II.** Clothing, individual equipment, tentage, organizational tool sets and tool kits, hand tools, and administrative and housekeeping supplies and equipment.
- **Class III.** Petroleum, oils, and lubricants.
- **Class IV.** Construction supplies.
- **Class V.** Ammunition.
- **Class VI.** Personal demand items (nonmilitary sales items).
- **Class VII.** Major end items: a final combination of end products that is ready for its intended use.
- **Class VIII.** Medical materiel, including medical-unique repair parts.

- **Class IX.** Repair parts and components.
- **Class X.** Materiel to support nonmilitary programs.

classification (maintenance)—Classification determines who repairs an item and where they make the repairs. When a user or maintenance activity evacuates an item to a higher level, the higher level repeats the inspection and classification process. Inspection and classification are also the last tasks that the maintenance activity performs before returning equipment. This inspection confirms that they have made the appropriate repairs. The owner of the equipment makes the final inspection and classification before placing the item back into service.

combat power—The total means of destructive and/or disruptive force which a Military unit/formation can apply against the opponent at a given time. (JP 1-02)

combat service support—The essential capabilities, functions, activities, and tasks necessary to sustain all elements of operating forces in theater at all levels of war. Within the national and theater logistic systems, it includes but is not limited to that support rendered by service forces in ensuring the aspects of supply, maintenance, transportation, health services, and other services required by aviation and ground combat troops to permit those units to accomplish their missions in combat. Combat service support encompasses those activities at all levels of war that produce sustainment to all operating forces on the battlefield. (JP 1-02)

combat service support area (CSSA)—An area ashore that is organized to contain the necessary supplies, equipment, installations, and elements to provide the landing force with combat service support throughout the operation. (JP 1-02)

combat service support detachment—A separate task organization of combat service support assets formed for the purpose of providing rearming, refueling, and/or repair capabilities to the Marine air-ground task force or designated subordinate elements; e.g., a battalion conducting independent operations or an aircraft squadron operating at a remote airfield. The combat service support element normally provides the command element of a combat service support detachment. (MCRP 5-12C)

combat service support element—The core element of Marine air-ground task force that is task-organized to provide the combat service support necessary to accomplish the Marine air-ground task force mission. The combat service support element varies in size from a small detachment to one or more force service support groups. It provides supply, maintenance, transportation, general engineering, health services, and a variety of other services to the Marine air-ground task force. It may also contain other Service or foreign military forces assigned or attached to the MAGTF. The combat service support element itself is not a formal command. Also called CSSE. See also aviation combat element; command element; ground combat element; Marine air-ground task force; Marine expeditionary force; Marine expeditionary force (Forward); Marine expeditionary unit; special purpose Marine air-ground task force; task force. (approved for the next edition of MCRP 5-12C)

command and control—The exercise of authority and direction by a properly designated commander over assigned and attached forces in the accomplishment of the mission. Command and control functions are performed through an arrangement of personnel, equipment, communications, facilities, and procedures employed by a commander in planning, directing, coordinating, and controlling forces and operations in the accomplishment of the mission. (JP 1-02)

common contingency support package allowances—Consist of those Marine common assets that the rotary-wing or fixed-wing host intermediate maintenance activity (IMA) of an aviation combat element (ACE) provides to support all, or the majority, of assigned aircraft. A fixed-wing Marine common item is one that has application to at least the F/A-18 and AV-8B aircraft that are part of the ACE. A rotary-wing common item is one that has application to at least the CH-53E, CH-46E, and AH-2W aircraft that are a part of an ACE. Weight, cube, cost, reliability, and supportability are the primary considerations in making this determination. Host IMAs, one rotary-wing and one fixed-wing per ACE, are sourced from designated MAGs. For planning purposes, it is assumed that the fixed-wing and rotary-wing IMAs will be geographically separated.

concept of logistic support—A verbal or graphic statement, in a broad outline, of how a commander intends to support and integrate with a concept of operations in an operation or campaign. (JP 1-02)

concept of operations—A verbal or graphic statement, in broad outline, of a commander's assumptions or intent in regard to an operation or series of operations. The concept of operations frequently is embodied in campaign plans and operation plans; in the latter case, particularly when the plans cover a series of connected operations to be carried out simultaneously or in succession. The concept is designed to give an overall picture of the operation. It is included primarily for additional clarity of purpose. Also called commander's concept. (JP 1-02)

contingency plan—A plan for major contingencies that can reasonably be anticipated in the principal geographic subareas of the command. (JP 1-02)

contingency support package (CSP)—Consists of the common and unique intermediate-level logistical support required for the task-organized deployment of detachments and/or squadrons of particular type, model, or series aircraft with one exception. CSP aviation consolidated allowance list and/or coordinated ship-station allowance list allowances are the exception because they provide the spare and repair parts to support both organizational- and intermediate-level maintenance. The four distinct elements that make up a CSP are: **a.** personnel; **b.** support equipment (individual material readiness list); **c.** mobile facilities; and **d.** spare repair parts (aviation consolidated allowance list and/or coordinated ship-station allowance list). CSP allowances are computed at the combat flying hour rate for a 90-day endurance period and are supplemental

allowances to those identified in master allowance documents.

control—Authority which may be less than full command exercised by a commander over part of the activities of subordinate or other organizations. (JP 1-02)

coordination—The action necessary to ensure adequately integrated relationships between separate organizations located in the same area. Coordination may include such matters as fire support, emergency defense measures, area intelligence, and other situations in which coordination is considered necessary. (MCRP 5-12C)

countermobility—The construction of obstacles and emplacement of minefields to delay, disrupt, and destroy the enemy by reinforcement of the terrain. The primary purpose of countermobility operations is to slow or divert the enemy, to increase time for target acquisition, and to increase weapon effectiveness. (MCRP 5-12C)

D

demolition—The destruction of structures, facilities, or material by use of fire, water, explosives, mechanical, or other means. (JP 1-02)

depot—1. supply—An activity for the receipt, classification, storage, accounting, issue, maintenance, procurement, manufacture, assembly, research, salvage, or disposal of material. 2. personnel—An activity for the reception, processing, training, assignment, and forwarding of personnel replacements. (JP 1-02)

depot maintenance—That maintenance performed on materiel requiring major overhaul or a complete rebuild of parts, assemblies, subassemblies, and end-items, including the manufacture of parts, modifications, testing, and reclamation as required. Depot maintenance serves to support lower categories of maintenance by providing technical assistance and performing that maintenance beyond their responsibility. Depot maintenance provides stocks of serviceable equipment by using more extensive facilities for repair than are available in lower level maintenance activities. (JP 1-02)

disposal—The process of eliminating excess, obsolete, surplus, or unserviceable property. Disposal may include transfer, donation, sale, or abandonment. It does not include redistribution or reissue.

distribution—**1.** The arrangement of troops for any purpose, such as a battle, march, or maneuver. **2.** A planned pattern of projectiles about a point. **3.** A planned spread of fire to cover a desired frontage or depth. **4.** An official delivery of anything, such as orders or supplies. **5.** That functional phase of military logistics that embraces the act of dispensing materiel, facilities, and services. **6.** The process of assigning military personnel to activities, units, or billets. (JP 1-02) For the MAGTF, distribution is the issue of supplies and equipment to using units or to intermediate supply points for future issue. The distribution process has two steps. The first step is requisition. A requisition identifies the user's needs. The second step is issue. The supply activity issues supplies and equipment based on the commander's priorities and allocations.

distribution methods—The two usual methods of distribution are supply point distribution and unit distribution. **a.** Supply point distribution is the method of distributing supplies in which the receiving unit is issued supplies at a supply point (depot, airhead, navigation head, railhead, combat train site, distribution point) and moves the supplies in organic transportation. **b.** Unit distribution is the method of distributing supplies in which the receiving unit is issued supplies in its own area; the transportation is furnished by the issuing agency. The receiving unit is then responsible for its own internal distribution.

distribution point—A point at which supplies and/or ammunition, obtained from supporting supply points by a division or other unit, are broken down for distribution to subordinate units. Distribution points usually carry no stocks; items drawn are issued completely as soon as possible. (JP 1-02)

distribution system—That complex of facilities, installations, methods, and procedures designed to receive, store, maintain, distribute, and control the flow of military materiel between the point of receipt into the military system and the point of issue to using activities and units. (JP 1-02)

E

embarkation—The process of putting personnel and/or vehicles and their associated stores and equipment into ships and/or aircraft. (JP 1-02)

embarkation phase—In amphibious operations, the phase which encompasses the orderly assembly of personnel and materiel and their subsequent loading aboard ships and/or aircraft in a sequence designed to meet the requirements of the landing force concept of operations ashore. (JP 1-02)

engineer reconnaissance—The gathering of specific, detailed technical information required by supporting engineer forces in order to prepare for and accomplish assigned missions. (MCRP 5-12C)

expeditionary airfields—A prefabricated and fully portable airfield. The effort and assets (e.g., materiel, engineer support, operational guidance, security) required for the installation and/or operation of an expeditionary airfield can require the participation and/or support of all elements of the MAGTF. When deployed, it provides the capability to launch and recover MAGTF helicopters and fixed-wing aircraft under all weather conditions. Full expansion of expeditionary airfield facilities into a strategic expeditionary landing field (SELF) allows the support and maintenance for a complete wing-sized ACE. The SELF has parking and taxiways to accommodate Air Mobility Command and civilian reserve air fleet aircraft. Normally, responsibility for the construction of the expeditionary airfield rests with the engineer support battalion of the force service support group (FSSG) or the engineers of a Marine wing support squadron (MWSS), unless the construction effort exceeds their capability. The Navy mobile construction battalion will provide augmentation to the FSSG and/or MWSS, or it can assume full responsibility for construction of the expeditionary airfield if required.

explosive ordnance—All munitions containing explosives, nuclear fission or fusion materials and biological and chemical agents. (extract from JP 1-02)

explosive ordnance disposal—The detection, identification, on-site evaluation, rendering safe, recovery, and final disposal of unexploded explosive ordnance. It may also include explosive ordnance which has become hazardous by damage or deterioration. (JP 1-02)

F

firepower—The amount of fire which may be delivered by a position, unit, or weapon system. (JP 1-02)

floating dump—Emergency supplies preloaded in landing craft, amphibious vehicles, or in landing ships. Floating dumps are located in the vicinity of the appropriate control officer who directs their landing as requested by the troop commander concerned. (JP 1-02)

fly-in support package (FISP)—Organizational-level parts support packages designed to support the fly-in echelon (FIE) aircraft of an maritime prepositioning force and/or MAGTF aviation combat element. A FISP, flown in with the FIE aircraft, will be combined with organizational-level aviation support equipment and organizational-level parts to support the equipment offloaded from maritime prepositioning ships. This combination of assets is designed to provide readiness and sustainability for the deployed aircraft until the intermediate maintenance support capability arrives in the theater of operations aboard the aviation logistics support ship, by airlift, or by other means.

follow-on support package allowances—Equipment consisting of those items that, although not required to initiate the assault, are required to sustain the assault. These are items that, because of sealift and airlift constraints, must be phased into a deployment area by use of assault follow-on echelon or follow-up shipping.

force combat service support area (FCSSA)—The primary combat service support installation established to support MAGTF operations ashore. Normally located near a beach, port, and/or an airfield, it usually contains the command post of the combat service support element commander and supports other combat service support installations. (MCRP 5-12C)

force service support group—The combat service support element of the Marine expeditionary force (MEF). It is a permanently organized Fleet Marine Force command charged with providing combat service support beyond the organic capabilities of supported units of the MEF. If supporting a force of greater size, additional assets are necessary to augment its capabilities. Although permanently structured with eight functional battalions, task organizations from those battalions would normally support MEF operations over a wide geographic area. (MCRP 5-12C)

forward arming and refueling point—A temporary facility, organized, equipped, and deployed by an aviation commander, and normally located in the main battle area closer to the area of operation than the aviation unit's combat service area, to provide fuel and ammunition necessary for the employment of aviation maneuver units in combat. The forward arming and refueling point permits combat aircraft to rapidly refuel and rearm simultaneously. (JP 1-02)

freight and passenger transportation—Subfunctions of traffic management. Freight and passenger transportation includes the procurement of both Department of Defense and commercial transportation assets. It encompasses the movement of personnel, equipment, and supplies via all modes (i.e., air, bus, rail, truck, and water). It includes planning for troop movements on scheduled or chartered trains, aircraft, and buses in the continental United States and overseas. It also entails port calling of passengers for overseas movement.

function (motor transport)—Movements that fall into two general categories—administrative and tactical. The commander selects administrative movement when there is little or no likelihood of enemy contact. Administrative movements make maximum use of available vehicles. They optimize the economical use of vehicle cargo capacities. They may include both military and civilian vehicles. The commander selects tactical movement when unit integrity must be preserved for tactical purposes. The commander combat loads the vehicles to maintain security and to speed unloading at destination. When making tactical movements, the timely delivery of unit personnel and cargo is of greater importance than economical use of the vehicles.

G

general engineering—Intensive effort by engineer units which involves high standards of design and construction as well as detailed planning and preparation. General engineering support normally serves the whole MAGTF. It is that wide range of tasks in rear areas which serves to sustain forward combat operations.

graves registration program—A program which provides for search, recovery, tentative identification, and evacuation, or temporary interment. Temporary interment is only authorized by the geographic combatant commander. Disposition of personel effects is included in this program. (JP 1-02)

H

health maintenance—Those tasks to ensure that the unit and its personnel are medically ready for combat operations. Included are routine sick calls, physical examinations, preventive medicine and dentistry programs, records maintenance, and medical reporting.

horizontal and vertical construction—Deliberate engineering projects that normally involve time, manpower, materiel, and equipment-intensive tasks. These tasks usually relate to survivability and sustainability efforts.

I

inspection—The inspection process determines maintenance requirements and satisfactory maintenance performance. All levels of maintenance include inspections. Inspections are most effective when the inspector is not the same person as the one who performs the maintenance.

inspection and classification—The checking or testing of an item against established standards and the assignment of that item to a maintenance category based on established rules. Inspection and classification are the first and last tasks that a user and maintenance activity perform on a piece of equipment.

intermediate maintenance (field)—That maintenance which is the responsibility of and performed by designated maintenance activities for direct support of using organizations. Its phases normally consist of: **a.** calibration, repair, or replacement of damaged or unserviceable parts, components, or assemblies; **b.** the emergency manufacture of nonavailable parts; and **c.** providing technical assistance to using organizations. (JP 1-02)

L

landing force—A task organization of troop units, aviation and ground, assigned to an amphibious assault. It is the highest troop echelon in the amphibious operation. (JP 1-02)

landing force supplies—Supplies and equipment in the assault echelon and the assault follow-on echelon. They include the initial supply support needed before arrival of resupply in the amphibious objective area. Landing force supplies include basic loads, prepositioned emergency supplies, and remaining supplies.

landing support—The assistance provided to effect the efficient and responsive throughput of personnel, supplies, and equipment during the ship-to-shore movement phase of the amphibious assault or across beaches in support of operations ashore. It includes control of the flow of personnel and materiel across the beach and into landing zones. Landing support does not end when the MAGTF completes the amphibious assault but continues through landing of the assault follow-on echelon. Landing support includes the evacuation of casualties and enemy prisoners of war during early stages of the assault. The landing support function does not include all of the functions that the landing force support party (LFSP) performs. The LFSP is a task organization that performs many other combat service support (CSS) and non-CSS functions. A common misconception is that the landing support function includes tasks that, in actuality, are subfunctions of the other five CSS functions.

landing zone support area—A forward support installation which provides minimum essential support to the helicopter borne assault forces of the MAGTF. It can expand into a combat service support (CSS) area but it is most often a short term installation with limited capabilities, normally containing dumps for rations, fuel, ammunition, and water only; maintenance is limited to contact teams and/or support teams. (MCRP 5-12C) A landing zone support area is a CSS installation established to support helicopter borne assault elements. It is established by the CSS element when a buildup of supplies or other CSS capabilities is anticipated. When a logistic buildup is not planned, the supported unit is responsible for the helicopter support team operations associated with support of the helicopter borne force.

levels of maintenance—Organizational, intermediate, and depot are the three maintenance levels of the Marine Corps ground and aviation equipment maintenance systems.

lines of communications—A route, either land, water, or air, which connects an operating military force with a base of operations and along which supplies and military forces move. (JP 1-02)

logistics—The science of planning and carrying out the movement and maintenance of forces. In its most comprehensive sense, those aspects of military operations which deal with: **a.** design and development, acquisition, storage, movement, distribution, maintenance, evacuation, and disposition of materiel; **b.** movement, evacuation, and hospitalization of personnel; **c.** acquisition or construction, maintenance, operation, and disposition of facilities; and **d.** acquisition or furnishing of services. (JP 1-02)

logistics over-the-shore operations—The loading and unloading of ships without the benefit of fixed port facilities, in friendly or nondefended territory, and, in time of war, during phases of theater development in which there is no opposition by the enemy. (JP 1-02)

M

main supply route—The route or routes designated within an area of operations upon which the bulk of traffic flows in support of military operations. (JP 1-02)

maintenance (materiel)—1. All action taken to retain materiel in a serviceable condition or to restore it to serviceability. It includes inspection, testing, servicing, classification as to serviceability, repair, rebuilding, and reclamation. 2. All supply and repair action taken to keep a force in condition to carry out its mission. 3. The routine recurring work required to keep a facility (plant, building, structure, ground facility, utility system, or other real property) in such condition that it may be continuously used, at its original or designed capacity and efficiency for its intended purpose. (JP 1-02) The Marine Corps includes efforts to update and upgrade the capability of materiel as a function of maintenance.

Marine air-ground task force—The Marine Corps principal organization for all missions across the range of military operations, composed of forces task-organized under a single commander capable of responding rapidly to a contingency anywhere in the world. The types of forces in the MAGTF are functionally grouped into four core elements: a command element, an aviation combat element, a ground combat element, and a combat service support element. The four core elements are categories of forces, not formal commands. The basic structure of the Marine air-ground task force never varies, though the number, size, and type of Marine Corps units comprising each of its four elements will always be mission dependent. The flexibility of the organizational structure allows for one or more subordinate MAGTFs, other Service and/or foreign military forces, to be assigned or attached. Also called MAGTF. See also aviation combat element; combat service support element; command element; ground combat element; Marine expeditionary force; Marine expeditionary force (Forward); Marine expeditionary unit; special purpose Marine air-ground task force; task force. (approved for the next edition of MCRP 5-12C)

Marine Air-Ground Task Force Deployment Support System II (MDSS II)—A system that enables commanders at various echelons of a MAGTF to build and maintain a data base that contains force and equipment data reflecting how the MAGTF is configured for deployment. This data can be maintained during normal day-to-day garrison activities and updated during plan development and execution.

Marine Air-Ground Task Force II—A system that allows MAGTF planners to select and tailor MAGTF force structures, estimate sustainment, and estimate airlift and/or sealift requirements for plan feasibility.

Marine Air-Ground Task Force II/Logistics Automated Information System (MAGTF II/LOGAIS)—A family of coordinated, mutually supporting automated systems. MAGTF II/LOGAIS enables commanders at different levels to track asset availability. The system calculates sustainment requirements and processes requisitions both inside and outside the area of responsibility from Defense Automated Addressing System, the Defense Logistics Agency, and Marine Corps logistic bases. MAGTF II/LOGAIS provides the MAGTF with the necessary tools to support war planning in both deliberate and time-sensitive situations and execution from initiation of mobilization or deployment through employment in the area of responsibility.

Marine expeditionary brigade—A mid-sized Marine air-ground task force (MAGTF) that provides combatant commanders with an extremely flexible expeditionary force. Commanded by a general officer, it is normally built around a ground combat element of a reinforced infantry regiment. Its aviation combat element consists of a Marine aircraft group with fixed- and rotary-wing squadrons. The combat service support element is organized to provide the full spectrum of combat service support. As an expeditionary force, it is capable of rapid deployment and employment via amphibious shipping, strategic airlift and/or sealift, marrying with maritime or geographical prepositioning force assets, or any combination thereof. It is a complete fighting force—a MAGTF that has been task-organized for the mission and is capable of self-sustainment for 30 days. It can function alone, as a logical follow-on force to the Marine expeditionary unit, as part of a joint task force, or as the lead element of a Marine expeditionary force.

Marine expeditionary force—The largest Marine air-ground task force and the Marine Corps principal warfighting organization, particularly for larger crises or contingencies. It is task-organized around a permanent command element and normally contains one or more Marine divisions, Marine aircraft wings, and Marine force service support groups. The Marine expeditionary force is capable of missions across the range of military operations, including amphibious assault and sustained operations ashore in any environment. It can operate from a sea base, a land base, or both. It may also contain other Service or foreign military forces assigned or attached to the MAGTF. Also called MEF. See also aviation combat element; combat service support element; command element; ground combat element; Marine air-ground task force; Marine expeditionary force (Forward); Marine expeditionary unit; special purpose Marine air-ground task force; task force. (approved for the next edition of MCRP 5-12C)

Marine expeditionary unit—A Marine air-ground task force that is constructed around an infantry battalion reinforced, a helicopter squadron reinforced, and a task-organized combat service support element. It normally fulfills Marine Corps forward sea-based deployment requirements. The Marine expeditionary unit provides an immediate reaction capability for crisis response and is capable of limited combat operations. It may contain other Service or foreign military forces assigned or attached. Also called MEU. See also aviation combat element; combat service support element; command element; ground combat element; Marine air-ground task force; Marine expeditionary force; Marine expeditionary force (Forward); Marine expeditionary unit (special operations capable); special purpose Marine air-ground task force; task force. (approved for the next edition of MCRP 5-12C)

maritime prepositioning ships—Civilian-crewed, Military Sealift Command-chartered ships which are organized into three squadrons and are usually forward-deployed. These ships are loaded with prepositioned equipment and 30 days of supplies to support three Marine expeditionary brigades. Also called MPS. (JP 1-02)

materials handling equipment—Mechanical devices for handling of supplies with greater ease and economy. (JP 1-02) Effective use of available materials handling equipment is essential to movement control and maintaining the throughput of supplies and equipment. All subordinate elements of the MAGTF possess some amount of materials handling equipment capability. Some units hold materials handling equipment for their own dedicated use (e.g., artillery battalions). In other cases, combat service support units hold materials handling equipment for use throughout the MAGTF. Those that have materials handling equipment must use their own before seeking help from other sources. Those that do not have materials handling equipment must request it in advance. There is a limited amount of materials handling equipment in a MAGTF. This dictates careful management. As with most scarce assets, a central agency can best manage materials handling equipment assets. The best alternative is centralized control of the assets and decentralized execution of the specific tasks. The controlling agency must be able to anticipate requirements and shift assets to critical points as the priority of effort shifts. As a general rule, the agency that controls use of motor transport resources should also control materials handling equipment resources. Where circumstances per-

mit, commanders should use manual labor or other suitable alternatives. Rapid unloading and turnaround of available trucks increases hauling capabilities.

medical regulating—See JP 1-02. Medical regulating is a casualty management system designed to coordinate the movement of casualties from the site of injury or the onset of disease through successive levels of medical care to a medical treatment facility that can provide the appropriate level of care. The medical regulating system has three principal elements, each with its own specific responsibilities: **a.** Global Patient Movement Requirements Center (GPMRC)—Regulates movement of patients from medical treatment facilities outside continental United States (CONUS) to and between facilities in CONUS. **b.** Theater Patient Movement Requirements Center (TPMRC)—Each unified command establishes a joint medical regulating office. The TPMRC regulates movement of patients to and between medical treatment facilities within the commander in chief's (CINC's) area of responsibility. It also provides information to the GPMRC about patients who are ready for movement to CONUS. The CINC may also establish lower level joint patient movement requirements centers (JPMRC) for subareas within the CINC's command. **c.** task force medical regulating system—Each task force commander establishes a medical regulating system to coordinate movement of casualties to and between medical treatment facilities. The commander also notifies the appropriate medical regulating element, usually the JPMRC, when patients are ready for movement to theater or CONUS facilities. Consequently, medical regulating elements must have compatible communications. Plans must provide radio frequencies, communications security equipment, and radios for the medical regulating functions of both commander, amphibious task force, and commander, landing force.

medical treatment facility—A facility established for the purpose of furnishing medical and/or dental care to eligible individuals. (JP 1-02)

MEU service support group—The task-organized combat service support element of the

Marine expeditionary unit. Personnel and equipment are assigned from the permanent battalions of the force service support group. As required, it may be augmented by combat service support assets from the Marine division or Marine aircraft wing. (MCRP 5-12C)

military requirement—An established need justifying the timely allocation of resources to achieve a capability to accomplish approved military objectives, missions, or tasks. (JP 1-02)

mobility—A quality or capability of military forces which permits them to move from place to place while retaining the ability to fulfill their primary mission. (JP 1-02)

modification—The maintenance action to change the design or assembly characteristics of systems, end items, components, assemblies, subassemblies, or parts. The purpose of modifications is to improve equipment functioning, maintainability, reliability, or safety characteristics. Maintenance activities routinely modify otherwise operable equipment. However, in some circumstances, the item may be in an administrative deadline status to prevent possible damage or unsafe operation.

motor transport—Surface transportation using wheeled vehicles. It is the most versatile mode of transportation. It links the aerial ports, ocean ports, supply centers, rail, and inland waterway terminals. During combat operations, it links beach support areas, the force combat service support area, combat service support areas, and combat units. After air, motor transport is the most flexible mode. It is an all-weather mode that the MAGTF commander can use over any trafficable terrain, including off road. Motor transport units can move almost any type of cargo. They can provide either local, line, or zonal hauls. The commander may use organic, attached, or supporting motor transport assets to make moves. Commanders must establish priorities and allocate their assets based on the situation. Seldom does vehicle availability permit unlimited, uncontrolled movement. Management is the key to best use of limited vehicle assets. There are two ways to classify motor transport movements—by degree of control and by function.

movement control—The planning, routing, scheduling, and control of personnel and cargo movements over lines of communications. (Joint Pub 1-02)

N

naval beach group—A permanently organized naval command within an amphibious force comprised of a commander and staff, a beachmaster unit, an amphibious construction battalion, and an assault craft unit, designed to provide an administrative group from which required naval tactical components may be made available to the attach force commander and to the amphibious landing force commander to support the landing of one division (reinforced). (JP 1-02)

O

objective—The physical object of the action taken, e.g., a definite tactical feature, the seizure and/or holding of which is essential to the commander's plan. (JP 1-02)

obstacle—See JP 1-02. Any natural or manmade obstruction that canalizes, delays, restricts, or diverts movement of a force. The effectiveness of an obstacle is enhanced considerably when covered by fire. Obstacles can include antitank ditches, blown bridges, built-up areas, minefields, rivers, road craters, terrain, and wire.

obstacle removal—The physical relocation of any structure, facility, or material so it no longer exerts a negative influence on friendly activities.

operating forces—Those forces whose primary missions are to participate in combat and the integral supporting elements thereof. (JP 1-02) See also combat service support element.

operation—A military action or the carrying out of a strategic, tactical, service, training, or administrative military mission; the process of carrying on combat, including movement, supply, attack, defense and maneuvers needed to gain the objectives of any battle or campaign. (JP 1-02)

operational chain of command—The chain of command established for a particular operation or series of continuing operations.

operational level of war—The level of war at which campaigns and major operations are planned, conducted, and sustained to accomplish strategic objectives within theaters or areas of operations. Activities at this level link tactics and strategy by establishing operational objectives needed to accomplish the strategic objectives, sequencing events to achieve the operational objectives, initiating actions, and applying resources to bring about and sustain these events. These activities imply a broader dimension of time or space than do tactics; they ensure the logistic and administrative support of tactical forces, and provide the means by which tactical successes are exploited to achieve strategic objectives. (JP 1-02)

organizational maintenance—That maintenance which is the responsibility of and performed by a using organization on its assigned equipment. Its phases normally consist of inspecting, servicing, lubricating, adjusting, and the replacing of parts, minor assemblies, and subassemblies. (JP 1-02)

overhaul—The restoration of an item to a completely serviceable condition as prescribed by maintenance serviceability standards. (JP 1-02)

P

peculiar contingency support package allowances—Consist of those peculiar items required to provide level I support for a specific type, model, or series and quantity of aircraft and associated support equipment provided to a MAGTF aviation combat element. A peculiar item is an item that is used for a specific aircraft and/or support equipment application.

pipeline—In logistics, the channel of support or a specific portion thereof by means of which materiel or personnel flow from sources of procurement to their point of use. (JP 1-02)

port—A place at which ships may discharge or receive their cargoes. It includes any port accessible to ships on the seacoast, navigable rivers or inland waterways. The term "ports" should not be used in conjunction with air facilities which are designated as aerial ports, airports, etc. (JP 1-02)

prepositioned emergency supplies—The commander uses prepositioned emergency supplies for replenishment early in the ship-to-shore movement. They are available on call for immediate delivery to units ashore. This category is further broken down into floating dumps and prestaged helicopter-lifted supplies.

procurement—The process of obtaining personnel, services, supplies, and equipment. (JP 1-02)

R

rear area—For any particular command, the area extending forward from its rear boundary to the rear of the area assigned to the next lower level of command. This area is provided primarily for the performance of support functions. (JP 1-02)

rear area security (RAS)—The measures taken before, during, and/or after an enemy airborne attack, sabotage action, infiltration, guerrilla action, and/or initiation of psychological or propaganda warfare to minimize the effects thereof. (MCRP 5-12C)

rebuild—The restoration of an item to a standard as nearly as possible to its original condition in appearance, performance, and life expectancy. See also overhaul; repair. (JP 1-02)

rebuild and overhaul—Maintenance functions. Rebuild is a depot maintenance function, and depending on the item, overhaul may be either a depot or intermediate maintenance function. When rebuilding or overhauling items, the maintenance activity also performs modifications not previously made.

reclamation—Restoration of condemned, scrapped, abandoned, or damaged materiel, parts, and components. Reclamation action includes repair, refabrication, or renovation. The maintenance activity returns reclaimed items to the supply system. Reclamation is a depot function.

recovery and evacuation—The process of retrieving or freeing immobile, inoperative, or abandoned materiel from its location. It includes returning the material to operation or to a collection point for repair, evacuation, or disposal. Recovery is an owning-unit responsibility. Evacuation moves materiel from one combat service support (CSS) maintenance activity to another for repair or other disposition. It includes moving equipment between the owning unit's maintenance site and that of the supporting CSS element and/or Marine aviation logistics squadron. Evacuation is a CSS unit responsibility.

removal—The physical relocation of any structure, facility, or material so that it no longer exerts a negative influence on friendly activities.

reorder point—See JP 1-02. That point at which the combat service support (CSS) unit must submit a requisition to maintain the stockage objective. The reorder point is the sum of the safety level and the order and shipping time. For example:

- Safety level   =   5 days
- Reorder time   =   2 days
- Shipping time =   15 days
- Reorder point =   22 days

In this example, the CSS unit reorders when the on-hand balance reaches 22 days. The reorder quantity is the difference between the stockage objective and the on-hand balance (reorder point). To determine actual quantities, the CSS element multiplies the number of days by the daily usage rate.

repair—The restoration of an item to serviceable condition through correction of a specific failure or unserviceable condition. (JP 1-02)

repair and replenishment point—A combat service support installation, normally in forward areas near the supported unit, established to support a mechanized or other rapidly moving force. It may be either a prearranged point or a hastily selected point to rearm, refuel, or provide repair services to the supported force. (MCRP 5-12C)

repair cycle—The stages through which a reparable item passes from the time of its removal or replacement until it is reinstalled or placed in stock in a serviceable condition. (JP 1-02)

replenishment systems—These pull or push systems for provide supplies to supported units. These systems are subject to availability of supplies and distribution capabilities. Two concepts that must be considered in the process of determining the replenishment system to be implemented are available supply rate and required supply rate. **a.** Pull systems require that the consumer submit a request for the desired support. The request is a requisition. Pull systems provide only what the unit says it needs. Pull systems are not as responsive as push systems because they do not provide support in anticipation of need. **b.** Push systems use reports as the requesting document. For example, on-hand or usage reports serve as the basis for resupply. The combat service support element (CSSE) compares the report to the basic load or stockage objective then pushes the difference between the on-hand and desired quantity to the unit. Use of this method requires caution because push systems can contribute to excesses, burdening the user with more stock than can be handled. This can lead to waste, including waste of transportation capability. The MAGTF commander should specify the most appropriate replenishment system based on recommendations from the CSSE and/or aviation combat element. Compromises normally dictate a combination of the two based on the tactical situation and available resources.

requisition—**1.** An authoritative demand or request especially for personnel, supplies, or services authorized but not made available without specific request. (DOD) **2.** To demand or require services from an invaded or conquered nation. (JP 1-02)

resupply—The act of replenishing stocks in order to maintain required levels of supply. (JP 1-02)

S

salvage—**1.** Property that has some value in excess of its basic material content but which is in such condition that it has no reasonable prospect of use for any purpose as a unit and its repair or rehabilitation for use as a unit is clearly impractical. **2.** The saving or rescuing of condemned, discarded, or abandoned property, and of materials contained therein for reuse, refabrication, or scrapping. (JP 1-02)

security—Measures taken by a military unit, an activity or installation to protect itself against all acts designed to, or which may, impair its effectiveness. (JP 1-02)

selective interchange—The exchange of selected serviceable parts and/or components from a deadlined item of equipment for unserviceable repair parts and/or components from a like item.

serial—An element or a group of elements within a series which is given a numerical or alphabetical designation for convenience in planning, scheduling, and control. (JP 1-02)

serial number—A number allocated to each unit or grouping, including its equipment, that is— **a.** embarked entirely in one ship, **b.** landed as a unit on one beach or helicopter landing zone, and **c.** landed at approximately the same time.

servicing, adjustment, and tuning—Maintenance tasks for operable equipment. Servicing may include all repairs or maintenance, including adjustment and tuning. Tuning is a process of adjusting equipment to achieve precise functioning. Tuning often refers to engine adjustments. Engines, however, are not the only components needing adjustment.

ship-to-shore movement—That portion of the assault phase of an amphibious operation which includes the deployment of the landing force from the assault shipping to designated landing areas. (JP 1-02)

stockage objective—The maximum quantities of materiel that the combat service support element (CSSE) and/or aviation combat element (ACE) must have on hand to sustain current operations. It consists of the sum of stocks represented by the operating level and the safety level. The operating

level is the level required to sustain operations between submission of requisitions or between the arrival of successive shipments. These quantities are based on the established replenishment period (daily, monthly, quarterly). In combat, the replenishment period is more frequent than during peacetime operations. The safety level is the quantity required to continue operations if there are minor delays in resupply or unpredictable changes in demand. In combat, the safety level is more critical than during peacetime. The MAGTF commander prescribes the stockage objective for combat service support installations based on the recommendations of the CSSE and/or ACE commander. Selection of the proper stockage objective is critical for proper management of transportation. It is also critical for continued support of combat operations. Too high a stockage objective can place an excessive burden on handling and management systems. Too low a stockage objective can delay or even prevent combat operations.

storage—**1.** The retention of data in any form, usually for the purpose of orderly retrieval and documentation. **2.** A device consisting of electronic, electrostatic, electrical, hardware or other elements into which data may be entered, and from which data may be obtained as desired. (JP 1-02) Storage is the safekeeping of supplies and equipment in a ready-for-issue condition. The storage function includes the process of receipting for supplies and equipment from the source. It includes the responsibility to maintain accurate inventory controls. Similarly, care in storage is a responsibility of the activity holding the supplies and equipment.

strategic level of war—The level of war at which a nation, often as a member of a group of nations, determines national or multinational (alliance or coalition) security objectives and guidance, and develops and uses national resources to accomplish those objectives. Activities at this level establish national and multinational military objectives; sequence initiatives; define limits and assess risks for the use of military and other instruments of national power; develop global plans or theater war plans to achieve these objectives;

and provide military forces and other capabilities in accordance with strategic plans. (JP 1-02)

subordinate command—A command consisting of the commander and all those individuals, units, detachments, organizations, or installations that have been placed under the command by the authority establishing the subordinate command. (JP 1-02)

supply—The procurement, distribution, maintenance while in storage, and salvage of supplies, including the determination of kind and quantity of supplies. **a.** producer phase—That phase of military supply which extends from determination of procurement schedules to acceptance of finished supplies by the military Services. **b.** consumer phase—That phase of military supply which extends from receipt of finished supplies by the Military Services through issue for use or consumption. (JP 1-02)

supply point distribution—That method of distributing supplies in which the receiving unit is issued supplies at a supply point (depot, railhead, truckhead, distribution point) and moves the supplies in organic transportation. This method is the normal method of providing direct support ammunition supply service.

supply requirements—In logistic and combat service support (CSS) terms, supply requirements are the needs for those commodities that are essential to begin and sustain combat operations. There are three types of supply requirements: routine, preplanned, and long term. Routine and preplanned requirements are relatively near term. **a.** routine requirements—These requirements support normal daily operations. The combat service support element (CSSE) and/or aviation combat element supports these requirements with available resources or through redistribution of assets within the MAGTF. **b.** preplanned requirements—These requirements pertain to support for special missions or operations. Like routine requirements, the CSSE supports these requirements with available resources or through redistribution of assets within the MAGTF. There is not enough time to obtain new resources. **c.** long-range requirements—These requirements involve unusual or high-cost items. If this type of support is not correctly determined and programmed in a timely manner, resources may not be available to support requirements. Errors in forecasting long-term requirements can restrict operations. Support might not be available, the allocation of costly resources might exceed real requirements, or both.

support—**1.** The action of a force which aids, protects, complements, or sustains another force in accordance with a directive requiring such action. **2.** A unit which helps another unit in battle. Aviation, artillery, or naval gunfire may be used as a support for infantry. **3.** A part of any unit held back at the beginning of an attack as a reserve. **4.** An element of a command which assists, protects, or supplies other forces in combat. (JP 1-02)

survivability—The inherent capacity of the organization and its capabilities to prevail in the face of potential destruction.

sustainability—The ability to maintain the necessary level and duration of operational activity to achieve military objectives. Sustainability is a function of providing for and maintaining those levels of ready forces, materiel, and consumables necessary to support the military effort.

T

tactical level of war—The level of war at which battles and engagements are planned and executed to accomplish military objectives assigned to tactical units or task forces. Activities at this level focus on the ordered arrangement and maneuver of combat elements in relation to each other and to the enemy to achieve combat objectives. (JP 1-02)

task force—**1.** A temporary grouping of units, under one commander, formed for the purpose of carrying out a specific operation or mission. **2.** Semi-permanent organization of units, under one commander, formed for the purpose of carrying out a continuing specific task. **3.** A component of a fleet organized by the commander of a task fleet or higher authority for the accomplishment of a specific task or tasks. (JP 1-02)

task organization—1. In the Navy, an organization which assigns to responsible commanders the means with which to accomplish their assigned tasks in any planned action. 2. An organization table pertaining to a specific naval directive. (JP 1-02)

terminal operations—The reception, processing, and staging of passengers, the receipt, transit storage and marshaling of cargo, the loading and unloading of ships or aircraft, and the manifesting and forwarding of cargo and passengers to destination. (JP 1-02)

testing and calibration—Maintenance tasks for precision instruments. The instruments may be components of larger items or may be maintenance test equipment. The testing process compares the accuracy of the instrument to an established standard. Calibration is the adjustment of precision instruments that deviate from the standard.

throughput—The average quantity of cargo and passengers that can pass through a port on a daily basis from arrival at the port to loading onto a ship or plane, or from the discharge from a ship or plane to the exit (clearance) from the port complex. Throughput is usually expressed in measurement tons, short tons, or passengers. Reception and storage limitation may affect final throughput. (JP 1-02)

traffic management—The direction, control, and supervision of all functions incident to the procurement and use of freight and passenger transportation services. (JP 1-02)

train—A service force or group of service elements which provides logistic support, e.g., an organization of naval auxiliary ships or merchant ships or merchant ships attached to a fleet for this purpose; similarly, the vehicles and operating personnel which furnish supply, evacuation, and maintenance services to a land unit. (JP 1-02)

transportation—The movement from one location to another by means of railways, highways, waterways, pipelines, oceans, and airways. It includes movement by military and/or commercial assets. For the MAGTF, transportation support is that support required to place sustainability assets (personnel and materiel) in the proper locations at the proper times to initiate and maintain operations.

Transportation Coordinator's Automated Information for Movements System (TC-AIMS)—This system provides the MAGTF commander with an automated capability to plan, coordinate, manage, and execute MAGTF movement from the point of origin to the air and sea port of embarkation and from the port of debarkation to the final destination. During the planning and execution phase of an operation, TC-AIMS updates MAGTF Deployment Support System II, and the Defense Transportation System with movement requirements and status.

transportation operating agencies—Those Federal agencies having responsibilities under national emergency conditions for the operational direction of one or more forms of transportation. (JP 1-02)

type/model/series (T/M/S) aircraft—An alphanumeric code used to identify a particular group of aircraft. Example: F/A-18C: F/A = fighter/attack, 18 = model, C = series.

U

unified command—A command with a broad continuing mission under a single commander and composed of significant assigned components of two or more Military Departments, and which is established and so designated by the President, through the Secretary of Defense with the advice and assistance of the Chairman of the Joint Chiefs of Staff. (JP 1-02)　　　　**(reverse blank)**

Appendix F

References and Related Publications

Department of Defense Instruction (DODI)

3020.37   Continuation of Essential DOD Contractor Services During Crisis

Department of Defense (DOD) Publication

4500.9-R   Defense Transportation Regulation, Parts I, II, and III

Joint Publications (JPs)

0-2   Unified Action Armed Forces (UNAAF)
1   Joint Warfare of the Armed Forces of the United States
2-0   Doctrine for Intelligence Support to Joint Operations
3-0   Doctrine for Joint Operations
3-02   Joint Doctrine for Amphibious Operations
3-02.1   Joint Doctrine for Landing Force Operations
3-02.2   Joint Doctrine for Amphibious Embarkation
3-05   Doctrine for Joint Special Operations
3-07   Joint Doctrine for Military Operations Other Than War
3-07.2   Joint Tactics, Techniques, and Procedures for Antiterrorism
3-07.3   Joint Tactics, Techniques, and Procedures for Peace Operations
3-07.4   Joint Counterdrug Operations
3-10   Doctrine for Joint Rear Area Operations
3-57   Doctrine for Joint Civil Affairs
4-0   Doctrine for Logistic Support of Joint Operations
4-01   Joint Doctrine for the Defense Transportation System
4-01.1   Joint Tactics, Techniques, and Procedures for Airlift Support to Joint Operations
4-01.2   Joint Tactics, Techniques, and Procedures for Sealift Support to Joint Operations
4-01.3   Joint Tactics, Techniques, and Procedures for Movement Control
4-01.6   Joint Tactics, Techniques, and Procedures for Joint Logistics Over the Shore (JLOTS)
4-02   Doctrine for Health Service Support in Joint Operations
4-02.2   Joint Tactics, Techniques, and Procedures for Patient Movement in Joint Operations
4-06   Joint Tactics, Techniques, and Procedures for Mortuary Affairs in Joint Operations

Chairman of the Joint Chiefs of Staff Manual (CJCSM)

3122.03   Joint Operations Planning and Execution System, Volume II, Planning Formats and Guidance

Naval Doctrine Publications (NDPs)

4	Naval Logistics
5	Naval Planning
6	Naval Command and Control

Naval Warfare Publications (NWPs)

1-14M	The Commander's Handbook on the Law of Naval Operations (dual designated as MCWP 5-12.1)
3-02.1	Ship-to-Shore Movement (dual designated as FMFM 1-8 to be updated as MCWP 3-31.5)
3-02.14	The Naval Beach Group (dual designated as FMFM 4-2 to be updated as MCRP 4-11.3D)
3-02.21	Military Sealift Command in Support of Amphibious Operations (dual designated as FMFM 1-15 to be updated as MCRP 3-31A)
3-02.3	Maritime Prepositioning Force (MPF) Operations (dual designated as FMFM 1-5 to be updated as MCWP 3-32)
4-02	Operational Health Service Support
4-02.2	Patient Movement, Part A, Naval Expeditionary Forces Medical Regulating
4-02.4	Part A, Deployable Heath Service Support Platforms—Fleet Hospitals
6-01	Basic Operational Communications Doctrine
80	Strategic Sealift Planning and Operations Doctrine of the U.S. Navy (dual designated as FMFM 1-16 to be updated as MCRP 4-13.1B)

Marine Corps Doctrinal Publication (MCDPs)

1	Warfighting
1-1	Strategy
1-2	Campaigning
1-3	Tactics
2	Intelligence
3	Expeditionary Operations
4	Logistics
5	Planning
6	Command and Control

Marine Corps Warfighting Publications (MCWPs)

0-1.1	Componency
2-1	Intelligence Operations
3-17	MAGTF Engineer Operations
3-24	Assault Support
4-1	Logistics Operations
4-11.1	Health Service Support Operations
4-11.4	Maintenance Operations

4-11.5	Seabee Operations in the MAGTF (dual designated as NWP 4-04.1)
4-11.6	Bulk Liquids Operations
4-11.7	MAGTF Supply Operations
5-1	Marine Corps Planning Process
6-22	Communications and Information Systems

Marine Corps Reference Publications (MCRPs)

| 5-12C | Marine Corps Supplement to the Department of Defense Dictionary of Military and Associated Terms |
| 5-12D | Organization of Marine Corps Forces |

Fleet Marine Force Manuals (FMFMs)

2-6	MAGTF Rear Area Operations (under development as MCWP 3-41.1)
3-1	Command and Staff Action
3-61	Ministry in Combat (under development as MCWP 6-12)
4-3	MAGTF Landing Support Operations (to be incorporated into MCWP 4-11.3)
4-9	Motor Transport (to be incorporated into MCWP 4-11.3)
5-40	Offensive Air Support (under development as MCWP 3-23)
5-50	Antiair Warfare (under development as MCWP 3-22)
6	Ground Combat Operations (under development as MCWP 3-1)
6-21	Tactical Fundamentals of Helicopterborne Operations (under development as MCWP 3-11.4)

Fleet Marine Force Reference Publication (FMFRPs)

| 1-18 | Amphibious Ships and Landing Craft Data Book (under development as MCRP 3-31B) |
| 5-71 | Aviation Planning Documents (under development as MCRP 5-11.1A) |

Marine Corps Order (MCO)

| P1700.27 w/ch 1 | Marine Corps Morale, Welfare, and Recreation Policy Manual |

U.S. Army Field Manuals (FMs)

8-55	Planning for Health Service Support
10-27	General Supply in Theaters of Operations
10-52	Water Supply in Theaters of Operations
10-67	Petroleum Supply in Theaters of Operations
27-10	The Law of Land Warfare (dual designated as MCRP 5-12.1A)
34-130	Intelligence Preparation of the Battlefield (IPB) (dual designated as FMFRP 3-23-2 to be updated as MCRP 2-12A)

54-40	Area Support Group
55-9	Unit Air Movement Planning
55-10	Movement Control in a Theater of Operations
90-31	Army and Marine Corps Integration (AMCI) (dual designated as MCRP 3-38)
100-16	Army Operational Support
100-19	Domestic Support Operations
100-23-1	HA Multiservice Procedures for Humanitarian Assistance Operations (multi-Service designated as FMFRP 7-16 to be updated as MCWP 3-33.6)
101-5-1	Operational Terms and Graphics (dual designated as MCRP 5-12A)
700-80	Logistics
701-58	Planning Logistics Support for Military Operations